THE NAVY

Other National Historical Society Publications:

THE IMAGE OF WAR: 1861-1865

TOUCHED BY FIRE: A PHOTOGRAPHIC PORTRAIT OF THE CIVIL WAR

WAR OF THE REBELLION: OFFICIAL RECORDS OF THE UNION AND CONFEDERATE ARMIES

OFFICIAL RECORDS OF THE UNION AND CONFEDERATE NAVIES IN THE WAR OF THE REBELLION

HISTORICAL TIMES ILLUSTRATED ENCYCLOPEDIA OF THE CIVIL WAR

CONFEDERATE VETERAN

THE WEST POINT MILITARY HISTORY SERIES

IMPACT: THE ARMY AIR FORCES' CONFIDENTIAL HISTORY OF WORLD WAR II

HISTORY OF UNITED STATES NAVAL OPERATIONS IN WORLD WAR II by Samuel Eliot Morison

HISTORY OF THE ARMED FORCES IN WORLD WAR II by Janusz Piekalkiewicz

A TRAVELLER'S GUIDE TO GREAT BRITAIN SERIES

MAKING OF BRITAIN SERIES

THE ARCHITECTURAL TREASURES OF EARLY AMERICA

For information about National Historical Society Publications, write: The National Historical Society, 2245 Kohn Road, Box 8200, Harrisburg, Pa 17105

THE ELITE
The World's Crack Fighting Men

THE NAVY

Ashley Brown, Editor

Jonathan Reed, Editor

Editorial Board

Lisa Mullins, Managing Editor, NHS edition

A Publication of
THE NATIONAL HISTORICAL SOCIETY

Published in Great Britain in 1986 by Orbis Publishing

Special contents of this edition copyright © 1988 by the
National Historical Society

Library of Congress Cataloging-in-Publication Data
The Navy / Ashley Brown, editor, Jonathan Reed, editor.
   p.   cm.—(The Elite ; v. 5)
   ISBN 0-918678-43-9
   1. Navies.   2. Naval history, Modern—20th century.
I. Brown, Ashley.   II. Reed, Jonathan.   III. Series: Elite
(Harrisburg, Pa.) ; v. 5
VA10.N39   1989
359'.00904—dc20

                                                    89-3399
                                                    CIP

CONTENTS

INTRODUCTION

From the dim reaches of the distant past down to the twentieth century, while the armies have defended homelands and marched across nations in conquest, it has been the navies of the world that have taken warfare to the far-flung shores of the enemy. Restrained by nothing more than the depth of the deep blue beneath them, the warships, landing craft and submarines could bring the conflict to an enemy thousands of miles away and, by controlling the seas, change the destiny of millions. And with the coming of the air age, those navies could take dominion of the skies with them. Wherever they have faced heavy odds, on ship, under the water, ashore or in the air, the navies have often had to call upon those who could dare more and achieve, their ELITE.

Who could be more daring than the Italian frogmen who became, almost literally, human torpedoes? The Underwater Division of the 10th MAS Flotilla put two men aboard a torpedo mounted in front of a submerged motorized "chariot" and sent them into enemy harbors to attack Allied shipping. They claimed 28 vessels, but suffered terrible losses themselves. Or the daring Aussies aboard their disguised little steamer *Krait*, who donned sarongs, dyed their faces, and sailed for 33 days in Japanese-controlled waters, virtually within sight of enemy patrol boats, to attack enemy shipping at Singapore. Or the intrepid airmen of the German Naval Airship Division in World War I, men who took their zeppelins over London to bomb time after time, or even made voyages of up to 4,000 miles as did the L59, taking supplies to German East Africa.

The exploits of the naval ELITE of the world span the century, right up to the conflict in the Falklands, Viet Nam, and the air spats with Libya. The great ships, themselves members of "the few," are heard from time and again—the *Bismarck*, the *Yorktown*, the *Warspite*. Their adventures, the cruise of the German *Emden* in 1914, the launch of the naval air wave with the cry "Tora, Tora, Tora," that heralded the Pearl Harbor attack, and much more, all make up the unexcelled story of brave men and mighty machines of war, all joining to rise above themselves to leave a special mark upon the records of their conflicts.

The mark of the ELITE.

HMS WARSPITE

The grand old lady of the Royal Navy, HMS Warspite, pulverised the Italian fleet at the battle of Cape Matapan in the eastern Mediterranean

AS DARKNESS fell on the night of 28 March 1941, the British Mediterranean Fleet, consisting of three battleships, an aircraft carrier, and supporting cruisers and destroyers, was steaming southwest of Cape Matapan in the eastern Mediterranean. The Commander-in-Chief, Admiral Sir Andrew Browne Cunningham, DSO, GCB, was on the compass platform of his flagship, the battleship HMS Warspite. In line abreast to port were the battleship HMS Valiant, the carrier HMS Formidable and the third battleship, HMS Barham.

Cunningham, who had already shown himself to be an aggressive commander, had only one ambition: to defeat the Italian battlefleet by whatever means came to hand. He had taken his own battlefleet out of Alexandria on the evening of 27 March after he had received warning of an Italian sortie against Crete. British forces were using Crete as a staging post for reinforcing Greece, and the Italians hoped to intercept or at least halt the convoys carrying troops and equipment from Egypt to Greece. Cunningham ordered Vice-Admiral

By the outbreak of World War II, HMS Warspite had been in service with the Royal Navy for nearly a quarter of a century. As the fourth ship of the 'Queen Elizabeth' class, she was launched in November 1913 and, after sea-trials, was ready for war in May 1915. Warspite was assigned to the Grand Fleet for most of World War I and fought as part of Vice-Admiral Beatty's force at the Battle of Jutland in May 1916.

During the inter-war period, the battleship was modified on two separate occasions to keep pace with developments in the field of naval technology.

By 1939, Warspite's main armament consisted of eight 15in guns in four turrets and eight 6in guns; and eight 4in, 32 two-pounder and 16 0.5in anti-aircraft guns.

Between 1939 and 1945, the Warspite gained a further 13 battle honours to add to the one won in 1916. After the battle at Narvik in April 1940, she became the flagship of Admiral Cunningham in the Mediterranean, and took part in actions off Calabria and Matapan.

Badly damaged during the evacuation of Crete in May 1941, she underwent repairs in the US, before returning to the Mediterranean in 1942. The Warspite went on to support the Allied landings in Europe and, although nearly sunk on one occasion, stayed in service until late 1945.

Above: HMS Warspite's badge.

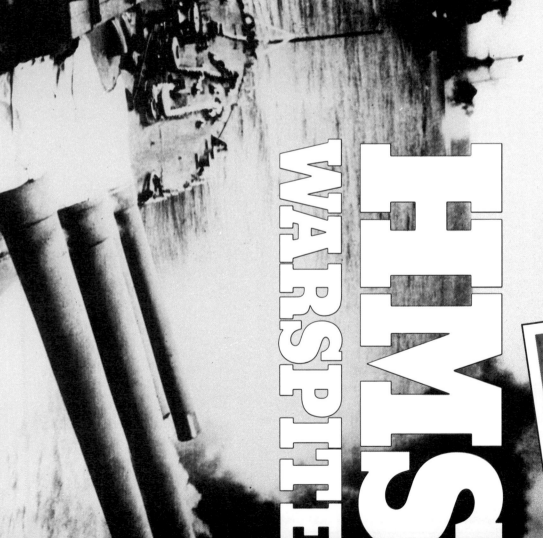

Pridham-Wippell to concentrate his force, consisting of four cruisers and four destroyers, south of Crete and await developments, while he took the main battleforce into the area.

At first light on 28 March, the *Formidable* had launched the first of a series of reconnaissance aircraft, and both the carrier aircraft and Pridham-Wippell's ships soon reported sightings of enemy vessels. Although the British did not yet know it, they had encountered the fast battleship *Vittorio Veneto* and two cruiser squadrons totalling eight ships. By 1230 hours Pridham-Wippell, on HMS *Orion*, had joined the main force, and it was clear to Cunningham that if the carrier's torpedo-bombers did not slow the Italians down, there was little chance of bringing them to battle before they reached home waters.

Cunningham was known for his 'caged-tiger act': pacing up and down the narrow admiral's bridge, just below the compass platform. As the morning passed, Cunningham continued to pace up and down the starboard side of the bridge, listening to the stream of sighting reports coming from the ships and aircraft of his fleet. Occasionally, he would go into the charthouse, where his staff were plotting

Below left: British battleships open fire. Left: An Italian Belzano-class cruiser under torpedo attack. Below: Two Zara-class cruisers head for destruction.

both friendly and enemy movements. At 1510 one of the carrier aircraft reported that a solitary torpedo hit had been obtained on the Italian battleship, but it was soon clear that the *Vittorio Veneto*'s speed had been only slightly reduced. Still convinced that the Italians could be brought to action, Cunningham had ordered another air strike, and just as the sun was setting, at about 1930, came the welcome news that a torpedo-bomber had penetrated heavy anti-aircraft gunfire and scored a hit on a Zara-class heavy cruiser.

Aboard the *Warspite*, the question was whether to risk a night action to sink the damaged cruiser, or to wait until daylight. Cunningham had almost certainly made up his mind to attack, but went through the motions of consulting his staff. When one or two pointed out the risks and uncertainty of a night action, the diminutive Cunningham is said to have retorted: 'You're a pack of yellow-livered skunks. I'll go and have my supper now, and after supper see if my morale is higher than yours.' True or not, the words reflect 'ABC's' determination not to let the Italians escape. At 2100, after Pridham-Wippell passed on a radar contact with a stationary ship, Cunningham went to the compass platform and gave a series of orders to bring his fleet into line ahead.

The various control positions reported that they had sighted the targets and that the armaments were ready to fire

The three battleships and the carrier made a 40 degree turn together into line ahead to close with the target. At 2200, the second in line, HMS *Valiant*, the only ship in the battle squadron equipped with radar, detected a stationary target only eight miles away on the port bow. In total darkness, the big ships drew closer and closer, reducing the range to four-and-a-half miles. A solitary British destroyer on the port bow was in the line of fire, and was given a curt order to 'get to hell out of it' as Cunningham turned his ships into quarter-line.

Suddenly the admiral's chief-of-staff, Commodore John Edelsten, saw more darkened ships crossing ahead of the British ships. As the alarm bells sounded, the twin 15in gun turrets swung onto a fresh bearing. For the next few moments, the *Warspite's* bridge was silent, with only the lap of her wash and the hum of machinery audible. Then, the various control positions reported that they too had sighted the targets and that the various armaments were ready to fire. Just before the *Warspite's* captain gave the order to open fire, the destroyer *Greyhound* switched on her searchlight, revealing two Italian heavy cruisers.

Cunningham later remembered the action on board the *Warspite* before her guns opened fire:

'In a dead silence, a silence that could almost be felt, one heard only the voices of the gun-control personnel putting the guns onto the new target. One heard the orders repeated in the director tower behind and above the bridge. Looking forward, one saw the turrets swing and steady when the 15in guns pointed at the enemy cruisers.'

Moments later, the ship's main armament was pointing at the two targets from a range of no more than 4000 yards. The main armament opened fire two minutes later. The ringing of the ship's fire gongs was followed an instant later by blinding flashes and the shattering concussion of a six-gun salvo of 15in shells. From the *Warspite*, one eyewitness remembered

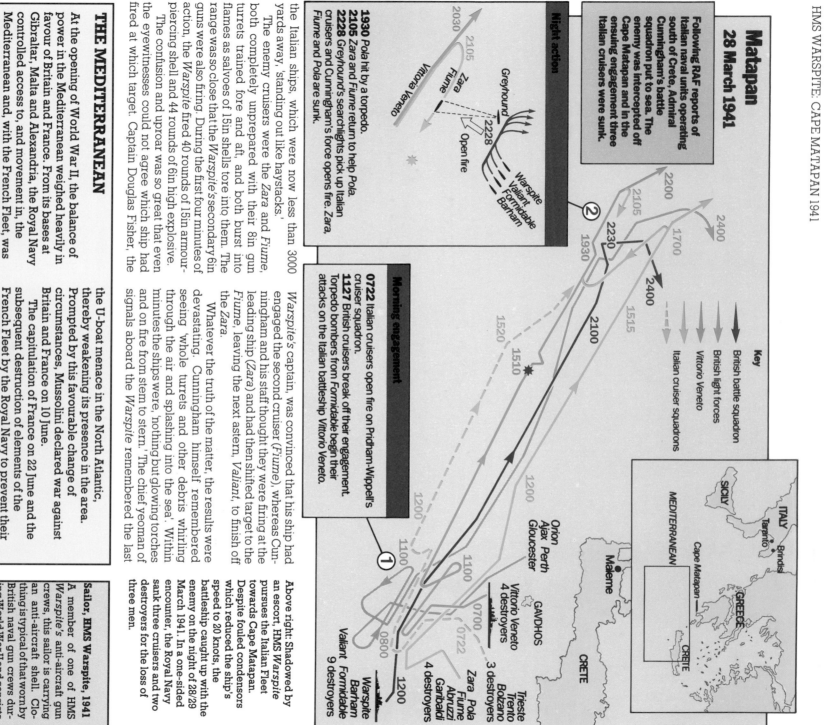

Matapan
28 March 1941

Following RAF reports of Italian naval units operating south of Crete, Admiral Cunningham's battle squadron put to sea. The enemy was intercepted off Cape Matapan and in the ensuing engagement three Italian cruisers were sunk.

Night action

1930 *Pola* hit by a torpedo.
2105 *Zara* and *Fiume* return to help *Pola*.
2228 *Greyhound's* searchlights pick up Italian cruisers and Cunningham's force opens fire. *Zara, Fiume* and *Pola* are sunk.

Greyhound

2030
2105
Zara
Fiume
Vittorio Veneto
2228
Open fire
Warspite
Valiant
Formidable
Barham

Morning engagement

0722 Italian cruisers open fire on Pridham-Wippell's cruiser squadron.
1127 British cruisers break off their engagement. Torpedo bombers from *Formidable* begin their attacks on the Italian battleship *Vittorio Veneto*.

Key

British battle squadron
British light forces
Vittorio Veneto
Italian cruiser squadrons

ITALY
Taranto
Brindisi
SICILY
MEDITERRANEAN
Cape Matapan
GREECE
CRETE
Maleme
GAVDHOS

2200
2105
2230
1930
2400
1700
1515
2400
2100
1520
1510
1200
1200
1100
1200
1100
0700
0722
0800
1200

Orion
Ajax
Perth
Gloucester
Vittorio Veneto
4 destroyers
Trieste
Trento
Bolzano
3 destroyers
Zara
Pola
Fiume
Abruzzi
Garibaldi
4 destroyers
Warspite
Barham
Valiant
Formidable
9 destroyers

Above right: Shadowed by an escort, HMS *Warspite* pursues the Italian Fleet towards Cape Matapan. Despite fouled condensors which reduced the ship's speed to 20 knots, the battleship caught up with the enemy on the night of 28/29 March 1941. In a one-sided encounter, the Royal Navy sank three cruisers and two destroyers for the loss of three men.

---

the Italian ships, which were now less than 3000 yards away, 'standing out like haystacks.'

The enemy cruisers were the *Zara* and *Fiume*, both completely unprepared with their 8in gun turrets trained fore and aft, and both burst into flames as salvoes of 15in shells tore into them. The range was so close that the *Warspite's* secondary 6in guns were also firing. During the first four minutes of action, the *Warspite* fired 40 rounds of 15in armour-piercing shell and 44 rounds of 6in high explosive.

The confusion and uproar was so great that even the eyewitnesses could not agree which ship had fired at which target. Captain Douglas Fisher, the

Warspite's captain, was convinced that his ship had engaged the second cruiser (*Fiume*), whereas Cunningham and his staff thought they were firing at the leading ship (*Zara*) and had then shifted target to the *Fiume*, leaving the next astern, *Valiant*, to finish off the *Zara*.

Whatever the truth of the matter, the results were devastating. Cunningham himself remembered seeing 'whole turrets and other debris whirling through the air and splashing into the sea.' Within minutes the ships were, 'nothing but glowing torches and on fire from stem to stern.' The chief yeoman of signals aboard the *Warspite* remembered the last

THE MEDITERRANEAN

At the opening of World War II, the balance of power in the Mediterranean weighed heavily in favour of Britain and France. From its bases at Gibraltar, Malta and Alexandria, the Royal Navy controlled access to, and movement in, the Mediterranean and, with the French Fleet, was poised to close the sea lanes through which flowed 80 per cent of Italy's imports. With the exception of Italy and Italian Libya, most of the adjacent countries were either neutral or in Allied hands. Under such circumstances the Italian leader, Benito Mussolini, shied away from initiating hostilities and played a waiting game.

Following the German conquest of northern Europe in 1940, the situation in the basin changed dramatically: the Royal Navy was forced to withdraw several key ships to combat

the U-boat menace in the North Atlantic, thereby weakening its presence in the area. Prompted by this favourable change of circumstances, Mussolini declared war against Britain and France on 10 June.

The capitulation of France on 22 June and the subsequent destruction of elements of the French Fleet by the Royal Navy to prevent their use by the Axis, further weakened the British position in the Mediterranean, and the fight for the control of the sea intensified.

Both sides wished to dominate the sea; the British to protect convoys from their Far East colonies, to secure the Middle East's oil supply and threaten the 'soft underbelly' of Europe. For their part, the Axis powers believed that control of North Africa and force British convoys to travel the long route around Africa via the Cape of Good Hope.

NIGHT ACTION

The Royal Navy's success at Matapan owed much to Admiral Cunningham's order to pursue the Italian Fleet as it withdrew under cover of darkness. It was not a decision taken lightly; night actions at sea were regarded as highly dangerous.

At the beginning of the war many of the navy's ships were poorly equipped for nightfighting. Few carried radar, and those that did were only able to identify other craft up to a range of 12,000 yards, a distance well within the range of a broadside.

One of the most serious problems was that friendly ships might blunder into each other or open fire in the belief that they were engaging the enemy. Visual identification at night was difficult, often relying on the keen sight and judgement of the men on watch duty. At close ranges, searchlights were used to pick up targets.

Darkness also favoured the enemy who, by taking advantage of a confused chase, could shake off the pursuers by a sudden change of course or speed.

It was also possible to double back, get through the other fleet's screen of destroyers and launch a torpedo attack against its vulnerable capital ships.

Target identification was a major problem for gunnery officers. Although range and direction could be judged from radar plots, it was difficult to gauge the fall of shot and correct a mistake. In this respect, the British use of flashless cordite did have one major advantage: it allowed the Royal Navy to fire unseen at an enemy whose gunfire illuminated the night sky.

few seconds before firing started; he had been ordered by Captain Fisher to signal the night challenge on his Aldis lamp but, before he could start the signal, Cunningham arrived on the compass platform and said, 'Challenge my foot – shoot.'

The same chief yeoman was blown over the chart table by the blast of the *Warspite's* first salvo of 15in shells. After he had recovered his senses, he looked out on the disengaged side and saw, silhouetted in one of the ship's searchlights, what appeared to be another Italian ship, so he called out the bearing: 'Green 60, enemy cruiser.' Fortunately, Cunningham, who was close by, took a quick look and said, 'Don't be a bloody idiot. It's the *Formidable*.'

The commander-in-chief was well aware of the risks inherent in a night action, and had previously ordered his carrier to leave the battle line to reduce the risk of becoming involved in the gun action. However, the destroyer HMS *Havock* had an even closer escape, when she was straddled by a salvo of 15in shells, before being identified as friendly.

A little after 2230 hours, Italian destroyers were sighted and engaged, and Cunningham ordered his own destroyers to sink the crippled cruisers and any destroyers they could find. At 2245 gunfire and starshell were seen to the southwest, and shortly afterwards the British battle squadron and all units not engaging the enemy were ordered to withdraw to the northeast to reduce the confusion and give the destroyers a free hand in attacking the enemy.

As the *Warspite* and the other heavy ships steamed clear of the action, the destroyers hunted down any Italian ships they could find. The Australian ship HMAS *Stuart* sank the *Alfieri* and HMS *Havock* sank the *Carducci*, hitting her with a torpedo and finishing her off with gunfire. Just after midnight, *Havock* reported what she thought was a battleship, and, to Cunningham in the flagship, it seemed that the *Vittorio Veneto* might be brought to action after all. Unfortunately, the destroyer's identification proved over-enthusiastic, and an hour later the *Havock's* captain amended the sighting report to say that it was another heavy cruiser.

The target was the luckless *Pola*, sister to the *Fiume* and *Zara*. She had been the unwitting cause of the catastrophe, for when she had been crippled by the *Formidable*'s torpedo-attack at dusk, the Italian Commander-in-Chief, Admiral Angelo Iachino, had sent Vice-Admiral Cattaneo with two more cruisers to cover her retreat or take her in tow. It was these cruisers which had been surprised just three hours earlier.

The sailors whose ship had been lying crippled less than eight miles from the centre of the fierce battle can be forgiven for wanting no further part in it. As the British and Australian destroyers trained their searchlights on her, their crews saw a scene of total confusion. Many panic-stricken sailors had jumped overboard, but the *Jervis*'s captain was able to run his ship alongside and take off as many men as he could, before pulling clear and firing a salvo of torpedoes into her.

Large patches of oil, boats, life-rafts and floating corpses covered the surface of the sea

The sinking of the *Pola* at 0410 on the 29th, brought the battle to an end. Dawn patrols, flown from the *Formidable* and by shore-based aircraft from Greece and Crete, revealed that the *Vittorio Veneto* had escaped during the night. As the fleet crossed the scene of the battle, evidence of the scale of the Italian defeat was visible everywhere: large patches of oil, boats, life-rafts and floating corpses covered the surface of the sea. There were also scattered groups of Italian survivors but, with German aircraft shadowing, the risk was too great for the Mediterranean Fleet to undertake large-scale rescue operations. Instead, an aircraft was ordered to signal the whereabouts of the boats and rafts to the Italians. In all, 900 survivors, mostly from the *Pola*, were rescued during the night. An Italian hospital ship saved another 150, and a flotilla of Greek destroyers found another 110 sailors. The British lost no more than a single aircrew, making Matapan one of the cheapest naval victories on record.

Despite sporadic air attacks during the afternoon

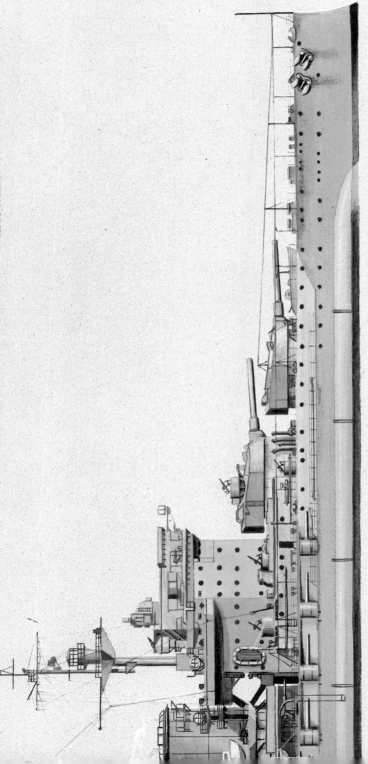

Above: The *Warspite*. Although laid down during World War I, the ship was extensively modernised in the inter-war period. The Supermarine Walrus aircraft was used for air-sea rescues and reconnaissance missions. Below right: Shrouded in dense clouds of smoke from a broadside, the *Warspite* undergoes sea-trials. Above left: The *Fiume* along with the *Pola* and *Zara* (left bottom), were the most up-to-date cruisers in the Italian Fleet at the outbreak of hostilities. At Matapan, however, their crews' lack of nightfighting experience allowed the Royal Navy to reduce these ships to shell-blasted hulks. Centre left: Aircraft from the carrier *Formidable* were the eyes of Cunningham's force. One scored a direct hit on the *Vittorio Veneto*, the pride of Mussolini's navy, with a torpedo.

of 29 March, Cunningham's ships suffered no damage, and the *Formidable*'s fighters had no difficulty in breaking up most of the attacks. The ships entered Alexandria harbour early the following evening, and two days later Cunningham ordered all ships to hold a Thanksgiving Service, following the tradition established by Nelson after the Battle of the Nile in 1798.

Despite the magnitude of the defeat inflicted on the Italians, Cunningham remained modest about his accomplishments. Speaking ten years later, he said: 'It was hardly a battle – just a long pursuit of the Italian Fleet followed by two minutes of fierce night action, which was much more like murder than anything else.

'At sea it has always been one of the principal objections to a pursuit by night that the pursuer always laid himself open to what might be a series of highly dangerous attacks by the enemy's light forces. The Italians must have known this quite well. They had some 18 destroyers and a considerable number of cruisers with which they might have launched a night attack upon us. They didn't do so, their argument being that as it was so highly dangerous for a Fleet to pursue at night that the British wouldn't attempt it. Therefore what was the good of sending their light forces to attack something that wouldn't be there?'

The Italians' poor showing at Matapan was caused partly by their navy's poor training in night-fighting. Whereas the British had learned their lesson at Jutland in 1916 and had tightened up their night-fighting drill, the Italians had not even introduced flashless cordite – which did not produce the tell-tale flash when a gun was fired. Nor was the enemy willing to exercise at night. Indeed, Cunningham's attacks had bred an understandable timidity in the enemy fleet, which in turn robbed its ships of the chance to develop the skills needed to match the British.

For the Italians, Matapan (or the Battle of Gaudo Island, as it is known to them) was a bitter blow, and the only consolation was the escape of the *Vittorio Veneto*. The death of Vice-Admiral Cattaneo and the loss of more than 2000 men as well as three large cruisers and two destroyers deepened the mood of pessimism at Supermarina, the Italian Navy's headquarters, brought about by the attack on Taranto in November 1940. Cunningham had clearly demonstrated that, with aggressive handling, his fleet could outfight and outmanoeuvre the larger Italian forces.

THE AUTHOR Anthony Preston is naval editor of the military magazine *Defence* and author of numerous publications including *Battleships*, *Aircraft Carriers* and *Submarines*.

Built at Clydebank in 1941, HMS *Onslow* was an 'O'-class destroyer with a displacement of 1610 tons and a complement of 217 men. The *Onslow* was powered by two-shaft geared turbines which produced 40,000 ship horse-power and a maximum speed of 36¾ knots – a typical speed for a fast-moving escort destroyer of the period. Armament comprised four 4.7in guns – fitted in single mountings, two forward, two aft – one 4in AA gun, four 2-pounder guns and eight 21in torpedo tubes. The *Onslow* had a long and distinguished career in World War II, serving as a convoy escort with the Home Fleet for much of the war although she also saw action in the Mediterranean and during the Normandy landings. After the war the *Onslow* was refitted for the Pakistan Navy, becoming the *Tippu Sultan*, although she returned to Britain in 1957 to be converted to an anti-submarine frigate.

FIGHT OF THE ONSLOW

To save the convoy it was escorting, the British destroyer HMS *Onslow* made a heroic attack on the German heavy cruiser *Hipper* on New Year's Eve 1942

ON THE LAST day of 1942 the 1610-ton British destroyer HMS *Onslow* was steaming through moderate seas, leading the escort screen of convoy JW51B, 12 merchant ships laden with war material for the Soviet Army. Convoy JW51A had reached the Soviet port of Murmansk on 25 December and the convoy's two cruiser escorts, *Sheffield* and *Jamaica*, had turned round to steam south in support of JW51B. Under the command of Rear Admiral Robert Burnett the two cruisers were less than 50 miles north of the convoy on the morning of 31 December.

Visibility was quite good for the conditions of an Arctic winter – five to six miles – but frequent snow showers could blot out everything, reducing visibility to zero. Conditions for the ships' crews were hell: the sub-zero temperatures made the simplest operations extremely difficult; exposed metal fittings could rip the skin of a man's bare hand:

lookouts regularly suffered from severe exposure and any man overboard was assumed lost, dead within minutes in the icy seas of the Arctic Ocean. The escort destroyers were themselves affected by the cold as it froze the spray swept over the ships, making it difficult to operate the forward guns.

After more than three years of constant warfare the Royal Navy had developed into a highly effective fighting force, with the main brunt of the action being borne by its escort destroyers. Apart from the constant danger of U-boat attack, the Arctic convoy destroyer commanders had to contend with the threat of German surface ships. The British realised that they would have to throw their escort vessels against any enemy surface ships, regardless of loss, in order to keep the convoys safe. And the performance of the *Onslow* at the battle of the Barents Sea was to prove an outstanding example of the aggressive spirit of the Royal Navy.

The crews of the escort ships were keyed-up for action as everyone in the convoy knew that the German Navy's powerful surface forces stationed in northern Norway would make every attempt to destroy the convoy. The Admiralty had intercepted and decoded German signals, and the commanding officer of the 17th Destroyer Flotilla, Captain Robert Sherbrooke, DSO, RN had been told to expect an attack by major surface units.

Tension increased when at 0820 hours on 31 December, the corvette *Hyderabad*, on the starboard side of the convoy, sighted two destroyers. Believing them to be Russian destroyers from Murmansk she did not report them, but 10 minutes later the destroyer *Obdurate* sighted them again, crossing the stern of the convoy. Her commanding officer immediately transmitted the sighting report to Sherbrooke and, when it was confirmed that they were German, he prepared the *Onslow* for action.

As three of the screening destroyers took up their pre arranged formation astern of the *Onslow*, the fifth destroyer, HMS *Achates*, started a zigzag course astern of the convoy, laying a smokescreen by altering the oil-air mixture in her boiler furnaces and making chemical smoke on her quarterdeck.

The two destroyers played their deadly game of cat and mouse

Not until 0939 did the lookouts in the bridge wings of the *Onslow* get a sight of the enemy, but their report was highly alarming, for the unmistakable control tower of a large German ship could be seen to the east of the two 'mystery' destroyers. Two minutes later the *Onslow* transmitted a signal to Rear Admiral Burnett that an enemy heavy unit was engaging the convoy. It was the *Admiral Hipper* – with three large destroyers in support – under the command of Vice-Admiral Kummetz; and, unknown to the British at the time, Kummetz also had at his disposal the pocket battleship *Lützow* and another three large

destroyers. His plan was to engage the convoy escorts from the north, driving them back into the arms of the *Lützow*, which was moving into position to the south.

The two destroyers *Onslow* and *Orwell* showed no hesitation in firing at the 14,000-ton *Admiral Hipper*, despite the fact that their armament (4.7in and 4in guns) was greatly outranged by the eight 8in guns of the heavy cruiser. What they had, however, were torpedoes which could sink the *Admiral Hipper*, if she should get too close.

For half-an-hour the two destroyers played their deadly game of cat and mouse, slipping in and out of snow showers and patches of smoke to avoid the *Admiral Hipper's* guns. Sherbrooke would not permit the convoy to be left unprotected, and so denied his other two destroyers, and *Obdurate* and *Obedient*, the chance to reinforce *Onslow* and *Orwell*. Suddenly the *Onslow's* luck ran out, when at 1020, three out of a straddle of four 8in shells from the *Admiral Hipper* burst on the forward part of the ship.

The German shells had caused terrible damage. Two hits knocked out the A and B 4.7in guns, leaving many of their crews dead and dying, while splinters killed and wounded many more below. The third shell hit the funnel, sending its deadly splinters to kill and maim people crowded on the bridge and putting both radar and radio sets out of action. Captain Sherbrooke received a terrible face wound from a splinter, which knocked his left eye out of the socket, leaving it hanging on his cheek. Sherbrooke remained conscious in spite of his wound, and in the finest tradition of the Royal Navy he refused to leave the bridge. Damage control and fire-fighting parties were despatched to report on the extent of damage.

Left: The most famous destroyer of World War II – HMS Onslow, seen here ploughing across the wintry seas of the Arctic Ocean (with HMS Ashanti in the background). Below left: the cruiser HMS Jamaica steams southwards to the aid of the beleaguered convoy JW51B. The Jamaica was armed with 12 6in guns, and, with HMS Sheffield, formed Rear Admiral Burnett's cruiser force, which was to play a crucial role in the battle of the Barents Sea. Below: kitted out with steel helmets and anti-flash gear the crew of a 4in gun on an Arctic convoy destroyer prepare for action.

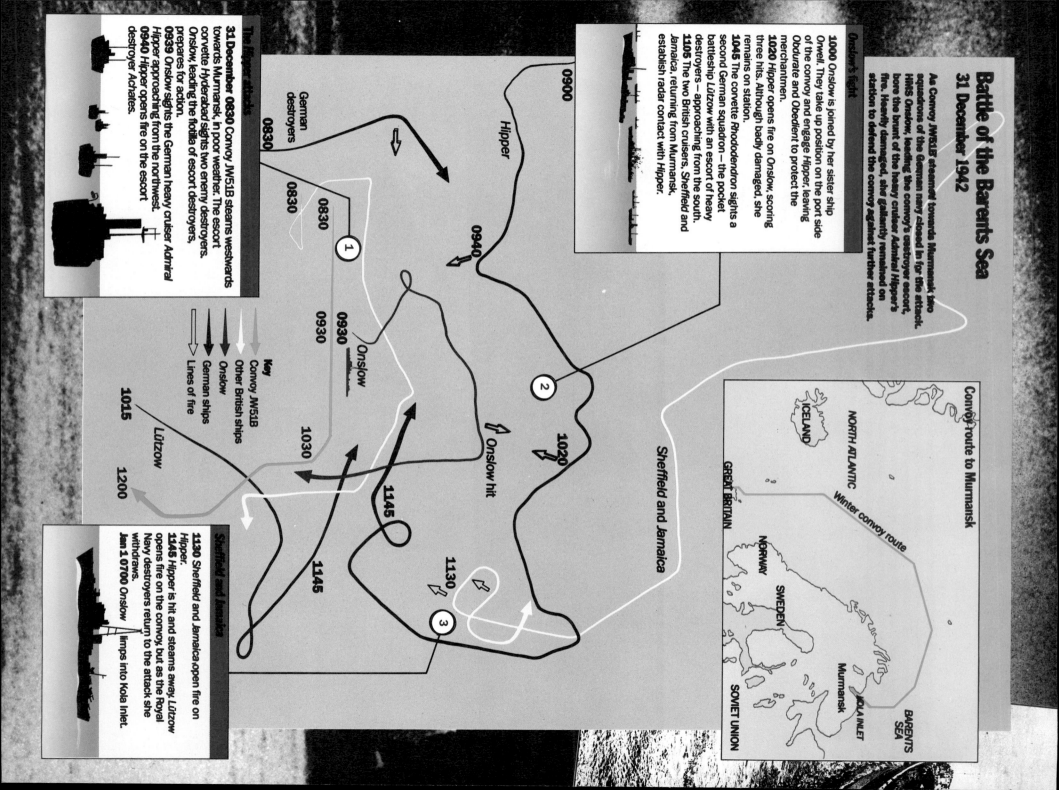

Battle of the Barents Sea
31 December 1942

Onslow's fight

1000 *Onslow* is joined by her sister ship *Orwell*. They take up position on the port side of the convoy and engage *Hipper*, leaving *Obdurate* and *Obedient* to protect the merchantmen.

1020 *Hipper* opens fire on *Onslow*, scoring three hits. Although badly damaged, she remains on station.

1045 The corvette *Rhododendron* sights a second German squadron – the pocket battleship *Lützow* with an escort of heavy destroyers – approaching from the south.

1105 The two British cruisers, *Sheffield* and *Jamaica*, returning from Murmansk, establish radar contact with *Hipper*.

As Convoy JW51B steamed towards Murmansk, two squadrons of the German navy closed in for the attack. HMS *Onslow*, leading the convoy's destroyer escort, bore the brunt of the heavy cruiser *Admiral Hipper's* fire. Heavily damaged, she gallantly remained on station to defend the convoy against further attacks.

The Hipper attacks

31 December 0830 Convoy JW51B steams westwards towards Murmansk, in poor weather. The escort corvette *Hyderabad* sights two enemy destroyers. *Onslow*, leading the flotilla of escort destroyers, prepares for action.

0939 *Onslow* sights the German heavy cruiser *Admiral Hipper* approaching from the northwest.

0940 *Hipper* opens fire on the escort destroyer *Achates*.

Sheffield and Jamaica

1130 *Sheffield* and *Jamaica* open fire on *Hipper*.

1145 *Hipper* is hit and steams away. *Lützow* opens fire on the convoy, but as the Royal Navy destroyers return to the attack she withdraws.

Jan 1 0700 *Onslow* limps into Kola Inlet.

Key

- Convoy JW51B
- Other British ships
- Onslow
- German ships
- Lines of fire

German destroyers

Hipper

Onslow

Onslow hit

Sheffield and Jamaica

Lützow

0900
0830
0830
0830
0930
0930
1030
0940
1020
1015
1200
1145
1145
1130

Convoy route to Murmansk

ICELAND
NORTH ATLANTIC
GREAT BRITAIN
NORWAY
SWEDEN
Winter convoy route
Murmansk
KOLA INLET
BARENTS SEA
SOVIET UNION

1
2
3

Captain Sherbrooke continued to remain on the bridge, refusing to have his wound dressed until he could satisfy himself that command of the flotilla had passed to Lieutenant David Kinloch of HMS *Obedient*. Only then was he persuaded by Surgeon Lieutenant Holland to go below to be treated.

The *Onslow* was to be spared further suffering, for the *Admiral Hipper* and her three destroyers now disappeared to the northeast. Admiral Kummetz still hoped to spring his trap, for the convoy had done exactly what he hoped. It had turned away from his attack, and would undoubtedly fall into the arms of the *Lützow* and her three destroyers, approaching from the south side. Pausing only to destroy the small minesweeper *Bramble*, which had blundered into the *Admiral Hipper's* path while searching for two convoy stragglers, Kummetz attempted to work his way round the escorts towards the convoy.

The battered *Onslow* took up station ahead of the convoy, with the *Achates*, while the other destroyers remained astern, ready to fend off the *Admiral Hipper* if she should re-appear. At around 1045 the corvette *Rhododendron*, on the port side of the screen, reported more enemy ships: the *Lützow* had made contact at last but at a crucial moment her captain lost sight of the convoy in a snow squall, and decided that he dare not take the risk of being torpedoed, choosing instead to keep his distance until the weather cleared.

The respite was a short one, however, for within a few minutes *Admiral Hipper* came into action once more, directing her fire at *Achates*, killing her captain and many of her crew in a hail of shell hits. The *Obedient* was hit next, but apart from suffering casualties from splinters and having her radio aerials shot away, she escaped serious damage. The *Obdurate* was also damaged by splinters but suffered no casualties. The *Achates* was now reduced to zigzagging slowly across the stern of the convoy, too slow to make her way to join the rest of the destroyers.

Under threat from the torpedoes of the British destroyers *Admiral Hipper* again withdrew but only

to come under fire from the fast-approaching *Sheffield* and *Jamaica* who had spotted the German ship at 1130 and had opened up with all their 24 6in guns at a range of 13,500m. Taking the Germans by surprise, they straddled the *Admiral Hipper* with four 6in salvoes, hitting her once and reducing her speed to 27 knots. She hauled round in a circle, heading for safety towards the south east, but as she broke away the *Sheffield* scored two more hits. Faced with this spirited assault, the German force withdrew, the cruisers following in hot pursuit. Another misfortune befell the Germans a few minutes later. The destroyers *Friedrich Eckholdt* and *Richard Beitzen* mistook the British cruisers for their own forces in the poor visibility. The British ships opened fire immediately and the *Sheffield* riddled the *Friedrich Eckholdt* at short range leaving her a burning wreck, although the second destroyer escaped unharmed.

Above inset: Armed with six 11in and eight 6in guns the pocket battleship *Lützow* heads out to sea. Completed in 1933, the *Lützow* had a displacement of 11,700 tons and a maximum speed of 26 knots. Main picture: In the midst of a German attack a British convoy steams forward towards Murmansk. The heavy black smoke of a torpedoed tanker is a grim reminder of the many perils of the Arctic run. The convoy vessels were vulnerable to attacks by surface ships, submarines and aircraft based in occupied Norway.

Sent down from the bridge as part of a damage control party, Leading Seaman Robinson was appalled by the sight that greeted him as he went below decks. Everywhere was in a shambles; amid the smoke and fire his shipmates lay dead and dying. One stalwart petty officer had both his legs blown off but managed to drag himself up a ladder in an attempt to gain the sick bay. Before dying he bitterly exclaimed, 'they will only give me bloody aspirins and no tot.'

The *Onslow* was in a sorry state, with 40 dead and wounded, both forward guns destroyed, a bad list to starboard and holes in the engine rooms and boiler rooms. Damage control parties gradually got to grips with the worst of the destruction, plugging the holes in the hull, shoring up bulkheads and putting out fires. Miraculously she was still able to steam and steer, and so could withdraw from the action, while her three sister ships tried to distract the *Hipper*.

Below: Captain Sherbrooke photographed at Buckingham Palace after his ordeal during the battle of the Barents Sea. For his heroic role in defending the convoy against a superior German force he was awarded the Victoria Cross; and of Sherbrooke's action First Lord A.V. Alexander wrote: 'There was never anything finer in the annals of the Royal Navy.' Below right: The battered HMS Onslow limps back to port in the United Kingdom after her epic defence of Convoy JW51B.

Sherbrooke's wounds were sufficiently severe to cause the doctor to consider them fatal

For convoy JW51B and its weary escorts there was still no rest. After a valiant struggle to save the ship, the *Achates* had to be abandoned, although 81 men out of the original 138 were rescued. Aboard the *Onslow* the damage control parties under the first lieutenant pumped out messdecks and compartments, checking shored bulkheads and restoring lighting and other essential services. The ship's doctor had been working with the sick-berth attendant in conditions of semi-darkness, performing amputations and coping with hideous wounds and burns. Sherbrooke's wound was sufficiently severe as to cause the ship's doctor to consider it fatal at first reaction; and the pain was such that a shot of morphine had little effect. The coxswain supervised a burial party, performing the traditional naval ritual of sewing the bodies into their hammocks before burial; 14 bodies would be tipped into the sea from the quarterdeck.

Worsening weather inflicted further suffering on the battered destroyer. By careful pumping and counter-flooding it proved possible to correct the list

and get the biggest hole in the starboard side clear of the sea. Eventually the *Onslow* was able to work up to 20 knots, and she then left the slow convoy to make her way direct to the Kola Inlet. She arrived at 0700 the next day and berthed at a pier in Murmansk but not before another three badly-wounded ratings had died. In all, 26 wounded men were sent ashore to recuperate in the primitive hospital made available by the Russians.

Sherbrooke returned to the United Kingdom in early January, still with a shell splinter in his face as medical conditions in Murmansk were considered too primitive for its removal. The *Onslow* was made ready and sailed on 29 January, arriving at Scapa Flow in the Orkneys on 4 February. Repairs to the ship took until mid-May when she rejoined her flotilla as escort leader.

The long-term results of the Barents Sea battle were much more important than Sherbrooke and his men could ever have imagined. When the news of the lacklustre performance of the *Admiral Hipper* and the *Lützow* was reported to Hitler he flew into one of his worst rages, and ordered the entire surface fleet to be scrapped and the guns sent ashore for use in coastal batteries. Although the order was later toned down, it precipitated the resignation of Grand Admiral Erich Raeder as Commander-in-Chief who gave way to Admiral Karl Dönitz. Although there was to be one last fatal sortie by the battlecruiser *Scharnhorst*, the Battle of the Barents Sea marked the end of serious attempts to stop British convoys from getting through to northern Russia.

THE AUTHOR Antony Preston is naval editor of the military magazine *Defence* and author of numerous publications including *Battleships, Aircraft Carriers* and *Submarines*.

While *Admiral Hipper* broke away, the *Lützow* came into action against the convoy, and opened fire at 14,000m range, firing salvoes of 11in shells at the merchant ships. The British destroyers once more hurled themselves forward to threaten *Lützow* with torpedo attacks, and after inflicting no more than splinter damage on a solitary merchant ship, the pocket battleship withdrew. Once again the threat of a torpedo attack was sufficient to make the German heavy ships keep their distance.

FIRESTORM AT JUTLAND

When the German and British fleets exchanged salvoes at the Battle of Jutland, the mighty guns of SMS *Derfflinger* found their mark

SMS *Derfflinger* was built at the Blohm und Voss shipyard in Hamburg. Laid down on 1 January 1912, it was launched on 12 July 1913 and completed after the outbreak of war in September 1914.

The *Derfflinger* displaced 26,180 tons, had a length of 210m and a beam of 29m. Main armament consisted of eight 305mm guns in four centreline turrets of two guns each. These guns fired an 893lb shell to a range of 20,500m. Twelve 150mm guns, in single casemate mountings along the upper deck, were provided to deal with attacks from light cruisers and destroyers. The main armour belt varied between 300mm and 100mm in thickness, and ran along the side of the hull from the fore to the aft turret. Four propeller shafts were driven by four German-built Parsons steam turbines giving 63,000 shp, and the power for these was generated by 14 coal-fired, and 4 oil-fired boilers. *Derfflinger*'s top speed was 26.5 knots.

The *Derfflinger* joined the High Seas Fleet in September 1914, and its first action was a raid on Scarborough, in company with other battlecruisers, in December 1914. On 24 January 1915, *Derfflinger* participated in the Battle of Dogger Bank and suffered some light damage from three 13.5in-shell hits. Shortly before Jutland, in April 1916, the *Derfflinger* took part in a raid on Lowestoft. The damage suffered at Jutland was not repaired until mid-October 1916, but the *Derfflinger* had seen its last action of the war. In November 1918, along with the rest of the High Seas Fleet, the *Derfflinger* was surrendered to the British and scuttled eight months later at Scapa Flow in June 1919.

Previous page. The victor and the vanquished. Seen here after the Battle of Jutland, SMS *Derfflinger* (main picture) has been modified to incorporate a heavy tripod in place of her original pole mast. Inset: Only 20 men from a crew of 1300 survived the death throes of HMS *Queen Mary*.

IT WAS THE NIGHT of 30/31 May 1916, and dusk had given way to a calm, clear evening sky. In the Schillig Roads of the German port of Wilhelmshaven – a relatively quiet sector of the Great War – the ships of the Imperial German High Seas Fleet lay at anchor. Yet for the German crews, the atmosphere was electric – they were preparing for battle. On 28 May, orders had arrived from the fleet commander, Vice-Admiral Reinhard von Scheer, for a sortie into the North Sea. Confirmation of this was given by Scheer two days later, when he signalled that the operation would commence in the early hours of 31 May. Anticipation of a major action with the British Grand Fleet spread throughout the entire High Seas Fleet.

At 0100 hours on 31 May, the battlecruisers of the 1st Scouting Group weighed anchor and set sail for the North Sea. They steamed through a swept channel in the minefields protecting the approaches to Wilhelmshaven in company with a squadron of light cruisers and three flotillas of destroyers. The big ships were led by SMS *Lützow*, flying the flag of the group's commander, Vice-Admiral Franz von Hipper. It was followed by the four other German battlecruisers: *Derfflinger, Seydlitz, Moltke* and *Von der Tann*. The *Derfflinger* was the sister-ship of the *Lützow* and a veteran of the Scarborough raid of 1914 and the Battle of Dogger Bank in 1915.

The *Derfflinger's* target was HMS *Princess Royal*, but the first five salvoes were all overs

Sunrise found the ships of the High Seas Fleet passing the fortified island of Heligoland, and the morning's clear weather permitted the men of the *Derfflinger* to see the battleships and escort forces of the main fleet some 30 miles astern. The gunnery officer of the *Derfflinger*, Georg von Hase, found his excitement mirrored by that of his comrades:

'At midday dinner, at which the officers of the watch were not present, there was great excitement and enthusiasm. Nearly everyone was agreed that this time there would be action . . . A few were pessimistic, and said we should soon turn about again without having accomplished anything. The Principal Medical Officer (PMO) always carried a large pocket compass about with him, which he used to place beside him on the table, for, as the wardroom scuttles were closed, and consequently the sea could not be seen, we could not tell when the ship altered course. We used to call him our between-deck strategist. He now kept a careful eye on his compass.'

At 1420, one of the light cruisers accompanying the 1st Scouting Group sighted clouds of steam to port. With two destroyers in company, it veered off and found a Danish steamer, the *N.J. Fjord*, blowing off steam from overheated boilers. The German ships

also discovered that they had been sighted by a British light cruiser from Vice-Admiral Sir David Beatty's battlecruiser force. A few shots were exchanged, and the Battle of Jutland had begun.

Hipper's ships, which had been steaming 347 degrees north in line abreast, now changed course to 190 degrees west in line ahead. German and British light forces were now engaged in a desultory skirmish as both sides waited for the arrival of their respective heavy forces, unaware of the nearness of the enemy's. After an hour's manoeuvring, the smoke of Beatty's battlecruisers was sighted by German lookouts, and the destroyers and cruisers retired behind the protection of their big ships. As the two battlecruiser forces closed on one another, von Hase ordered his gunners to load with armour-piercing shell. He observed the approaching British ships:

'I could now recognize them as the six most modern enemy battlecruisers . . . It was a stimulating, majestic spectacle as the dark-grey giants approached . . . The six ships, which had at first been proceeding in two columns, formed line ahead. Like a herd of prehistoric monsters they closed on one another with slow movements, spectre-like, irresistible.'

When the two forces had closed to 15,000m, the guns of the *Lützow* opened fire, followed by those of the other battlecruisers down the line of the 1st Scouting Group. The *Derfflinger's* target was HMS *Princess Royal*, but the first five salvoes were all overs. Finally, the sixth salvo straddled the target and von Hase gave the order for rapid fire:

'Then began an ear splitting, stupefying din. Including the secondary armament, we were firing on an average one mighty salvo every seven seconds . . . Dense masses of smoke accumulated round the muzzles of the guns, growing into clouds as high as houses, which stood for seconds in front of us like an impenetrable wall and were then driven by the wind and their weight over the ship. In this way we could often see nothing of the enemy for seconds at a time as our forecontrol was completely enveloped in thick smoke.'

At 1558 hours the *Derfflinger* hit the *Princess Royal* twice. One shell penetrated into the port forward reserve coal bunker, causing slight damage, while another blew up on impact with the armour belt. The shock of these two hits temporarily damaged *Princess Royal's* fire control systems, but a third hit two minutes later was even more serious: eight men were killed and 38 wounded when a shell exploded inside the ship. At about the time that the *Derfflinger* scored its third hit on the *Princess Royal*, the first ship was sunk. When the *Von der Tann* struck HMS *Indefatigable* on the forecastle and forward turret,

HIGH SEAS STRATEGY

From the outset of World War I, the course of the naval conflict was dictated by the relative geographical relationship between the German Empire and Britain. Essentially, Britain was able to impose a near total blockade on Germany, and the Grand Fleet's considerable numerical superiority prevented Vice-Admiral Scheer's High Seas Fleet from attempting to break this blockade without risk of total destruction. The Germans sought to rectify this situation by luring out a part of the Grand Fleet, hoping to destroy it in the naval engagement that would follow. Before Jutland, three previous attempts at implementing this strategy had failed – one ending in the German defeat at Dogger Bank on 24 January 1915.

Jutland was originally intended to be a combined operation involving U-boats to ambush the Grand Fleet as it left its bases at Scapa Flow, Cromarty and Rosyth, and airships to scout far in advance of the German fleet. However, the airships proved unable to participate in the action and the U-boats were an abysmal failure. Despite far heavier material losses, the Grand Fleet eventually won the Battle of Jutland.

The High Seas Fleet had failed to break the blockade, or even to redress the balance of forces between the two fleets. The blockade proved instrumental in the defeat and ultimate destruction of the German Empire in November 1918, when the combination of military collapse on the Western Front and starvation on the home front forced it to seek an armistice.

Above left: Vice-Admiral Franz von Hipper, who commanded the German battlecruisers of the 1st Scouting Group during the Battle of Jutland. Left: Battleships from the 3rd Battle Squadron of the High Seas Fleet steam across a calm sea in line ahead.

the British ship exploded in sheets of flame; there were only two survivors from a crew of 1017 men.

Fortuitously, the *Derfflinger* spent the first 10 minutes of the battle unengaged, and it was not until 1617 that HMS *Queen Mary* began to concentrate fire on the German battlecruiser. The *Derfflinger* accordingly shifted fire from the *Princess Royal* to the *Queen Mary*. Von Hase could follow the course of the huge 1400lb shells fired from the British 13.5in guns:

'With each salvo fired by the enemy I was able to see distinctly four or five shells coming through the air. They looked like elongated black spots. Gradually they grew bigger, and then – crash! They exploded on striking the water or the ship with a terrific roar. After a bit I could tell from watching the shells fairly accurately whether they would fall short or over, or whether they would do us the honour of a visit. The shots that hit the water raised colossal splashes. Some of these columns of water were of a poisonous yellow-green tinge from the base to about half their height; these would be lyddite shells. The columns stood up for quite five to ten seconds before they completely collapsed again ... The *Queen Mary* was firing less rapidly than we, but usually full salvoes ... I had to admit that the enemy was shooting superbly.'

'Finally nothing but a thick, black cloud of smoke remained where the ship had been'

At 1624 hours the *Derfflinger* recommenced rapid fire. Six salvoes straddled the *Queen Mary* in succession, and one of the shells of the sixth smashed into her front turrets and detonated one of the magazines. The whole forepart of the ship was utterly destroyed and a fire began to spread through a magazine amidships. Not long after, the remainder of the ship blew up. Von Hase recalled:

'First of all a vivid red flame shot up from her forepart. Then came an explosion forward which was followed by a much heavier explosion amidships, black debris of the ship flew into the air, and immediately afterwards the whole ship blew up with a terrific explosion. A gigantic cloud of smoke rose, the masts collapsed inwards, the smoke cloud hid everything and rose higher and higher. Finally nothing but a thick, black cloud of smoke remained where the ship had been.'

The triumphant *Derfflinger* shifted its fire, its target once again the *Princess Royal*, but, despite three more hits being scored during the next five minutes, only minor damage was caused. Meanwhile, a fierce action between light forces had erupted on the seas

between the two groups of big ships. The secondary armament of the *Derfflinger* engaged the British destroyers, which were making a torpedo attack on the German battlecruisers. In addition, the 5th Battle Squadron, containing the most modern battleships in the British Grand Fleet, was closing on the 1st Scouting Group from the north, and already causing damage to the rear two battlecruisers, the *Von der Tann* and the *Moltke*. But the action drew the British battlecruiser force towards the main part of the German High Seas Fleet, which was approaching from the south. Beatty, on receiving reports of the German main force, ordered his ships to retire north at top speed. Visibility had now become very poor and the smoke of battle added to the confusion. Initially, the 5th Battle Squadron was unable to see Beatty's signal and continued south for some time before retiring. The *Derfflinger* engaged HMS *Barham* at about 1700 hours, but, with the range never less than 18,000m, only four hits were scored and none caused serious damage. *Derfflinger* itself was hit by a 15in shell from one of the British battleships at 1719, ripping a large hole in the forward section and starting several fires. The Ger-

The Battle of Jutland
30 – 31 May 1916

From the outbreak of the First World War, the British Grand Fleet — far superior to the German High Seas Fleet — was able to impose a maritime blockade on Germany. Several unsuccessful attempts to end the blockade had already been made by 1916.

At 2030 on the evening of 30 May 1916, the British Grand Fleet, comprising 24 Dreadnought battleships, three additional battleships, 20 cruisers and some 52 destroyers, under the command of Admiral Lord Jellicoe, put to sea from Scapa Flow in the Orkneys. It was followed after a short interval by the 2nd Battle Squadron from Moray Firth. A smaller fleet under Vice-Admiral Sir David Beatty, consisting of the 5th Battle Squadron and the 1st Battlecruiser Fleet, numbering six battlecruisers and four Dreadnought battleships, left at about 2300 from Rosyth on the Firth of Forth.

The German High Seas Fleet under Vice-Admiral Rheinhard von Scheer, with a strength of 16 Dreadnoughts, six older battleships, and screening forces, put to sea at 0100 on 31 May. Beatty's battlecruiser force speeded ahead and and at 1515 engaged the battlecruisers of the German Scouting Groups. The main fleets drew closer and at 1817 began to exchange fire. At 1835 the German fleet disengaged, turning away to the southwest. By 1900, Scheer was heading east towards and the British battle fleet which opened fire again at 1910. Eight minutes later, the German fleet disengaged for the second time, and under threat from a torpedo attack the British turned westwards at 1923. Chased by British destroyers, the German High Seas Fleet fled for home.

man battlecruiser was now shipping water. At 1724, Beatty, confident that the Grand Fleet was just over the horizon, turned his battlecruiser force east, intending to cross the "T" of the German ships. The two sides exchanged salvoes intermittently as Hipper manoeuvred his ships in an attempt to prevent the British from crossing his bows. The *Derfflinger* was hit a second time at 1755, by one or perhaps two 15in shells. These ploughed through the armour belt in the bows, destroying two 4in armour plates and letting in some 250 tons of water. Unlike the first hit, no internal damage was caused. Simultaneously, the ships of the Grand Fleet entered the action and the battlecruisers of the 3rd Squadron engaged the German 2nd Scouting Group of light cruisers, disabling the *Wiesbaden*.

The 1st Scouting Group now turned away to the east, under torpedo attack from British destroyers. This action probably saved the group from total destruction as it had almost sailed into the midst of the Grand Fleet. The 1st Scouting Group resumed its old course at 1812, by which time the Grand Fleet had deployed into a line ahead that stretched almost seven miles. *Derfflinger* was unwittingly steaming into a crescent moon of 33 British battleships and battlecruisers. Von Hase observed the dangerous position that the German battlecruisers now found themselves in: 'At 8.15 p.m. [Berlin time] we came under heavy fire. It flashed out on all sides. We could

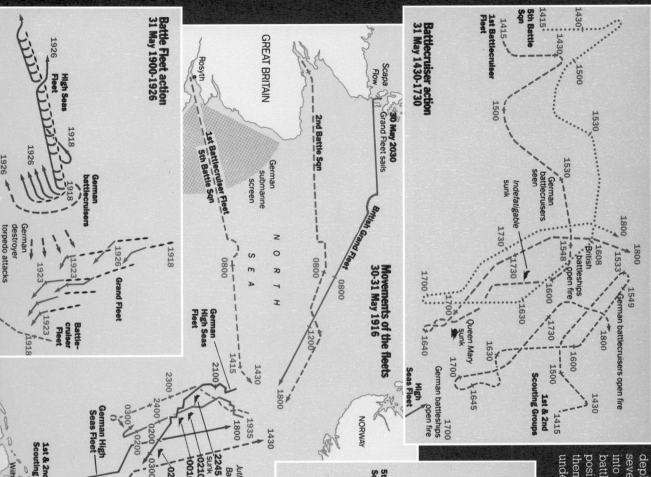

Battlecruiser action
31 May 1430-1730

1415
1430
1500
1500
1530

1st Battlecruiser Fleet
5th Battle Sqn

1500
1415
1415
1430
1430

German battlecruisers seen

Indefatigable sunk

1730
1530
1530

British battleships open fire

1548
1533
1608
1800
1549
German battlecruisers open fire

1700
1640
1730
1730
1600
1630
1800
1600
1500
1415
1430

Queen Mary sunk
1700
1630
1645

1700
German battleships open fire

High Seas Fleet
1st & 2nd Scouting Groups

Movements of the fleets
30-31 May 1916

Scapa Flow
Rosyth
GREAT BRITAIN

1st Battlecruiser Fleet
5th Battle Sqn

German submarine screen

2nd Battle Sqn

30 May 2030 Grand Fleet sails

0800
0800
1200
1415
1430
1800

NORTH SEA

British Grand Fleet

German High Seas Fleet

NORWAY

DENMARK
Jutland Bank
Horns Reef
Wilhelmshaven

1935
1800
1430
2100
2300
2400
0300
0200
0300
0200
0300
0200

German High Seas Fleet
1st & 2nd Scouting Groups

2245 *Frauenlob* sunk
0210 *Elbing* sunk
1010 *Black Prince* sunk
0210 *Pommern* sunk
1918

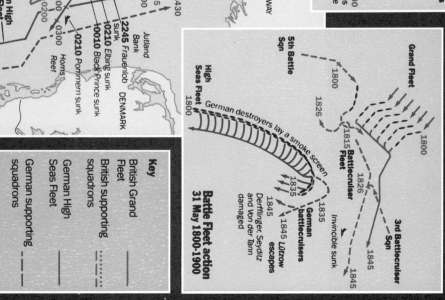

Battle Fleet action
31 May 1800-1926

1926
1918
1918
1926
1926
1926

High Seas Fleet

German battlecruisers

German destroyer torpedo attacks

1918
1926
1923
1923
1923
1918
1926

Grand Fleet
Battle-cruiser Fleet

Battle Fleet action
31 May 1800-1900

5th Battle Sqn

1800
1826

High Seas Fleet
1800

Battlecruiser Fleet

German destroyers lay a smoke screen

1815
1826
1835
1835
1835
1845
1845
1845
Lützow escapes
Derfflinger, *Seydlitz* and *Von der Tann* damaged

German battlecruisers

Invincible sunk

Grand Fleet

1826
1800
1845
1845

3rd Battlecruiser Sqn

Key

British Grand Fleet	
British supporting squadrons	
German High Seas Fleet	
German supporting squadrons	
German submarine screen	

Main picture: Battle practice for Britain's Grand Fleet.
Above: Sighting a British light cruiser. Inset below: HMS
Invincible succumbs to the crashing salvoes of SMS
Lützow and *Derfflinger*.

only make out the ships' hulls indistinctly, but as far as I was able to see, enemy ships were all round us.'

At first, the *Derfflinger* engaged several British armoured cruisers currently enjoined in the battle of light forces that raged in the sea between the two main fleets. After HMS *Defence* was sunk by fire from the *Lützow* and two German battleships, the *Derfflinger* turned southeast and began to trade salvoes with the ships of the 3rd Battlecruiser Squadron. Although the British ships badly damaged the *Lützow* and scored three minor hits on the *Derfflinger*, at 1832 hours HMS *Invincible*, under fire from both the *Lützow* and the *Derfflinger*, blew up. Von Hase was firing his guns at medium range – 9000 metres – when he saw it happen.

'As with the other ships there occurred a rapid succession of heavy explosions, masts collapsed, debris was hurled into the air, a gigantic column of black smoke rose towards the sky, and from the parting sections of the ship, coal dust spurted in all directions. Flames enveloped the ship, fresh explosions followed, and behind this murky shroud our enemy vanished from sight.'

Despite this success, Vice-Admiral Scheer recognised the predicament of his fleet. He ordered his ships to perform a 180 degree turn, hoping that the manoeuvre would turn the tide of battle in the Germans' favour. It was carried out perfectly, and there was now a 20 minute lull in the action as the High Seas Fleet steamed away from the Grand Fleet, the latter being unaware of the position of German ships. The *Lützow* now retired from the action due to battle damage, and Admiral Hipper boarded a destroyer to transfer his flag. The *Derfflinger* found itself at the front of the 1st Scouting Group when Admiral Scheer inexplicably ordered his ships to turn about again, straight into the jaws of the enemy. As the British fire once more gained in intensity, Scheer realised his mistake. He promptly ordered his battleships to retreat, while the 1st Scouting Group was instructed to 'attack with everything'. Captain Hartog of the *Derfflinger* ordered the other battlecruisers to follow his ship at top speed.

Beatty ceased fire at 2040 hours, and the *Derfflinger's* role in the Battle of Jutland came to an end

Known as the battlecruisers' 'Death Ride', the charge almost lived up to its name. Between 1915 hours, when the charge began, and 1937 when this phase of the battle ended, the *Derfflinger* was hit by 14 shells. The most serious hits struck both aft turrets, killing over 150 men and reducing the gun positions to smouldering ruins. The last shell struck the conning tower, and, while it failed to pierce the armour, Von Hase and his men in the gunnery control position were forced to wear gas masks until the poisonous fumes from the explosion had dissipated. The closest the *Derfflinger* got to the whole of the Grand Fleet during the 'Death Ride' was 8000m.

There now followed another lull in the action until 2022 hours, when the battlecruisers of Beatty's force and the 1st Scouting Group exchanged salvoes. The

German Naval Officer, Jutland 1916

In line with the standard dress for all German executive officers, this Kapitänleutnant has the Imperial Crown over the rings on his left sleeve. He wears a blue officer's cap with a black mohair surround, upon which is the Imperial cockade with crown and oak wreath.

Below: HMS *Indefatigable* (right of picture). After the damage sustained at Jutland, the *Derfflinger's* boat deck (right), required extensive repair, and much of the 150mm secondary armament (below right) had to be replaced. Above: The *Derfflinger* is scuttled at Scapa Flow in June 1919.

High Seas Fleet was heading south-southeast in an attempt to retire on Wilhelmshaven, with the 1st Scouting Group on the flank nearest the Grand Fleet. *Derfflinger*'s only functioning turret was put out of action during this exchange of fire. The situation was desperate, since only the *Moltke* possessed functioning armament capable of piercing the armour of the British battlecruisers. Fortunately for the ships of the 1st Scouting Group, the six pre-dreadnoughts of the High Seas Fleet now interposed themselves between the two forces of battlecruisers, fending off the British long enough for Hipper to take his ships round to the other side of the High Seas Fleet. Beatty ceased fire at 2040 hours, and the *Derfflinger*'s role in the Battle of Jutland came to an end.

A confused night action between light forces followed, but, of the ships comprising the 1st Scouting Group, only the *Lützow* was lost, abandoned shortly before 0100 hours on 1 June when it became obvious that battle damage was fatal. When the sun rose on 1 June, the crew of the *Derfflinger* could not see any sign of the Grand Fleet. By 1200, the *Derfflinger* was safely in port at Wilhelmshaven, a battered survivor of the largest battleship action the world would ever see.

THE AUTHOR P. M. Szuscikiewicz is an American writer, based in London, who has published several articles on naval and military affairs.

THE FALL OF SINGAPORE

When Japan entered World War II in December 1941, the island of Singapore, lying at the tip of the Malayan peninsula, was Britain's greatest naval base in the Far Eastern theatre. Well defended along its seafront by powerful guns in concrete emplacements, the port was, nevertheless, almost defenceless on its landward side.

On 8 December 1941, troops of the Japanese Twenty-Fifth Army landed on the east coast of Malaya at Kota Bharu, and on the eastern shores of Thailand at Singora and Patini. Singapore itself was subjected to repeated intensive air attacks.

Opposed only by the 3rd Indian Corps, the Japanese advance down the peninsula was rapid, forcing a hasty evacuation of British troops to Singapore island that was completed by 31 January 1942.

In the face of Japanese air and sea superiority (the capital ships of Singapore's Force Z, HMS Prince of Wales and Repulse, had been sunk on 10 December) Lieutenant-General Arthur Percival, Commander of Malaya Command, organised the defence of Singapore. The Japanese began to land on 8 February on the island's northwest corner. A wedge was struck into the defensive perimeter and the well-trained, well-armed Japanese soon compressed the British force into the port area. With ammunition and fresh water running low, Percival surrendered on 15 February. In 73 days the Japanese had taken Malaya from a force that outnumbered them by 20,000 men. The Allies had lost 9000 killed or wounded and 130,000 were made prisoner. Japanese losses were 9284, of which 3000 were killed. It was Britain's most humiliating defeat of the war.

In September 1943 a small Australian sabotage team penetrated Japanese-occupied Singapore and crippled nearly 40,000 tons of enemy shipping

WHEN LIEUTENANT Ted Carse of the Royal Australian Navy Volunteer Reserve first set eyes on Krait, he was not impressed. She was 78ft long with a beam of only 10ft, and had served as a Japanese spy-boat when the Japanese Navy had been preparing the capture of Singapore. In those days she had been called Kofuku Maru, and her deck had been given a bullet-proof coating of pitch six inches thick. Captured by the Allies, she had been used to carry refugees out of Singapore, first to Sumatra and thence to Bombay.

It was this inconspicuous craft which had been selected for the transport of a team of volunteers back to Singapore, now an important Japanese stronghold. Their mission, codenamed Operation Jaywick, was to enter the Singapore Roads and, operating from two-man Folbot canoes, cripple Japanese merchant shipping lying at anchor with limpet mines. The use of Krait, and Operation Jaywick itself, were both ideas of Major Ivan Lyon, a Gordon Highlander who had served as an intelligence officer at Singapore Headquarters before the Japanese occupation. Driven from the city, he had vowed to return and make an assault on the harbour.

THE KRAIT RAID

ROYAL AUSTRALIAN NAVY: SINGAPORE RAID 1943

Bottom left: Japanese troops exult at their lightning capture of Singapore island. Left: Some of the men of Operation Jaywick: front row – Carse, Davidson, Lyon, Campbell (who assisted in the organisation of the raid), and Page. Second row (in naval uniform) – Crilly, Cain, McDowell and Young; back row – Berryman, Marsh, Jones and Huston. Below: In her modern livery, Krait forges through a heavy swell.

His wife and small son were even then behind barbed wire in Singapore. Lyon and his second-in-command, Lieutenant Donald Davidson of the Royal Navy, a physical-fitness fanatic, who could track animals in the jungle as well as any native, were both going on the mission.

To raise personnel for the operation, volunteers were sought among recruits of the Australian navy, all of whom were about 18 years old, had never been to sea, and had been in the Navy for only a few months. Like the men of Australia's Independent Companies, the volunteers soon began commando training, and in the early months of 1943 they spent 18 hours a day working up to operational readiness at Refuge Bay, north of Sydney. They learned to strip weapons and climb ropes in the dark, and to kill with cord, hand, cosh, knife and machete. They canoed long distances in the surf of Sydney's northern beaches, and at night they practised camouflage and blind manoeuvres. Eventually the 40 volunteers were thinned down to 17, and of these, five were finally selected for the mission. A former Welsh coalminer, Corporal R. G. Morris of the Royal Army Medical Corps, also joined them.

Meanwhile, Ted Carse was busy recruiting his crew and preparing Krait for her mission. A naval stoker joined as engineer, and a 16-stone seaman from the merchant service arrived from Queensland. Captain Bob Page of the Australian Army, whose father had died while a prisoner of the Japanese, was recruited, along with a young naval telegraphist called Horrie Young and a naval cook named Crilley, whose speciality soon had him nicknamed 'Pancake Andy'. Ted Carse then sailed the *Krait* to Cairns in northern Queensland, where she was given a new six-cylinder Gardiner engine and her armament was taken aboard. The weapons included two Lewis guns, two Brens, eight Sten and eight Owen sub-machine guns, and enough revolvers to go round. Several hundred hand grenades were taken aboard, with stabbing knives and throwing stilettos. With the stowing of four Folbot canoes and the strike force's plastic explosives and limpet mines, the boat was ready to sail.

On 9 August 1943, Ted Carse took the *Krait* out of Cairns harbour to sail the 2400 miles to Exmouth Gulf on the far side of Australia where Operation Jaywick would begin. Aboard were 14 men – four soldiers and 10 sailors. The going was uneventful and, with stores fully replenished, *Krait* soon set sail again from the American base. American sailors on the depot ship *Chanticleer* called out, 'You'll never make it to Fremantle. We'll see you again soon.' But *Krait* was going north, not south.

Once out of harbour, Major Lyon immediately ordered that no debris at all should be tossed overboard. Everything had to be collected in tins and sunk. All the men were given sarongs and dark dye to spread on their skin to give them the appearance of Pacific islanders. Then up went a soiled Japanese flag, the sort of ensign one would find on a grubby fishing boat.

Captain Page showed him the capsules. 'They go under the tongue,' he said, 'You'll be dead in five seconds. They're cyanide.'

Between the Indonesian islands of Bali and Lombok lies the Lombok Strait, in places only 12 miles wide, but 4000ft deep, a channel which links the Indian Ocean with the Java Sea. Carse had been warned of strong tides there, but they turned out to be much stronger than he had expected, and for a time *Krait* made no headway at all. The boat, they knew, was already under observation from Japanese posts ashore. At last, as the tide began to change, *Krait* was able to move on.

Ted Carse later recalled a moment when Captain Page, who had joined the army from medical school, showed him the capsules that the canoeists were to take with them. 'They go under the tongue,' he said, 'You'll be dead in five seconds. They're cyanide.' Then he confided that the cyanide wasn't foolproof. Since the men would almost certainly be tortured by the Japanese, Lyon and Davidson were going to shoot the team, then themselves, if capture became inevitable.

In most cases, the Japanese ensign flying from *Krait* was enough to scare away the fishing-boats that they encountered as they continued north. Japanese seaplanes were often sighted overhead and patrol boats made regular passings. On the islands on either side, searchlights and clearings on the hilltops indicated the positions of observation posts. Finally, they saw a glow of lights low on the horizon. The journey from Cairns to Singapore had taken 50 days. Lieutenant Davidson now took command. He gave orders that only three canoe teams would make the

strike; the fourth would be held in reserve. The canoe teams would comprise Lyon with Able Seaman Huston, Davidson with Able Seaman Falls, and Page with Able Seaman Jones. The 17ft black Folbots were loaded with limpets, ammunition, food and water. Each canoe carried three sets of limpets and a spare, primer cord, timing pencils, two magnetic hold-fasts, and a short broomstick with which to apply the magnetic limpets below the waterline. The weapons men again dyed their skin, then donned a suit of black waterproof japara silk over a khaki shirt, securing it tight at the ankles and the wrists. Each man was given a .38 revolver with 100 rounds, a knife, a rubber cosh, a compass, and a medical kit that included morphia. Finally, the men were given the cyanide capsules, but without letting them know that it represented only the second line of defence in the event of imminent capture.

The rendezvous between the canoes and *Krait* was set for midnight on 1/2 October. Lyon and Davidson were familiar with the Singapore region and for the rendezvous point they chose an island called Pompong, one of the Rhios archipelago which stretches from Malaya almost to Borneo. Although the island was 50 miles from Singapore, a long paddle for the canoeists who had inevitably softened up after 50 days of enforced idleness, 14 of them spent in tropical heat, it was chosen as a safe refuge for *Krait*. Lyon wished *Krait* to sail for Australia directly after the deadline had passed, but Ted Carse insisted that he would return 24 hours later if any team had not been accounted for. This point agreed, the canoeists and the crew-members gripped hands and the Folbots disappeared into the darkness. Ted Carse said later, 'Suddenly I found my eyes were stinging badly. Fancy an old man and a bloke who had been at sea for so long standing there in the dark and letting the tears flow.'

At midnight on 26/27 September, the Folbots pulled into a rocky, uninhabited island to sleep. The current had been particularly strong and they had averaged only about two miles an hour, getting nowhere near their intended forward operational base on the island of Dongas, eight miles from Singapore. While four of the men slept, two remained on watch for Japanese patrols and aircraft. They were also observing the Singapore Roads for target ships, and that night they saw a

Operation Jaywick

Key
→ Route followed by the Krait during Operation Jaywick

BURMA
THAILAND
FRENCH INDO-CHINA
MALAYA
SARAWAK
Singapore
SUMATRA
JAVA
Exmouth Gulf
INDIAN OCEAN
Perth
Fremantle
AUSTRALIA
Melbourne
Sydney
Cairns
PAPUA
NEW GUINEA
CELEBES
PHILIPPINES
CAROLINE IS.
PACIFIC OCEAN

convoy assembling, 13 big ships in all. They realised that they might not get such a chance again.

Next night, the canoes were carried down to the water's edge and loaded up. After four hours of paddling it was obvious that they would not reach Singapore. Two miles from the Roads, they were paddling across the tide and the canoes were constantly sheering from their course, forcing the men to expend extra effort to right them. At midnight Davidson gave his whistle and they were ordered to make their way independently back to Dongas, which they had passed that evening. By now the men were weary, their backsides chafed, their hands were blistered and their legs were cramped from being so long in the narrow, laden canoes. Some of them were now suffering from saltwater boils.

As a preliminary move on the following night, the canoes headed for a barren island closer inshore, and there they divided up the targets. First to paddle out were Davidson and Falls, whose targets were the furthest away. The others followed half an hour later. Close to Singapore island a searchlight probed the sea ahead of them, edging across the water and turning it silver. They were then dazzled in the light's full beam, and, hearts in their mouths, they counted the seconds. Then the light snapped off.

Soon the teams were close to the wharves, and welders above them were shedding an eerie, flickering light over the water. The boats were now seeking their targets. Page and Jones paddled into the shadow of a big freighter and Jones fitted the magnetic holdfast as quietly as he could. Page readied the limpets, fixing the first onto the broomstick and sliding it four feet under the surface. Two more were placed as Jones eased the canoe down the ship's side.

They had practised the manoeuvre a thousand times back in Australia and now, their work done, they hung on to the anchor chain while welders' sparks arced over them. Directly above, a Japanese sentry, his rifle slung on his shoulder, looked out to sea and spat into the water beside them. They knew that in an ideal limpet attack the boat should drift into the cover of the ship's bulging hull, but with a six-knot tide they had to propel themselves hard towards the next vessels. They attacked another freighter, then a tramp, so rusty that they had to scrape the rust away with their nails before the limpets gripped the steel. Then, just as Page was fitting the last limpet, he looked up to see a crewman's face staring down at them. Quickly, he felt for the emergency detonator, the one with the one-minute fuze, designed for use if they were discovered. But the face withdrew and they heard a cabin light snap on. Evidently, he thought they were a Malay fishing canoe.

Meanwhile, Lyon and Huston had not been so lucky. Confused by the lights on the shore they had paddled for two hours without locating a target. Finally, they found a big tanker, well down in the water, and they decided to use all their limpets on her. Davidson and Falls, for their part, were almost run down by a fast steam tug and they had had to paddle furiously to escape it. Over the water they heard the Japanese singing and whooping it up in the Singapore Yacht Club. Their first two ships had been too small to limpet, and the Empire Dock, though full of large vessels, was brightly floodlit. Narrowly avoiding a sampan, they

They attacked a tramp, so rusty that they had to scrape the rust away with their nails before the limpets gripped the steel

homed in on a line of ships lying off the commercial centre, attached all their limpets in quick succession, and then began the long paddle back. It had already been decided that, since they were the most likely team to make good time, they would paddle ahead and hold Krait for the others.

Next morning, the other two teams, now safely back on Dongas, heard dull explosions followed by wailing ships' sirens in Singapore harbour. Soon patrol boats were combing the approaches to the Roads and aircraft were racing down Singapore's runways. Almost 40,000 tons of Japanese shipping, including the 10,000-ton tanker Sinkoku Maru, had been destroyed.

After paddling for a full 33 hours, Davidson and Falls reached Pompong Island. They arrived 23 hours before the rendezvous with Krait, and for 15 hours they slept, exhausted, beside their concealed canoe. On Dongas Island, the other crews decided to risk paddling by daylight in order to reach Pompong in time, trusting that the Japanese would take them for fishing canoes. Although they were not challenged, no Malay that they passed was in any doubt as to their identity.

The Krait arrived half an hour late at the rendezvous. For her crew it had been a long, anxious wait, and Ted Carse had even ordered the ship's hull to be scraped during the period. Deciding that it didn't matter if the Japanese were waiting for them in the darkness, Ted Carse shouted out, 'Ship ahoy'. The whole crew was at action stations with Brens, Stens and Owens covering the beach. 'Don't fire unless fired on,' said Carse as a shadow moved over the water. Then Davidson slapped the guard-rail and said, 'It's good to be back'.

At first light the other crews looked out to see Krait already well down the strait. Close to exhaustion, they had landed on the wrong beach. If Krait didn't

Below: Singapore, the key naval base for operations in the Pacific, its harbour crammed with ocean-going freighters raising steam for the voyage out. The canoeists of Operation Jaywick benefited from the myriad of small Malayan boats in the area as in the darkness they were able to blend in with them and thus escape the notice of Japanese sentries aboard their targets. Right: A thick pall of smoke hangs over the Singapore waterfront. Bottom right: The leader of the raid, Major Ivan Lyon shows his exultation on the journey home.

return, Page resolved to commandeer a junk and sail her to Ceylon – he'd done it before. They were out of rations, and Lyon decided to make a trip into the interior to buy food from a Malay kampong. It was risky, but they needed the food.

That night, the men heard Carse's 'Ship ahoy' and they were soon aboard. Near Lombok Island, a Japanese destroyer kept pace with them for half an hour. They all went to action stations, preparing to put into effect the emergency plan, which was to pull alongside, start firing, and then explode *Krait*, themselves, and the Japanese vessel. However, the destroyer eventually pulled away, making for Bali.

On 19 October *Krait* anchored in the American base at Exmouth Gulf. She had been at sea for 72 days and had covered 5000 miles. Of those days, 33 had been spent in Japanese-controlled waters within sight of enemy patrols and observation posts. Years later, the *Krait* was found working as a timber barge in Borneo. She was bought by public subscription, restored, and now sails on Pittwater near Sydney.

Not all the men were so lucky. Major Ivan Lyon went on to plan another raid on Singapore, naming it *Rimau*, the Malay word for the snarling tiger he had tattooed across his chest. In this operation 23 men took part, mostly from the Australian Army and Navy. They included six of the Jaywick party, namely Davidson, Page, Falls, Marsh, Huston and Lyon. Not one man survived: they all died in combat with the Japanese, or were executed on a vacant strip of ground off Singapore's Reformatory Road.

THE AUTHOR Pat Burgess is an Australian writer and broadcaster. He has compiled several programmes from his extensive researches into the history of Australian prisoners in World War II.

HUMAN TORPEDOES

Slipping through the defences of Alexandria harbour, Italian frogmen, mounted on human torpedoes, made a daring attack on two battleships, *Queen Elizabeth* and *Valiant*, of the Royal Navy's Mediterranean Fleet

WITHIN MINUTES of the Italian submarine *Scirè* slipping from her base on the occupied Greek island of Leros, an illicit radio transmitter was tapping out the information to the British. Her commander, Captain Count Julio Borghese, knew only too well that the departure to the enemy. The *Scirè* had three large cylindrical containers built into her deck, each containing an SLC (*siluro a lenta corsa*, or slow-running torpedo), weapons known to their operators as 'maiali', or pigs. The departure of his submarine with its distinctive silhouette would mean only one thing to British Intelligence—a maiali attack on Alexandria. It was the night of 17 December 1941.

Clear of Leros, Borghese ordered full speed ahead and the *Scirè* rapidly built up speed to 17 knots, her phosphorescent bow wave lifting high as she cut through the silent darkness towards Alexandria. He was anxious to get as close to the Egyptian base as possible during the hours of darkness, knowing that orders would already have been issued by the enemy for anti-submarine sweeps, and that he would soon have to take the submarine to a safe depth. Normally, the shallow waters around Alexandria made the detection of submerged boats almost inevitable, but the raid had been planned to coincide with the Nile flood which muddied the sea for miles beyond the delta. The raid had been meticulously planned from the very beginning; months had been spent poring over a detailed model of the Royal Navy base, and all training had been carried out in secret near the 10th MAS Flotilla's headquarters at La Spezia in Italy. The security had been totally effective; the British had received no early information of the coming attack.

Starting from their humiliating defeats at Taranto in November 1940 and at Cape Matapan in March 1941, the Italian Navy was desperate to redress the balance of naval power in the Mediterranean and lift the plummeting morale of the fleet. Thus a daring plan had been devised to sink two of the three remaining British battleships in the Mediterranean as they lay in harbour at Alexandria, HMS *Queen Elizabeth* and HMS *Valiant*. Although they were not to know it, the third battleship, HMS *Barham*, had already been sunk by a German U-boat.

At 2000 hours on 18 December, Borghese brought the *Scirè* up to periscope depth, made a swift search through 360 degrees, and then gave the order to 'blow all ballast'. As the compressed air roared into the tanks, driving out the sea water, he gently eased the boat up to conning-tower height, the water remaining waist high on the narrow upper deck of the submarine. Nervously he and the look-outs scanned the horizon. A lightening of the skyline off the port side fixed Alexandria as being about 10km away. Borghese wondered whether the noise of the compressed air had carried across the still water. He hurried the six frogmen of the attack group down the conning-tower ladder to the deck, where they unplugged the leads which had been charging the electric motors of their maiali from the *Scirè*'s batteries, and then dragged the craft from the containers. Dressed in floppy, rubberised canvas suits, with heavy goggles pulled down over their pointed helmets and their breathing apparatus strapped to their chests, they resembled beings from an alien planet. The group leader, Lieutenant-Captain Luigi de la Penne, was a man who had shown a passion for submarines since boyhood, but who was still considered too young to command one. He had therefore grasped eagerly at the opportunity to join the MAS when it was offered, and at 24 he had already gained a reputation for daring and initiative. Having lost a maiale on his latest, unsuccessful attack, he was anxious to redeem himself and had resolved to sink the British battleships.

The frogmen hastily mounted their craft and directed them towards Alexandria, the silence of the

Attack on Alexandria Harbour
10th MAS Flotilla, Royal Italian Navy, 18-19 December 1941

On the night of 18 December 1941, the Italian submarine *Scirè* released three two-man SLC-type human torpedoes near Alexandria. Some hours later the underwater teams succeeded in penetrating the British naval base at Alexandria. At 0600 hours on 19 December their charges exploded, putting the battleships *Queen Elizabeth* and *Valiant* out of action and seriously damaging the oil tanker *Sagona* and the destroyer *Jervis* which was moored alongside.

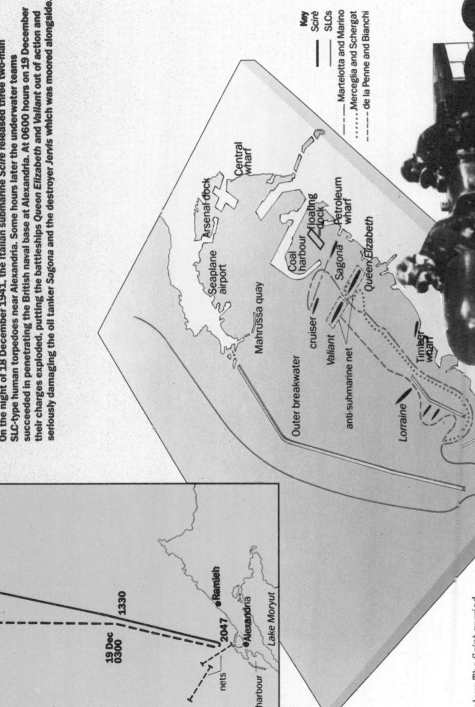

Key
— *Scirè*
— SLCs
--- Martelotta and Marino
····· Merceglia and Schergat
--- de la Penne and Bianchi

Arsenal dock
Central wharf
Seaplane airport
Coal harbour
floating dock
Petroleum wharf
Mahrussa quay
Sagona
Queen Elizabeth
cruiser
Valiant
anti-submarine net
Timber wharf
Outer breakwater
Lorraine
Quarantine wharf

18 Dec 0515
0715
1330
19 Dec 0300
2047
•Ramleh
•Alexandria
Lake Moryut
nets
harbour

Below: The *Scirè* carried three torpedo housings, one forward and two mounted aft of the conning tower.

Above: Human torpedo raids were a serious danger to Allied shipping at anchor.

bitterly cold, pitch-black December night broken only by the muted hum of electric motors and whirling propeller blades. Behind them a whispered 'Good luck' was followed by the thud of the conning-tower hatch slamming shut. Borghese had no intention of dallying for long in such an exposed position. Another submarine, the *Topazio*, would lie off Rosetta the following night to pick up the frogmen, if they managed to escape out to open sea.

Linked together by a cable that kept them only centimetres apart, their heads barely above the water, the frogmen of the three maiali crept slowly towards the harbour entrance. Months of planning were being put into operation and they knew exactly what they had to do, but the bitter cold of the sea water was worse than they had expected, in spite of their rubberised suits. The leader, de la Penne, and his diver, Leading-Seaman Emilio Bianchi, had *Valiant*, a 32,700-ton battleship, as their target; Captain Antonio Marceglia and Leading-Seaman Spartaco Schergat were to sink her sister ship, *Queen*

THE 'HUMAN' TORPEDO

Unlike conventional torpedoes, the 'human' torpedo was devised primarily as a means of transporting a heavy charge to a defended naval target without detection. Cigar-shaped, it consisted of a motorised underwater chariot on which the two-man crew of a pilot and diver sat astride. The whole of the fore section was a 300kg high-explosive warhead fitted with a time fuse. At the target ship it was detached by releasing an airscrew and then held against the target's hull by steel cables secured with magnetic clamps.

The chariot's twin screws were driven by a virtually silent battery-powered electric motor, and it achieved little more than two knots over a range of 24km. Its maximum working depth was 25m, below which its thin metal plates buckled under the pressure of the water. Depth was maintained by control of diving tanks fore and aft, and a third lever-operated crash-diving tank; but it was designed to travel just below the surface. The craft was steered by a control column that also operated the diving and horizontal-plane rudders. Following a magnetic compass, the pilot and diver crouched behind protective housings on the chariot. The men wore skin-tight rubberised suits as insulation against the cold water, and oxygen respirators enabled them to spend long periods below the surface.

The torpedo was fitted with net-cutters and net-lifters to enable the crew to penetrate light harbour defences. Their job done, the men then had a chance of escape astride the chariot, but in the event few succeeded in evading capture.

In December 1941 the battleships *Queen Elizabeth* (seen left at Alexandria) and *Valiant*, each carrying eight 15in guns, were the pride of Britain's Mediterranean fleet. Both were crippled for several months by Italian human torpedoes.

Elizabeth. The third maiale with Captain Vincenzo Martelotta and his diver, Frogman-Sergeant Mario Marino, who were to attack a fully-laden oil tanker, was carrying incendiary bombs.

After two seemingly endless hours crawling through the icy water, the beam from Ras-al-Tin lighthouse suddenly pierced the dark and swept across the frogmen; involuntarily they ducked, before realising that with only their heads above water there was little chance of their being spotted. Nerves jangling, de la Penne called a halt. They wolfed down the provisions they carried in watertight containers, then re-started the motors and pressed forward.

One hour later, as they skirted the jetty wall towards the harbour entrance, they heard a distinct crack directly ahead. Peering into the darkness, the Italians could just make out a faint line of phosphorescence – a boat was coming towards them. Three minutes later there was a far sharper crack, and then a much louder one which caused the maiali to shudder. A guard boat was approaching, lobbing 10kg bombs over the side at regular intervals on the off-chance of destroying any frogmen in the area. A bomb exploded 50m away and the maiali reared wildly; the next would certainly destroy them. And if the warheads went up, the guard boat would be obliterated as well. De le Penne later wrote:

'I remember that I was all huddled up; I closed my eyes, I put my hands over my ears, I heard the explosion – then I opened my eyes and saw that my companions still near me, and I saw that the boat had turned round!'

At last, reaching the three lines of steel anti-submarine nets, they dived and searched for gaps, but there were none. Attempts to manhandle the maiali over the nets proved hopeless – it looked as if the raid was doomed to ignominious failure. Then, as de la Penne puts it, 'It was at that moment that the miracle occurred.' As if by magic, on the stroke of midnight the floodlights came on and lit up the treacherous sandbanks of the harbour mouth. The nets were dragged open and three sleek destroyers, part of the patrol on watch for the *Scirè*, steamed slowly into the channel. In a trice the Italians were alongside, hardly a metre from the destroyers' grey hulls, spluttering and gasping in the wash. Had they been wearing their masks, the reflections from the glass goggles could well have betrayed their presence to the British.

Once inside the harbour, de la Penne gave the signal for the individual assaults to begin, the cable was slipped and he and Bianchi made for the *Valiant*. Italian agents in Alexandria had pin-pointed the position of the battleship and they could see her vast bulk looming less than a kilometre away, a steady half-hour's journey through the oil-slicked, litter-strewn, filthy waters of the harbour. A jangling sound gave them the position of *Valiant*'s anti-submarine net in the choppy water, a rope affair lined with 20cm steel balls. Manhandling the maiale over the net created an appalling racket, but everything was as silent as the grave aboard the British ship, and they had obviously not been alerted. Submerging to a depth of five metres, de la Penne steered straight for the centre of *Valiant*'s hull. They hit it with a dull thud; it seemed impossible that no one should have heard it. The group leader, his hands stiff with cold, found that he was unable to turn off the motor and his maiale plunged 17m to the bottom, spun round once, and then settled in the harbour mud. His diver, Bianchi, had already kicked away from his seat and was

Below: A human torpedo of the type carried by *Scirè*. Bottom: *Scirè* was modified during 1940-41 by the addition of three watertight containers, one forward and two aft, to carry SLC-type torpedoes.

SLC-type human torpedo

Length 6.7m
Diameter 53.3cm
Weight 1200kg
Propulsion 1.6hp electric motor
Maximum speed 4.5 knots
Range 24km at 2.3 knots
Maximum working depth 25m
Warhead 300kg high-explosive
Crew 2

Scirè

making for the other side of the ship to attach his magnetic clamp.

Up to his chest in slimy ooze, de la Penne looked round in the murky water, but there was no sign of Bianchi. He could only assume that at that depth the pure oxygen had caused him to faint and float to the surface. Kicking free of the mud, the maiale commander swam upwards, and quickly glanced around; Bianchi was nowhere to be seen. He saw that it was still quiet aboard *Valiant*, and slipped silently under again. The maiale, all 1200kg of it, was completely immersed in the ooze, its propeller fouled by a steel cable. Frantically he hauled at the torpedo, desperately attempting to manoeuvre it beneath the keel of the battleship, but it looked hopeless. Then it moved, just a centimetre, but it moved. 'I made another strenuous effort,' wrote de la Penne in his account, 'and thus, centimetre by centimetre, working at it for an hour and homing in on the noise of a pump on board, I could hear that I was under the ship.'

Blinded by sweat pouring down his face, and made euphoric by his oxygen at that depth, he took off his mask to clear it; immediately it filled with water. There was nothing else for it, and he was forced to gulp down the noxious harbour water to empty it. In a daze he set the time fuse, covered up the maiale's glowing instrument panel with mud and, sick and half-fainting, struggled to the surface. He was met by a stream of bullets from the now alerted *Valiant*, but struck out for the ship's mooring buoy and found Bianchi crouching astride it. Minutes later *Valiant's* whaler came alongside, the Italians were roughly bundled in, and they were brought before the Officer of the Watch. To their intense relief he mistook them for parachutists and sent them ashore for interrogation. Once ashore, their luck deserted them. Interviewed by Commander 'Buster' Crabbe, himself an eminent frogman (who in the 1950s was to disappear in mysterious circumstances whilst diving beneath a brand new Russian cruiser on a

THE AUTHOR Bernard Brett left the Royal Navy at the end of World War II, and has since written several books on ships, sea power and naval warfare. He is currently preparing a history of modern sea power.

Below: Lieutenant-Captain Luigi de la Penne, leader of the team of frogmen that attacked Alexandria on 18 December 1941. After Italy's surrender, de la Penne took part in British raids on German naval bases in his country. Background: Allied shipping at anchor in Alexandria, sitting targets for Italy's underwater bombers. Inset: The bizarre spectacle of a torpedo team, their deadly weapon humming almost silently below the surface.

courtesy visit at Portsmouth), de la Penne was recognised. Sent back to the *Valiant*, the Italians were closely questioned by her commander, Captain Morgan. De la Penne, giving no more information than required by the Geneva Convention – 'I am Lieutenant-Captain de la Penne of the Italian Royal Navy, and more than that I cannot tell you' – was taken below to an ammunition locker and kept under guard. To his horror he realised that the locker was directly above the maiale's fused warhead.

With hardly 15 minutes to go, acutely conscious of the bomb ticking away beneath his feet, de la Penne asked to be taken to the captain. After informing him of the imminent explosion, the Italian then refused to give the position of the warhead, and was taken back to the ammunition locker and battened down. Bianchi was no longer there. In an agony of suspense that he was never to forget, he waited. 'I thought of a whole host of things, and I prayed, very quickly. And then came the moment, while I was praying I think, that I heard the explosion.' When he regained consciousness he was enveloped by the acrid stench of high-explosive fumes. Miraculously he was alive, and furthermore the magazine hatch had been blown off. In an instant he was scrambling up ladders towards the confusion of the upper deck. He was happy to be alive, and aware that it was going to be a glorious day. As the sun came up behind the *Queen Elizabeth*, moored 500m ahead, there was a sudden flash and the roar of an explosion raced over the water towards them – Marceglia and Schergat had succeeded. That team made its way to the crumbling steps of the old port and actually reached Rosetta, but there the men were arrested trying to cash the British banknotes with which they had been issued. Unknown to Italian Intelligence, they were invalid in Egypt.

The third torpedo team attached their warhead to the oil tanker *Sagona*, but by now the port had been alerted and Martelotta and Marino were picked up as they landed at the old steps. The *Queen Elizabeth*

settled on the bottom, her deck a foot or so above the water. The *Valiant* heeled over as if to capsize, but to de le Penne's chagrin she righted herself and also settled on the bottom.

The *Topazio* waited in vain off Rosetta. The Italian frogmen were interrogated and then shipped off to a prisoner-of-war camp in Palestine. Ironically, reconnaissance photographs did not reveal the extent of the damage they had caused; and the Italians did not press their advantage. Nevertheless, the frogmen had avenged the agonising defeats of Taranto and Matapan, putting the two battleships that remained of Britain's Mediterranean force out of commission for many months to come.

Diving out of the sun, pilots from the Japanese naval air arm pressed home a devastating attack on the US Pacific Fleet at Pearl Harbor

ON 26 NOVEMBER 1941 the six aircraft carriers of the Imperial Japanese Navy's First Air Fleet set sail from Tankan Bay in the Kuriles. Their objective was the US Pacific Fleet's base at Pearl Harbor on the island of Oahu, in the Hawaiian group. The strike force had been assembled under conditions of the greatest secrecy, the carriers and their attendant warships leaving the Inland Sea in groups of two or three in order to avoid any suspicion of hostile activity. For the same reason, their course towards the Hawaiian Islands was shaped across an area of the North Pacific rarely frequented by merchant shipping. Such careful attention both to detail and the needs of security was typical of the meticulous, yet audacious, planning that characterised the entire operation. Its conception owed a great deal to the brilliant Commander-in-Chief of the Combined Fleet, Admiral Isoruku Yamamoto. The actual execution of the raid, however, was in the hands of Vice-Admiral Chuichi Nagumo, flying his flag in the carrier Akagi.

The Pearl Harbor attack was the first major action to be fought by the air arm of the Imperial Japanese Navy. It was to set the pattern for the naval battles of the Pacific war, most of which were fought at long range by the carrier air groups – with the ships themselves rarely, if ever, coming within sight of the enemy fleet. In common with the naval air arms of the other major powers during World War II, Japanese naval aviation had been something of a Cinderella branch of the service during its early years. In competition with the other service arms, it had been forced to fight hard for resources and equipment. However, the Washington Naval Treaties of 1922 had, by limiting the number of battleships allowed to the Japanese Navy, turned its commanders' attention to the aircraft carrier as a substitute for conventional warships. The first Japanese naval pilots had completed their training as early as 1912, and the first Japanese carrier, the Hosho, was completed 10 years later. During the 1920s and 1930s, naval airmen took part in a number of minor actions against Chinese forces. When a full-scale conflict erupted with China in 1937, the Imperial Japanese Navy was able to test its aircraft, crews and tactics under operational conditions. By the time of the Pearl Harbor attack, therefore, Japan's naval air arm had grown to a strength of some 3000 aircraft, almost half of which were serving with frontline combat units.

A Japanese agent on Oahu had reported that nine battleships and 30 other ships were in harbour

The pick of the naval airmen were assigned to the carriers of the First Air Fleet. The carrier forces were grouped into carrier divisions, each comprising two ships and their air groups. Division 1 comprised Akagi and Kaga, Division 5 Zuikaku and Shokaku. The two ships of Division 5 had only recently joined the First Air Fleet, and their aircrews had not had the opportunity to train to the same high standards as their comrades in the other two divisions. Consequently, they were assigned to attacks on the airfields on Oahu, rather than the more difficult warship targets.

The composition of each carrier's air group was broadly similar to that of Akagi, comprising 21 A6M Zero fighters, 18 D3A Val dive bombers and 27 B5N Kate torpedo bombers. The standard of aircrew training and experience was extremely high. Most Japanese pilots were ratings, and a few officers had been selected for a more intensive training course to prepare them for their role as tactical leaders. On completion of eight months' instruction, aircrews had been assigned to a land-based air group. Only after completing this initial assignment, and being assessed as of above average ability, were they considered eligible to join the carrier air groups.

On the evening of 6 December, when the First Air Fleet reached a position some 500 miles to the north of Pearl Harbor, Vice-Admiral Nagumo paraded Akagi's complement on the flight deck to witness the ceremonious hoisting of the 'Z' Flag that Admiral Togo had flown during his famous victory over the Russian fleet at Tsushima in 1905. Once this ritual was over, the carriers altered course and raced south-

ADMIRAL YAMAMOTO'S 'WAR GAME'

The attack on Pearl Harbor was the brain-child of Admiral Isoruko Yamamoto, Commander-in-Chief of the Japanese Combined Fleet (above). As a former naval attaché in Washington, DC, Yamamoto initially opposed the idea of attacking the United States. However, his scepticism disappeared when the opening of hostilities began to look inevitable.

Yamamoto appreciated that Japan would have to destroy the US Pacific Fleet at the outset, and in the naval air arm he recognised a well-honed weapon that was capable of performing this task. He therefore ordered his staff to develop plans for a carrier-borne air strike on Pearl Harbor as one of the opening blows of the war.

The concept was revolutionary in that it departed from the conventional doctrine of carriers as a protective force for battleships. Instead, they were to be deployed as an offensive air weapon. By the spring of 1941, the plans had been drawn up.

Four Japanese carrier air groups began intensive training for their mission in the spring of 1941. In Kagoshima Bay they found an area that closely resembled the anchorage of the US Pacific Fleet. The plan was also evaluated as a 'war game' at the naval war college.

In early November 1941 Yamamoto issued the operational orders for the attack, assigning all six of the navy's carriers to the mission. The carriers came together for the first time later that month, and performed a final dress rehearsal prior to the attack on 7 December.

wards. They were heading towards a point 230 miles short of their objective. From here, the initial strike would be launched early the following morning. As the flight deck crews worked to prepare the aircraft, pilots, observers and radio-operator/gunners completed their final briefings for the mission that lay ahead. Each crew was provided with a chart of the main anchorage at Pearl Harbor. Incorporating the latest intelligence information, received from Tokyo that same day, the chart showed the locations of the US Navy's warships. A Japanese agent on Oahu had reported that nine battleships and 30 other ships were in harbour, but that the American aircraft carriers were not present. Last-minute information on any changes in the enemy's dispositions would be provided by the crews of four E13A Jake reconnaissance floatplanes, which were launched from the seaplane cruisers *Tone* and *Chikuma* shortly before dawn on 7 December.

Page 37 : As a swarm of Zero escort fighters warm up on the flight deck of the *Akagi*, a pilot from the Japanese naval air arm poses for the camera (right). Far left, below: Cheered on by the officers and men of *Akagi*, a Zero sets off on its 200-mile journey to Pearl Harbor. Above: The Imperial Navy's attack on the US Pacific Fleet was preceded by months of careful planning. While pilots honed their dive-bombing techniques, a miniature mock-up of 'Battleship Row' was used by Admiral Yamamoto to evaluate the overall strategy of the raid. Below: A B5N Kate.

At 0600 hours on 7 December, the six Japanese carriers turned into the wind and began to launch the 213 aircraft that made up the first wave of the strike force. In the lead was the B5N Kate of Commander Mitsuo Fuchida, responsible for directing the initial attack. The 89 B5N Kates in the first wave were to carry out the attacks on the US Navy's warships; 40 of them were armed with torpedoes, and the remainder with 1760lb armour-piercing bombs. Both of these weapons had been specially adapted for the Pearl Harbor mission. The standard Japanese Type 91 17.7in torpedo was modified with a wooden 'air tail' that broke off as the weapon entered the water. This improvement meant that the torpedo could be dropped in the comparatively shallow waters of an anchorage, since its initial plunge after release took it only slightly below its standard running depth. Without the air tail it was liable to dive down and hit the bottom. A further modification, dictated by the torpedo's planned use in the confined waters of a fleet anchorage, was the reduction in its effective minimum range. This was made possible by resetting the arming propeller. The armour-piercing bomb was an improvisation,

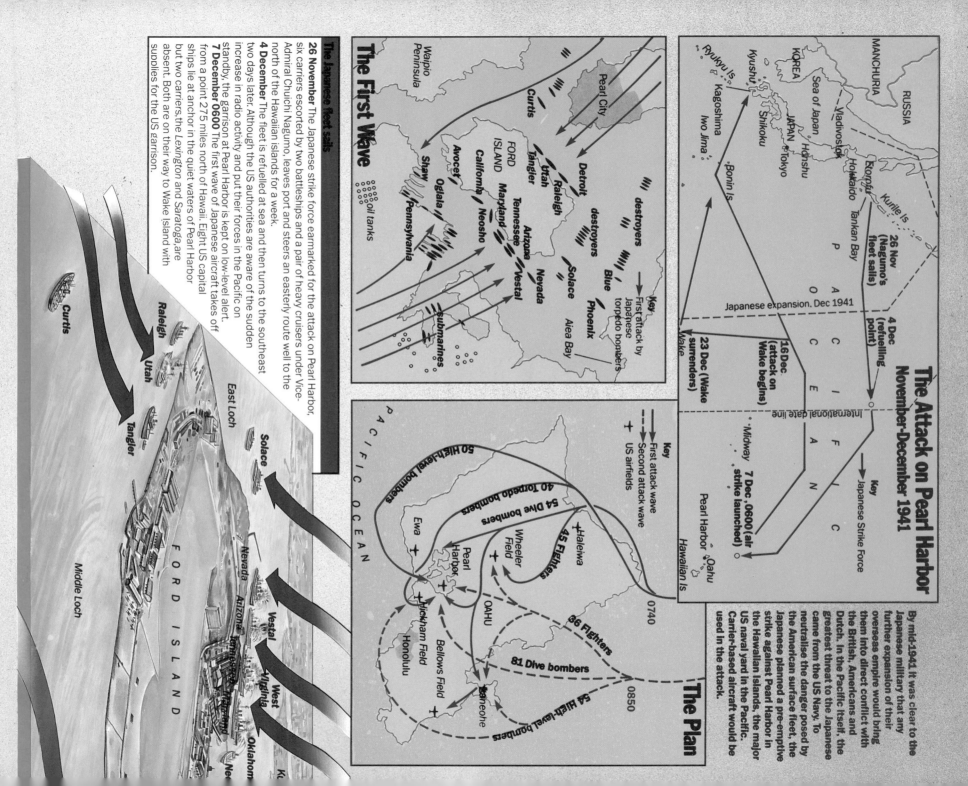

The Attack on Pearl Harbor
November–December 1941

MANCHURIA
RUSSIA
KOREA
JAPAN
Vladivostok
Hokkaido
Honshu
Tokyo
Sea of Japan
Shikoku
Kyushu
Kagoshima
Iwo Jima
Ryukyu Is.
Kurile Is.
Tankan Bay
Etorofu

26 Nov (Nagumo's fleet sails)
4 Dec (refuelling point)

Bonin Is.

Japanese expansion, Dec 1941

International date line

16 Dec (attack on Wake begins)
23 Dec (Wake surrenders)
Wake
'Midway

Key
→ Japanese Strike Force

7 Dec, 0600 (air strike launched)
Pearl Harbor
Oahu
Hawaiian Is

P A C I F I C   O C E A N

By mid-1941 it was clear to the Japanese military that any further expansion of their overseas empire would bring them into direct conflict with the British, Americans and Dutch. In the Pacific itself, the greatest threat to the Japanese came from the US Navy. To neutralise the danger posed by the American surface fleet, the Japanese planned a pre-emptive strike against Pearl Harbor in the Hawaiian Islands, the major US naval yard in the Pacific. Carrier-based aircraft would be used in the attack.

The First Wave

Waipio Peninsula
Pearl City
Curtis
Detroit
Raleigh
Tangier
Utah
FORD ISLAND
California
Maryland
Tennessee
Arizona
Vestal
Nevada
Neosho
Solace
Shaw
Ogala
Avocet
Pennsylvania
Blue
Phoenix
destroyers
submarines
oil tanks
Alea Bay

Key
→ First attack by Japanese torpedo bombers

The Plan

P A C I F I C   O C E A N

50 High-level bombers
54 Dive bombers
40 Torpedo bombers
Ewa
Haleiwa
45 Fighters
Wheeler Field
Pearl Harbor
36 Fighters
OAHU
Hickham Field
Bellows Field
Honolulu
81 Dive bombers
Kaneohe
54 High-level bombers
0740
0850

Key
– – – First attack wave
——— Second attack wave
+ US airfields

The Japanese fleet sails

26 November The Japanese strike force earmarked for the attack on Pearl Harbor, six carriers escorted by two battleships and a pair of heavy cruisers under Vice-Admiral Chuichi Nagumo, leaves port and steers an easterly route well to the north of the Hawaiian islands for a week.

4 December The fleet is refuelled at sea and then turns to the southeast two days later. Although the US authorities are aware of the sudden increase in radio activity and put their forces in the Pacific on standby, the garrison at Pearl Harbor is kept on low-level alert.

7 December 0600 The first wave of Japanese aircraft takes off from a point 275 miles north of Hawaii. Eight US capital ships lie at anchor in the quiet waters of Pearl Harbor but two carriers, the *Lexington* and *Saratoga*, are absent. Both are on their way to Wake Island with supplies for the US garrison.

Curtis
Raleigh
Utah
Tangier
Solace
East Loch
Middle Loch
Nevada
Arizona
Vestal
West Virginia
Oklahoma
FORD ISLAND

since no such weapon existed in the naval air arm's inventory. It consisted of a 14in shell fitted with stabilising fins. Since the bomb's weight was similar to that of the torpedo, a B5N Kate could carry one of these weapons as an alternative payload. It could be delivered from level flight against stationary ships, although dive bombing was preferred against ships that were underway. The D3A Val had been developed specifically for that role. However, since its

standard bomb load was no more than a single fuselage-mounted 550lb bomb, plus two 130lb bombs underwing, the 81 D3As launched in the first wave of the Pearl Harbor attack were assigned to airfield targets rather than the warships. Fighter escort was provided by 43 agile and well-armed A6M Zeroes. These were responsible for securing air superiority over the target, and, if no fighter opposition was encountered, their secondary mission was to strafe enemy airfields.

As the last aircraft of the first attack wave left the flight decks, formed up in formation and set course for Oahu, the cheering sailors who had waved them off set about preparing to launch a second group of aircraft. This was launched one hour later, and comprised 50 B5N Kates, 80 D3A Vals and 40 A6M Zero fighter escorts. The formation was led by Lieutenant-Commander Shigekazu Shimazaki. A further 39 Zero fighters were held back in reserve to provide an air-defence umbrella for the carriers. Meanwhile, the first attack wave was nearing its target, using the broadcasts of the commercial Hawaiian radio stations as homing beacons. Two variants of the plan of attack had been prepared, one to be used if complete surprise was achieved,

Above: The Japanese naval aviation collar patch. The schedule for the extensive Japanese air, naval and amphibious operations against Malaya, Siam, the Philippines and Hong Kong was largely governed by the fact that it was the custom of the US Pacific Fleet to be at anchor in Pearl Harbor each Sunday afternoon. The result of the Japanese attack was devastating, with not a single US battleship escaping unscathed. Top: A flight of B5N Kates. Despite its vulnerability, the Kate proved its worth during the attack on Pearl Harbor.

and the other if the defences had been alerted. If the Americans were caught unawares, the torpedo bombers would spearhead the attack on the warships, followed closely by the bomb-armed Kates. The D3A Val dive bombers would then attack the naval airfield on Ford Island, in the middle of the anchorage. If the approach of the Japanese aircraft had been detected, however, the initial priority would have been to neutralise Hawaii's air defences. An American radar station had, in fact, picked up the approaching formation, but its warning was ignored – the contact was thought to be a squadron of B-17 Flying Fortresses due in from California.

At 0740 hours, the leading Japanese aircraft broke cloud cover and sighted the northern coast of Oahu. Commander Fuchida fired a single flare, the signal to carry out the first attack option. When the fighter escort failed to respond to this signal, Fuchida mistakenly believed that his first flare had not been seen. He therefore fired a second. As two flares signified that the second attack option was to be implemented, the dive bombers and torpedo bombers attacked simultaneously, rather than in succession as had originally been intended. The D3A Val dive bombers split into two groups. The 26 aircraft from Shokaku, led by Lieutenant Kakuichi Takahashi, headed for the Naval Air Station on Ford Island and the nearby US Army Air Force base at Hickam Field. Directed by Lieutenant Akira Sakamoto, the 25 Vals of Zuikaku headed towards Wheeler Field, in the centre of the island, identified by Japanese intelligence as the hub of the Hawaiian air defences. Commander Fuchida's B5N Kate transmitted the radio message 'Tora, Tora, Tora' to inform Admiral Nagumo that surprise had been achieved and that the attack was imminent. By a freak of atmospheric conditions, the message was picked up not only by the Akagi, but also by Yamamoto's flagship off Japan.

Of the seven ships moored in 'Battleship Row', only two escaped the Japanese torpedoes

None of the Pacific Fleet's aircraft carriers was in harbour, and so the battleships became the focus of the B5N Kates' attack. Seven of these ships were moored alongside Ford Island in 'Battleship Row', and an eighth was in dry dock. (The ninth battleship reported by the Japanese agent was the former battleship Utah, which had been relegated to target-ship duties.) Lieutenant-Commander S. Murata led the torpedo-carrying B5N Kates into the attack. Of the seven ships moored in 'Battleship Row', only two escaped the Japanese torpedoes – these were moored on the inside of sister ships, and thus could not be reached by the deadly underwater weapons. Although the two ships were hit by armour-piercing bombs, they escaped serious damage. Of the five battleships exposed to torpedo attack, four were sent to the bottom. The fifth, USS Nevada, was hit by a bomb and a torpedo during the first wave of Japanese attacks. She nonetheless managed to get underway and headed for open water. The target ship Utah received a disproportionate share of attention from the torpedo bombers and was sunk. One of the bomb-carrying Kates scored a hit on the battleship USS Pennsylvania in dry dock, causing heavy damage.

The attack is launched

7 December 0740 The first attack aircraft break through the cloud cover over Oahu and form up into two attack waves.

0800 As dive bombers blast US airfields at will, torpedo bombers attack the ships at anchor in Pearl Harbor. Five of the US battleships, the West Virginia, Arizona, Nevada, Oklahoma and California, take hits.

A target ship, the Utah, also sustains damage.

0835 Supported by fresh waves of high-level and dive bombers, the Japanese pilots continue the attack. The West Virginia is sinking, Utah has capsized, the Tennessee is shrouded in flames, Arizona has settled on the bottom and Oklahoma has received a number of mortal blows.

0850 The Nevada is forced to beach.

0945 The attack ends. The Japanese have inflicted a crippling blow.

Southeast Loch

California

Waipio Peninsula

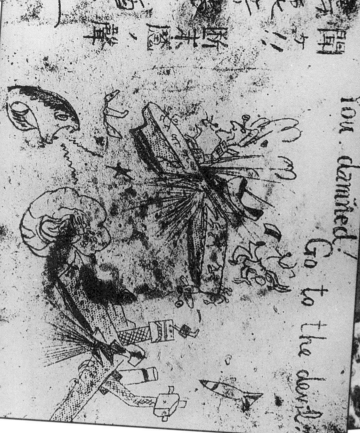

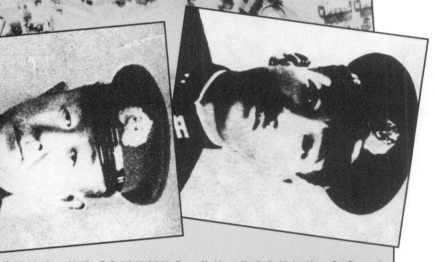

'BATTLESHIP ROW'

Commander Mitsuo Fuchida (left) described the attack on Pearl Harbor:

'As we approached, the sky cleared and through my binoculars I recognised the American battleships at their anchorage, eight in total, but to my great regret no aircraft carriers could be seen... Lieutenant-Commander Murata released his torpedo and scored the first hit on a battleship, the *West Virginia*, and an enormous fountain of water rose up beside it. Then, immediately, the second hit on target, the third, the fourth!

'Beginning my second attack I saw an enormous explosion beside our target. Scarlet flames and a gigantic column of black smoke began to rise into the air. It was, as I judged immediately, the ammunition magazine of a battleship, the effect of two penetration bombs dropped by No.2 Squadron from the *Kaga*. Through my binoculars I identified the victim as the *Arizona*. To the north, the *Nevada* was also in flames...

'Just to the south, the *Maryland* seemed undamaged and it was this battleship that I indicated to my leading pilot... I distinctly saw my four bombs falling towards the target... Holding my breath, I saw the bombs become smaller and smaller and finally disappear. Suddenly, there were two puffs of white smoke on the bridge of the ship, and I shouted "Two strikes on target!"'

Of the 143 serviceable USAAF aircraft on Oahu, less than one-third survived the Japanese attack

While leading a formation of nine A6M Zeroes on a strafing attack, Lieutenant Fusata Iida's fighter was damaged by anti-aircraft fire. Since the Zero was losing fuel rapidly, Iida knew that he had insufficient reserves to reach his carrier. He therefore deliberately crashed his aircraft into the Naval Air Station's hangars. The US Marine airfield at Ewa was similarly devastated, 33 of its 49 aircraft being utterly destroyed. On the main USAAF airfields – Hickam Field and Wheeler Field – aircraft were lined up wing-tip to wing-tip in neat rows so that they could be more easily guarded against sabotage. The result was inevitable. Of the 143 serviceable USAAF aircraft on Oahu, less than one-third survived the Japanese attack. Only 11 American fighters were able to take off and engage the enemy, five of them using a small training airfield at Haleiwa that Japanese intelligence had overlooked. Lieutenant Ken Taylor scored one of the defender's few aerial victories after he manoeuvred his Curtiss P-40 onto the tail of a

While the B5N Kates concentrated on the warships, the D3A Val dive bombers and strafing A6M Zeroes were wreaking havoc on Oahu's airfields. Ford Island was the first to feel the concussion of exploding Japanese bombs. This airfield housed 29 Consolidated PBY patrol flying boats, and within a few minutes all but one of them were destroyed. A further 27 of these aircraft were destroyed at the Naval Air Station at Kaneohe Bay, on the northeast of the island.

D3A Val:

'I let him have a short burst – I don't think I fired more than 15 rounds. As he flamed, he went into the most perfect slow roll I've ever seen. All I could see was his wheels sticking out of the smoke, and fire spurting from the ship. He hit the surf right off the beach.'

The second attack wave arrived over the target at about 0850 hours, but there was virtually no respite for the defenders between the two phases of the Japanese attack – A6M Zeroes from the first wave had continued to roam over the island. However, the second-wave aircraft were poorly equipped to deal with capital ships. The only remaining B5N Kates were the 50 aircraft from the inexperienced *Shokaku* and *Zuikaku* air groups. These were assigned to airfield targets, leaving the 80 D3A Val dive bombers from the four well-trained carrier groups to make follow-up attacks on the warships. The original planning had envisaged that the Vals, with their comparatively light bomb loads, would concentrate on finishing off the Pacific Fleet's aircraft carriers. Since the carriers had unarmoured flight decks, this part of the plan had seemed perfectly feasible. However, the Vals stood considerably less chance of inflicting a mortal blow against battleships. The main weight of their attack fell on the USS *Nevada*, which was attempting to get out to sea. Bombs showered all around her, and at least three hits were scored. This

damage, added to the effects of the earlier attack, were sufficient to cause the battleship to be beached, rather than risk her sinking and blocking the main channel leading from the anchorage to the open seas. By the time that the second wave of attackers arrived, however, the American defences were in action and 15 of the D3A Vals were shot down.

The operation had been an outstanding tactical victory for the Japanese Navy

By 1000 hours the Japanese aircraft had completed their mission and were withdrawing to the north. The last to leave the target area was a section of A6M Zeroes responsible for assessing the damage. Their pilots were able to report that four battleships were sunk, or were in the process of sinking, with four more damaged. Various other ships had been sunk or damaged, and a total of 188 aircraft destroyed. By 1330 hours the First Air Fleet had recovered its returning aircraft, and Vice-Admiral Nagumo set course for Japan. His losses, although far from negligible, had not been serious. Out of an attacking force of 350 aircraft, only 29 had failed to return. The operation had been an outstanding tactical victory for the Japanese Navy, thanks to the exemplary performance of the naval aircrews. The Pearl Harbor attack was the largest and most complex carrier air strike ever to be attempted, and it showed the world that the Japanese naval air arm had matured into a formidable fighting force.

THE AUTHOR Anthony Robinson was formerly on the staff of the RAF Museum, Hendon, and is now a freelance military aviation writer. His books include *American Air Power* and *Aerial Warfare*.

Far left: Taken in the aftermath of the Japanese attack, this aerial photograph shows five US battleships at anchor on the southern shore of Ford Island. They are, from bottom to top: USS *Arizona, Tennessee* and *West Virginia, Maryland,* and *Oklahoma* (capsized). **Inset left** (above): Commander Mitsuo Fuchida. **Inset left** (below): Vice-Admiral Chuichi Nagumo. **Bottom left:** One of the propaganda leaflets carried by Japanese airmen during the raid on Pearl Harbor. The drawing depicts a battleship exploding, together with a caricature of President Roosevelt emerging from the funnel of a stricken aircraft carrier. A further warning appears in the Japanese script: 'Listen to the voice of doom – open your eyes, blind fools.' **Below:** Billowing clouds of smoke and raging fires shroud *West Virginia* and *Tennessee*, providing testimony to the wrath of the Japanese dive bombers.

RUNNING THE GAUNTLET

Volunteers to a man, the valiant merchant-navy MGB crews braved the German blockade to bring vital war materials from Sweden to Britain

SIR ANDREW DUNCAN, a senior member of the British Iron and Steel Federation, wrote on 9 July 1940. 'It is of paramount importance that we receive the war stores now on order in Sweden. We MUST, repeat MUST, at all costs get them to England.' Without these vital supplies, he knew that Britain's war effort was likely to collapse.

The man to whom this tall order was given was George Binney, a 40-year-old metallurgist who had been sent to Sweden on the outbreak of the war to make contact with local industrialists. Ostensibly, Binney was working for the federation but, in fact, he had close contacts with the Ministry of Economic Warfare as well as military and naval intelligence. Binney himself was a rugged individualist who knew the Scandinavian countries well, having led several pre-war expeditions to the Arctic. He was tough and, on occasion, ruthless, yet he possessed considerable charisma.

Despite a number of successful runs between 1941 and 1942, Britain's need for the products of Sweden's steel industries remained urgent. Although, by this stage, there was a Swedish ban on any break-out attempts by interned ships, there was no reason why a British merchant ship could not sail to Sweden, collect a cargo and return to Britain. Binney argued that converted motor gun boats (MGBs), flying the Red Ensign, would be the most suitable craft. Such ships, with their high speed and shallow draught, had an excellent chance of avoiding detection and could

The sailors who spearheaded the blockade-running missions to Sweden during World War II under the leadership of George Binney, were experienced members of the Merchant Navy, well qualified to crew the fleet of motor gun boats (MGBs) used on many of the operations.

Their vessels, although primarily designed as small cargo ships, were ideally suited to Binney's needs. Some 117ft long with a beam of 10ft, their cargo-carrying capacity could be easily increased by the removal of accommodation areas fore and aft.

The MGBs, once converted, also carried an array of light defensive armaments: a pair of 20mm Oerlikon mountings, two Vickers machine guns on either side of the bridge and a quadruple Vickers aft of the bridge.

However, their true power lay below decks in the engine room. Each MGB was driven by three Davey Paxman Ricardo 16-cylinder diesels, each developing 1000 horsepower. The MGBs had a top speed of 23 knots, but even when loaded with a 40-ton cargo, they were able to travel some 1200 miles at an average speed of 17 knots. Unfortunately, despite these impressive figures, the engines themselves were prone to mechanical failure. An Admiralty survey had revealed the possible problems and had advised that suitable replacements be installed. However, any engineering work would have halted the clandestine trips to Sweden, so Binney opted to continue with the original engines and rely on his crews' skills to keep them running.

Above: The cap badge of a member of the Merchant Navy.

penetrate the enemy's temporary minefields with impunity. Hence the birth of Operation Bridford, using five gun boats, each of which could carry 40 tons of cargo. The plan was for the MGBs to enter the Skagerrak, a 100-mile wide channel between Denmark and Norway, at night under suitable weather conditions and with no moon. After entering Swedish territorial waters, they would head for the port of Lysekil, where they would load their cargoes. For the return journey, they would again select the right weather conditions, sail westwards through the night and be well into the North Sea by daylight, where RAF cover would be available. Two surviving ships from a previous mission, *Lionel* and *Dicto*, were anchored in Brofjord, near Lysekil, and would be used as depot ships for the MGBs.

On 25 April 1943 the Admiralty allocated Binney five MGBs that had been originally ordered by the Turkish government. The boats were handed over to Ellermans Wilson of Hull, who would manage them. Binney personally selected the crews, all of whom were experienced seamen from the company's merchant fleet. Each boat had a volunteer crew of 20 men and 80 per cent of them came from Hull. Binney named the five vessels the *Nonsuch*, *Hopewell*, *Master Standfast*, *Gay Corsair* and *Gay Viking*. By the middle of October 1943, everything was ready for the first trip.

On the evening of 26 October, the weather conditions were judged to be perfect and in the early evening the five boats proceeded slowly down the Humber and through the coastal minefields. Once clear of these obstacles, they increased speed and set course for the Skagerrak. It was only then that Binney told the crews of their real destination.

Shortly after clearing the minefields, *Gay Viking* became the first victim of the MGBs' notoriously unreliable engines and had to stop to repair a fault with her starboard motor, losing touch with the other four craft in the process. Repairs were quickly carried out, and the ship's master, Captain 'Whit' Whitfield, decided to press on alone, hoping to catch up with Binney and the rest of the flotilla early on the morning of the 27th. Meanwhile, the other four boats had been forging across the North Sea towards the Skagerrak, but during the day, Binney became alarmed at repeated sightings of German aircraft. His fears were increased when he had to alter course to avoid a Danish fishing fleet. He became certain that this mission had been compromised, and, at 1940 hours on the 27th, reluctantly ordered his four craft to return to Hull.

This left the *Gay Viking* tearing on alone towards the Skagerrak, the crew unaware that Binney had turned back. Whitfield was determined to get through and was not unduly worried when German aircraft flew over his ship. As *Gay Viking* entered the Skagerrak, Whitfield, to the disgust of his crew,

Below left: The mastermind behind the blockade-running missions, George Binney (centre), jokes with some of his men. Below: An early success. A tanker lies at anchor after a hair-raising dash across the North Sea in March 1941. As Binney's operations evolved, motor gun boats (MGBs), such as the *Gay Viking* (above left), made the run to Sweden. Main picture: Gunners on the *Nonsuch* blaze away. Top left: *Nonsuch*, skippered by Captain D. Stokes (right), returns to base with the *Hopewell*.

Although Binney's flotilla of blockade-busting vessels made great use of their speed to avoid detection, each motor gun boat was fitted with an array of defensive armaments that consisted of machine guns and anti-aircraft guns. Far left: Leslie 'Ginger' Brown mans quad-mounted Vickers guns beneath the *Nonsuch's* Red Ensign. The ship also carried 20mm Oerlikon guns, mounted fore and aft (below). Left: Some of the captains of the 'Grey Ladies'. Clockwise from top: George Holdsworth of the *Master Standfast*; Harry Whitfield to the *Gay Viking*; 'Jacko' Jackson of the *Gay Corsair*; and 'Ginger' Stokes of the *Hopewell*.

hoisted a Nazi flag, hoping that the ship looked sufficiently like a German E-boat for him to get away with it. At 0400 hours on 28 October, Whitfield was in Swedish territorial waters, where he ordered the dumping of all surplus ammunition, leaving only one pan for each gun, before pressing on toward Lysekil.

At the port, a small reception committee of British diplomats and officials from the Legation in Stockholm, together with friendly Swedes, was waiting on the cliffs above the harbour; they had been alerted by the SOE (Special Operations Executive) that the gun boats had sailed, and the cargoes were safely stored and waiting down on the jetty in the town below. Shortly after 0700, the *Gay Viking* roared into the harbour, flying an enormous Red Ensign from her mast, together with the Wilson Line flag. Practically the whole town turned out to welcome her. 'Have a drink', said Whitfield to Helge Fallquist, the local customs officer, who was the first man aboard.

During their stay at Lysekil, while the *Gay Viking* was loaded with cargo, its crew was accommodated ashore. On the evening of 29 October Whitfield sailed for England, arriving safely at Immingham on the morning of the 31st. Binney was elated at the success of the *Gay Viking*, but disappointed that all five boats had not made it. He was also being severely criticised for his decision to turn back, but was still determined to succeed. On the same evening as the *Gay Viking's* arrival, he resolved to return to Sweden with *Hopewell*, commanded by Captain 'Ginger' Stokes, Captain Jacko Jackson's *Gay Corsair* and the *Master Standfast* under Captain George Holdsworth. However, shortly after sailing, the *Gay Corsair* was forced to drop out with a faulty gearbox, leaving the other two ships to carry on. Early on the morning of 2 November, the *Master Standfast* became separated from the *Hopewell* and later stopped to fix her position by radio direction-finding. Unfortunately, the noise of her powerful diesels had been picked up by the hydrophonics of a German patrol craft, *Vp.1606*. Arthur Hannah, the *Master Standfast's* boatswain, saw the *Vp.1606* creeping up astern and correctly identified her as a Bremen-built

trawler, Tom Jardine, the mate, was not so sure; he thought that the ship was a Swedish pilot vessel.

The captain of *Vp.1606* initially identified the *Master Standfast* as another German patrol craft but then realised that it was far too small. Accordingly, his vessel's main armament was brought to bear and the *Master Standfast* was challenged. In an attempt to gain time, Holdsworth asked for a pilot, but the *Vp.1606* switched on her searchlight, blinding the crew of the gun boat. Some of his crew urged Holdsworth to make a high-speed run for the safety of Swedish waters, but it was not a practical proposition in view of the numerous rocks and islands that dotted the area. Al Brown, the SOE representative on board, switched on the navigation lights to show the 'Swedes' – if they were Swedes – that the *Master Standfast* was friendly, while other members of the crew prepared the vessel's scuttling charges. Meanwhile, the *Vp.1606* had steamed round the *Master Standfast* and was 70yds on her starboard beam, steering a parallel course.

Vp.1606 had already fired one burst of gunfire as a warning, but a second burst demolished the wireless mast and the aerials, severing all communications and wrecking the bridge, and severely wounding some of the crew, including Holdsworth, in the process. While the unharmed members of the crew attempted to aid the wounded, the Germans boarded the MGB and removed the crew to their own craft, and thus took the *Master Standfast* in tow to Frederickshavn in Denmark, where the crew were landed as prisoners of war and where Holdsworth later died of his wounds.

The *Hopewell* had continued to Lysekil, arriving at 0615 hours on 2 November. After taking on 40 tons of cargo, *Hopewell* was delayed by the weather and began the return journey to Britain on 10 November. Just after clearing Swedish waters, *Hopewell's* main gearbox seized up and the ship was forced to put back to Lysekil; a replacement was quickly sent to Gothenburg by Dakota. The repairs required could not be carried out at Lysekil, so the ship steamed slowly round to Gothenburg, where her arrival caused a sensation as the Swedes turned out to cheer the first British merchant ship seen in the city for nearly four years. After the repairs had been completed, the *Hopewell* returned to Lysekil, where she re-embarked her cargo, before making a swift pas-

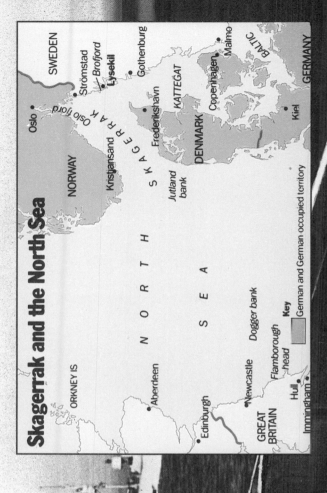

Skagerrak and the North Sea

Key

German and German occupied territory

INDUSTRIAL LIFELINE

The German occupation of Norway, Denmark and much of western Europe, and the material losses associated with the evacuation from Dunkirk in 1940, placed enormous strains on Britain's industry during the subsequent drive to rearm. Starved of raw materials and facing a massive demand for equipment, key firms were brought to the point of collapse.

In particular, shortages of the high-quality products of Sweden's iron and steel plants caused great government concern. With enemy forces firmly in control of both Denmark and Norway, the only feasible sea route to Sweden, through the 100-mile wide Skagerrak, appeared a risky proposition. However, George Binney, the key figure behind blockade running, believed that, given the right weather conditions, ships might be able to force a passage and reach British shores.

In January 1941, after several months of fighting for official backing, Binney was given the go-ahead to test out his theory. Binney's plan, codenamed Rubble, called for five Norwegian merchantmen to escape from the Swedish ports where they had been interned since the early days of the conflict.

Although fraught with danger, the mission was highly successful, with some 25,000 tons of raw materials and engineering equipment being transported back to England.

With mounting confidence, Binney then planned a second break-out attempt, codenamed Performance. However, the operation went disastrously wrong: of the 10 ships that took part, six were sent to the bottom of the sea, two others returned to Sweden and only the remaining pair reached England.

The failure of Performance led Binney to drop any further break-outs. Henceforth, he would lead a flotilla of motor gun boats to bring out the vital war supplies.

sage back to Hull. While Hopewell was at sea on her return voyage, the other three gun boats, Gay Viking, Gay Corsair and Nonsuch, set out again for Sweden but the attempt was abandoned because of heavy weather.

Two days later Gay Corsair, commanded by Captain Bob Tanton, set out alone and, despite rough weather, succeeded in reaching Lysekil, returning to Hull on Christmas Eve 1943 with 40 tons of ball-bearings.

Hopewell and Gay Viking arrived at Lysekil on 28 December. Throughout this period the Swedish Navy had been keeping a close eye on the activities of the gun boats but had not actively interfered. However, while Hopewell and Gay Viking were at Lysekil, the Swedish Navy attempted to confiscate parts of their radar equipment, claiming that the items in question were incompatible with the boats' status as merchant ships. The matter was quickly settled after a strong protest had been made by the British Legation in Stockholm, but the incident served to show that the 'neutrality' of the Swedes could not be taken for granted.

The first two weeks of 1944 saw operations suspended because of appalling weather conditions. However, on 16 January the Gay Viking left for England, leaving the Hopewell behind. The Germans were aware that there were two blockade runners at Lysekil and were determined to stop them. Three ships of the 6th Destroyer Flotilla had been sent to Kristiansand to stop the 'Grey Ladies', as the Germans called the blockade runners. When the local weather conditions favoured a break-out, the Germans planned to put their destroyers on two-hour notice for sailing.

As the Gay Viking sped across the Skagerrak, her radar detected numerous German aircraft, but by reducing speed to lessen its phosphorescent wake, she avoided detection. The night was clear with visibility about a mile, but the swell and an adverse wind prevented Whitfield from going at full speed. Then, out of the darkness, came a challenge from a signal lamp. Whitfield did not hang around to find out whether it was the Swedes or the Germans who were challenging him; he reversed course until he was out of sight of the other vessel.

With complete cloud cover there was little chance of enemy aircraft finding the MGB

At such a critical time, when he knew the Germans were looking for him, Whitfield was dismayed to see that the Pole Star, which should have been on his starboard beam, was in fact on his starboard quarter. On his present course he was heading obliquely across the Skagerrak into the minefields off the Danish coast. He had a rough idea of his position by dead reckoning and knew that his cargo was likely to render his magnetic-compass unstable. He decided to disregard his compass and use his echo-sounder to follow the 50-fathom line off the Danish coast, keeping the Pole Star on his right and the line

Top right: Inside the engine room of the Nonsuch; its three diesels enabled the ship to reach speeds of up to 23 knots. Left: An MGB awaits a cargo at Lysekil; a normal load might include high-grade steel and ball-bearings. Below: The Hopewell, speeding across a placid North Sea, heads for home. Each of Binney's raiders had a crew of about 20, all volunteers from the Merchant Navy.

on his left. By dawn, *Gay Viking* had made good progress and was no more than 15 miles from her planned position. As she crossed the North Sea, her radar picked up numerous aircraft contacts but the little ship's luck held for, with complete cloud cover and visibility down to less than a mile, there was little chance of an aircraft finding the MGB. At 0745 on 18 January, she passed through the Humber boom to receive a tremendous welcome from the crews of the other gun boats, who had given her up for lost.

On 19 January the *Gay Corsair* left for Sweden and returned a month later with the *Hopewell*. Their arrival meant that, despite the mechanical problems and often severe weather conditions, the gun boats had completed six round trips and had brought out nearly 240 tons of ball-bearings and special equipment. Although this figure was well below the 400 tons demanded by the Ministry of Supply, it was considerably higher than the amounts brought back by the air service.

Left: Some of the *Gay Corsair's* crew pose for the camera. Under the expert leadership of Captain Bob Tanton (below), the vessel completed several journeys to Sweden. During Operation Bridford, the *Gay Corsair* and the *Gay Viking* survived mechanical failures to bring over 65 tons of ball-bearings back to Britain.

Bottom: With her look-outs scanning the horizon for signs of enemy aircraft and E-boats, the *Nonsuch*, accompanied by the *Hopewell*, approaches the Yorkshire coast. Once within range of RAF air cover, those members of the crew not on watch or tending the engines were able to snatch a well-earned break (below). Thanks to their dedication, Britain was never starved of the vital war materials produced by Sweden's steel industry.

Throughout the spring of 1944, the blockade-running operations continued, with the *Nonsuch*, on the flotilla's seventh round trip, arriving back at Hull on 19 February with 40 tons of ball-bearing manufacturing equipment and a Norwegian refugee, who had earned the title of the 'Butcher of Trondheim' for his activities with the Resistance. But the coming of spring meant longer days, and Binney had to face the prospect of suspending the trips for the summer.

On 18 March *Gay Viking* and *Gay Corsair* arrived back at Hull with another 67½ tons of ball-bearings to complete the last blockade-running operation. Their trip had been an engineering nightmare. On the outward journey, while trying to avoid a German merchant ship bound for Oslo and its three E-boat escorts, the input shaft on *Gay Corsair's* centre engine fractured, causing an engine-room fire. The fire was quickly extinguished but the ship had to be stopped and, during a time that Bob Tanton later described as an 'interesting interlude', the German convoy steamed right by them. The problem with the *Gay Corsair's* engines meant that the centre prop-

eller had to be removed at Lysekil and the ship sailed back to Britain using its wing engines only. On the voyage back, RAF cover never materialised and more trouble was in store for both vessels: off the Yorkshire coast, the *Gay Corsair* broke her starboard crankshaft and the *Gay Viking* her main gearbox input shaft on the port engine. Nevertheless, the total tonnage of equipment and ball-bearings brought to Britain by the Grey Ladies after their latest mission stood at 347½ tons.

The long summer days prevented the running of any more trips to Lysekil, but in the following winter a new use was found for the gunboats. Operation Moonshine, an SOE plan to smuggle arms to the Danish Resistance, involved three of the MGBs. Tragically, on 6 February 1945, the *Gay Viking*, the ship that had been the first to break the German blockade, was sunk after a collision with the *Hopewell*, though fortunately without loss of life. Yet, despite the loss of the *Gay Viking*, over 1000 carbines, 1000 Sten guns with four magazines each, four bazookas, 120 bazooka rounds, and two-and-a-half million rounds of smallarms ammunition were supplied to the Resistance. On the homeward trip, the *Nonsuch* and the *Hopewell* carried 63 tons of cargo between them, most of it high-grade steel that was unobtainable in Britain at the time.

It is for the blockade-running missions that the little ships will be best remembered. After their operations were wound up, Sir Duncan Sands, who had sent Binney to Sweden in 1939, wrote:

'This operation gives us a substantial part of the equipment for a vital ball-bearing factory we are putting up and which should enable us to maintain our own supply of ball-bearings. There is no need to exaggerate the importance of this.'

However, Sir Duncan Sands omitted to say that in the months leading to the invasion of Europe in the summer of 1944, when British industry was working flat out, all its requirements for ball-bearings and special steels were met by the Grey Ladies operating from the Humber. Unsung heroes of Britain's war effort, the MGBs had earned their place in the history of covert operations in World War II.

THE AUTHOR Paul Kemp is a photographic researcher at the Imperial War Museum and is the author of several articles on naval subjects.

AVENGER

In May 1982 HMS *Avenger* set sail for the South Atlantic, where she came up against both missile and air attack. Major Hugh McManners was on board, and tells the story of the frigate's fight for survival

THE BRITISH TYPE 21 Frigate HMS *Avenger* spent Christmas 1981 in New Orleans, after a tour of the Caribbean during which she visited Curacao. Be-

lize, Grand Cayman and the Virgin Islands. She was then due for a refit in dry dock. On the visit to Belize she had fired her 4.5 in gun on the naval gunfire range and had then taken the 148 Commando Forward Observation Battery team, who had been working with her, north with the ship's company for the seasonal festivities. The trip north to the mouth of the Mississippi river was enlivened by the queasy harmonium playing of the ship's surgeon, who had to retreat to the galley in mid-hymn to be sick if bad weather coincided with religious services.

The passage up the Mississippi took place at night, during which *Avenger* succeeded in astonishing the

Left: Avenger at sea. Commissioned in July 1978, she was in action less than four years later in the South Atlantic, where she survived the unwelcome attention of two Argentinian Exocets.

HMS AVENGER – F185

HMS Avenger is an Amazon Class (Type 21) frigate, built by Yarrow (Shipbuilders) Ltd of Glagow. Costing £28.3 million, she was launched on 20 November 1975 and was first commissioned on 19 July 1978.

Avenger displaces over 3250 tons at full load and is 384ft in length. Powered by two Rolls-Royce TM3B gas-turbines, she can steam at around 30 knots with an endurance of 1200 miles. She has two smaller gas turbines (Rolls-Royce Tyne RM1C) for cruising, giving her a range of 4000 miles at 17 knots without refuelling. The ship's company totals 176 men – 13 officers and 163 ratings – and she carries either a Lynx Mk2 or a Wasp helicopter.

For defence against submarines, Avenger relies upon helicopter-launched Mk46 lightweight homing torpedoes, although six torpedo tubes are to be fitted.

For above-water defence she is equipped with both missiles and guns: four MM 38 Exocet (single cells) surface-to-surface missiles and one quad launcher of Sea Cat surface-to-air missiles, with four 20mm Oerlikon single mounted cannon and one 4.5in Mk 8 gun. The 4.5in gun is able to fire both as artillery support for troops on shore (high explosive or starshell), or in defence of the ship during air attack (chaff or high explosive air burst).

It can also be used to engage surface ship targets. Her GWS 24 radar is used to control the Sea Cat missiles, while a Type 912 radar is used in conjunction with the 4.5in gun.

During the Falklands campaign, two Type 21s were lost, her sister ships Ardent and Antelope.

helmsman of an oil tanker, who was hogging the middle of the channel, by overtaking like a speed-boat in the darkness. After a busy but enjoyable tour, Avenger returned to Plymouth in March 1982 for DED (docking and essential defects) repairs. The ship's company was sent on leave on 1 April but told to stay near Plymouth. The next day, the Argentinians invaded the Falkland Islands.

Dry docking was due to last six weeks but the yard completed the task in 17 days – an achievement which impressed Avenger's captain, Hugo White: 'At times it was like an anthill. Dockyard maties actually running to get things done. The ship practically came together under my very eyes.'

After spending a long weekend in Plymouth storing, Avenger moved on to Portland for five days of solid operational sea training, which included damage-control exercises, 'lots of threat briefs on the Argentinians', and the firing of her 4.5in gun at St. Alban's Head.

Then, the news of the sinking of Sheffield reached them. The First Lieutenant Lieutenant Commander Tony Bolingbroke, remembered the effect of this blow:

'It was a shock which brought home to us the reality that the enemy were a capable and dangerous military force. An atmosphere of "trying to joke it off" was followed by all the preparations becoming very much more serious.'

Avenger spent a brief weekend in Plymouth and then steamed flat out for the South Atlantic.

'We spent the time practising the closing down for action routine to get it faster – it went from 15 minutes down to about two. We had to establish set routes through the ship for all those running to their action-station posts – one-way systems to avoid congestion. By Ascension this had improved immeasurably.'

Sam, the Chinese laundry man (a locally contracted civilian from Hong Kong) – somewhat against his better judgement – stayed on board. As the likelihood of Avenger going into action increased, so it got harder for Sam. He knew that, when on defence watches, the crew would not change out of their blue cotton denims and woolly-pullies and his laundry profits would plummet. But a suitable financial arrangement was made and he stayed – to become a very proud man at the end of it all.

Exercises with Harriers were conducted and stores and ammunition flown on board

Avenger had sailed south on 10 May with the group led by HMS Bristol, which included Active, Ambuscade, Cardiff, Andromeda, Minerva and Penelope, along with Royal Fleet Auxiliary Olna. Arriving off Ascension Island six days later, she sailed past at speed while exercises with Harriers were conducted and stores and ammunition flown on board. As Avenger left Ascension, a new atmosphere pervaded the vessel, what Tony Bolingbroke described as a 'tightening of the gut'.

On 22 May an Argentinian Boeing 707 reconnaissance aircraft overflew the fleet at great height, and for the first time on the voyage Avenger prepared for

Right above: On the bridge with the Officer of the Watch (left of picture). Right: A helicopter-pilot's view of Avenger under way. Far right: Avenger's Lynx lifts off from the flight deck, still attached to its communications cord.

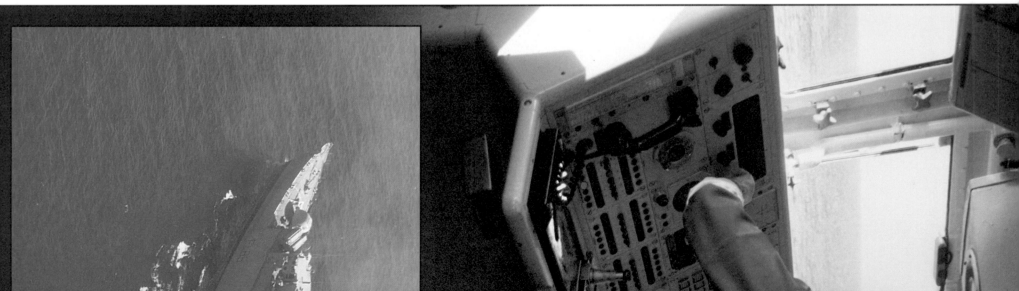

VICKERS 4.5IN MK 8 GUN

Based on the British Army's Abbott gun, the radar-controlled 4.5in Mk 8 gun is currently in service with the

Royal Navy in frigates and destroyers. The Mk 8 can fire at a rate of 24 rounds of high explosive or starshell per minute. As an air-defence system, it tracks incoming missiles and fires shells to detonate in their path. As a gunnery system – firing at other surface ships or, more usually, onto land targets in support of ground operations – the Mk 8 fires a 21kg shell to a range of 23km. Operating in the fire-support role, the gun's computer system locks onto a land feature and compensates for all movements of the ship – pitch, roll, yaw and any tidal or powered movement – when firing the gun. Two targets may be engaged simultaneously, plus one may be illuminated by starshell.

The fire from the gunship onto land targets is controlled by forward observers, operating on the ground, from 148 Commando Forward Observation Battery, Royal Artillery.

The Mk 8 saw extensive combat service during the Falklands conflict, culminating in the largest and final bombardment which took place on the night of 13/14 June. *Avenger, Active, Ambuscade* and *Yarmouth* shelled targets from a gunline in Berkeley Sound in support of the 7th Gurkha Rifles, 2 Para, 2nd Scots Guards and 3 Para who were attacking Argentinian positions around Stanley. During the bombardment 856 shells were fired.

Vickers 4.5in Mk 8 naval gun

Calibre 4.5in
No. of barrels 1
Elevation -10° to +55°
Muzzle velocity 870mps
Effective range (surface fire) 23km (anti-aircraft) 6km
Ammunition impact, proximity and delayed action HE; illuminating chaff; illuminating
Weight of projectile 21kg
Rate of fire 24rpm

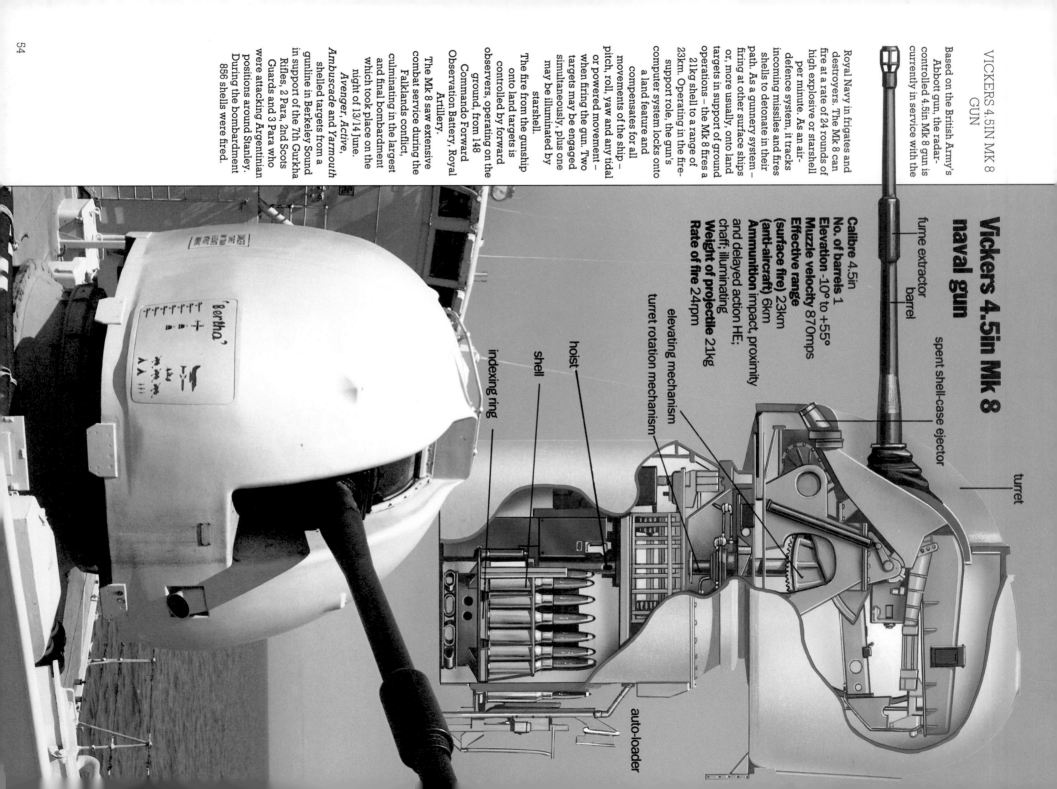

Firepower. *Avenger* is equipped with a Vickers Mk 8 4.5in gun, a weapon that saw extensive combat service during the Falklands conflict. Affectionately known as 'Bertha', *Avenger's* gun proudly displays her battle tally on the shield. In the right-hand column can be seen the A-4 Skyhawk shot down, and below it the Exocet that narrowly missed the ship and crashed into the sea during the attack on 30 May. Also registered are the successful shellings of Argentinian artillery batteries and troop concentrations. *Avenger's* armament also includes four 20mm cannon for close-in self-defence against air attack and other surface vessels (below right).

action in earnest. The Boeing, however, was out of range but HMS *Cardiff* still fired off two Sea Dart surface-to-air missiles (SAMs).

As the *Bristol* group reached the Total Exclusion Zone (TEZ), *Active* and *Avenger* were thrown ahead to join the Task Force. Although *Active* claims that *Avenger* pulled rank and slowed her down deliberately, *Avenger* gained the blue riband for the fastest run down by any ship – 15 days from Plymouth – entering the TEZ at 2015 GMT on 25 May and beating *Active* by half an hour. Joining the ships already on station in the TEZ, Captain White was very conscious of being 'a new boy in a sea of old hands':

'We then heard *Broadsword's* running commentary on the sinking of *Coventry*, and *Atlantic Conveyor* went down the following night. The first 24 hours in the TEZ was a really low day.'

The night of the 27th was to be *Avenger's* 'blooding' in action – a night bombardment of Stanley with HMS *Glamorgan* and *Alacrity*. As the new boy, *Avenger* was to be third into the shoreline to fire, observing the other two as they went in. *Glamorgan*, under the command of Captain Mike Barrow, was in charge of the operation and fired first. Sporadic and inaccurate flak from the Argentinian land-based artillery was falling around the ships and wetting them with the spray sent up by the incoming shells.

In action Captain White fought *Avenger* from the ops room, situated amidships below the bridge, in darkness except for the glow of the radar screens. There the shells could clearly be heard on the

underwater phones.

In the engine room, below the waterline, the exploding shells could be heard even more clearly. Engineering Officer Lieutenant Commander Nick Harry and his crew, with nothing to do but wait for something to go wrong with the engines, were having an intellectual discussion... 'an animated debate about whether or not the Royal Navy was a terminal experience'.

Meanwhile, Captain White was making jokes over the tannoy about the poor Argentinian shooting to cheer everybody up:

'We were aware that we were handing it out for the first time ever, but also that there was a risk of receiving some back. The ship ran itself and all I had to do was play Russian roulette with the shells landing – did I go toward where the last one landed, or away?'

From the bridge, Lieutenant Commander Doling broke could see flashes from the guns on the shore. He saw *Avenger's* gun firing – a bright flash – and then the shells landing on target:

'It was an eerie, detached feeling, in the warm – calm and quiet, except for the bang of the gun. On the shore there was the glow of starshell and the flash of the HE exploding. It was more like a night NGS exercise – except that we could hear the incoming fire'.

There were often 'goofers' (sightseers) from below on the bridge watching night firing:

'... seeing the fireworks and the red lines of tracer. It was very odd watching people killing each other, with a hot cup of coffee in your hand.

'Between broadcasts it was very quiet, the claustrophobia of incarceration – and very frightening. The fear was the worst on that first night because no-one knew what to expect.'

It was also on the night of 27 May that *Avenger* got her first taste of a weapon that, since the sinking of *Sheffield*, had become the nightmare of the Royal Navy – the awesome Exocet. By late May, the Argentinian forces in Stanley were equipped with Exocet missiles, mounted on the backs of lorries parked in the southeast of the town. That night they fired the first – at *Avenger*. In the ops room Captain Hugo White heard a 'whoosh and a strangled cry' from aft over the tannoy'. Sub Lieutenant Carl Walker, the Flight Deck Officer and the Captain's Secretary, announced that a 'bloody great missile' had just flown over the flight deck. His voice was raised in pitch and pretty loud. In contrast, everyone in the ops room was being calm and professional, assuming that this sort of thing was usual.

Sub Lieutenant Walker and his flight-deck crew had seen a hard, white light, getting brighter and larger by the second as it came towards them from the direction of Stanley. Walker is well over six feet in height and in the final stages of the missile's approach decided to get down – the crew threw themselves to the deck. Later, they estimated that the Exocet had passed five feet above the flight deck and 15ft aft of the hangar under powered flight – level and going hard, skimming the surface of the sea. Inside the ops room the noise of the missile was audible without headphones. The Exocet vanished to seaward, veering to the right.

Captain White was annoyed, and said sharply: 'Tell the flight deck not to make such hysterical reports. If the missile missed it is no longer a problem – we are fighting a war up here.'

Afterwards he was amused at his own response to the near miss:

'Because it was our first night in action we were keeping a furiously stiff upper lip and thought that Exocets overflying the flight deck were par for the course!'

Captain White regards the Exocet launch – on the last of three gunships coming close into the shore in order to fire – as a piece of Argentinian opportunism that very nearly paid off:

'Sheer luck, because had we known there was an Exocet there, we wouldn't have been anywhere near for all the tea in China!'

Lieutenant Commander Bolingbroke was amused

by his captain's reaction:

'...in other words, an Exocet missing you by two or three feet is trivial. Down in the ops room they assumed that the flight-deck crew had misinterpreted the sound of a shell – people were scared later on when they realised what it actually had been!'

That night, despite the close shave with the Exocet, *Avenger* fired 100 high-explosive shells and nine starshells in support of 3 Commando Brigade.

Two days later, on 29 May, a combined Special Boat Squadron and 148 Battery special forces team flew onto *Avenger* to be taken south for an insertion into the area of Volunteer Lagoon, to the north of Stanley. I was a member of this team and it was good to return to *Avenger*; there was a warm welcome from Hugo White and the other, now white-hooded, survivors of Christmas in New Orleans in the dim glow of radar screens on the dark bridge.

We had intended to land that night, then reconnoitre and attack a reported Argentinian position on Mount Brisbane. Over the next 10 days we were to clear the high ground to the north of Berkeley Sound. But, by the time we had all arrived on board, it was too late to make the landing and attack before first light on the following day.

The 30th was choppy, and I was seasick, remaining horizontal on a bunk except for meals. We were out in the TEZ with the *Hermes/Invincible* group which we would leave after dark to steam south to our drop-off point.

The atmosphere on *Avenger* was tense. Throughout the day there were constant air raids with the ship's company continually going to Air Raid Warning State Red. Racing from messdecks to action stations, they pulled on long, white anti-flash gloves and hoods while strapping respirators and 'once-only suit' packs (immersion suits) round their waists.

At their action stations the surgical team was in the wardroom, surrounded by oxygen bottles, stretchers

Action stations! Kitted out in white anti-flash gloves and hoods, the ship's company go about their crucial tasks. **Far left, top:** The 4.5in gun control console in the ops room. The console is divided into two sections – the nearer operative working the gun in its anti-aircraft mode, while the far side is used for naval gunfire support on land targets. **Far left, below:** A firefighter awaits the call to action. **Bottom left:** In the 'tiller flat', above *Avenger*'s twin screws. In combat this is a particularly dangerous position to be in since the frigate's commander will try to turn the stern of the ship into any incoming missile attack. **Bottom centre:** Down in the engine room. **Bottom right:** The Engineering Officer (in white) looks on as crew members monitor the ship's operation in the Ship Control Centre.

ARGENTINA

SOUTH ATLANTIC

Total Exclusion Zone

FALKLAND IS

Site of engagement ★

Incoming attack force

Key
Argentinian attack force

Exocet

Four A-4 Skyhawks

1 Argentinian A-4 Skyhawk shot down by Sea Dart from HMS Exeter.

3 A-4 Skyhawk shot down by anti-aircraft fire from Avenger's 4.5in gun.

HMS Avenger

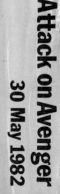

2 Incoming Argentinian Exocet launched from a Super Etendard deflected by Avenger's chaff. The missile runs out of fuel and crashes into the sea.

Attack on Avenger
30 May 1982

and boxes of instruments. First-aid teams and the fire and damage-control crews were sprawled out on the floors of the main corridors, the fire-fighters wearing their stiflingly hot asbestos suits, trying to read paperbacks in the red glow of the emergency lighting. In the ops room, crew were hunched tensely over the glowing screens of their radars, while down in the bowels of the ship the engineers were making macabre jokes about being hit by an Exocet – the batting order of who would be first out of the small hatch in their roof bulkhead. Throughout the ship, the stewards were making their interminable rounds with 'action snacks' – sandwiches and sausage rolls and flasks of hot, sweet tea to fill the mugs that everyone carried tied to their respirator belts.

But it was down below, away from the ops room and the bridge, that the tension was greatest. The engineers had work to do which helped take their minds off it. The technical repair teams, the general support – cooks and stewards – and first aid parties, however, had nothing to do except wait for the first action damage – with the accompanying fires and casualties. Those whose action-station jobs entailed

waiting endured the worst stress. They were allowed, in turn, to go on deck and man smallarms. This was purely psychological – firing SMGs, LMGs and SLRs at incoming air raids as a token gesture in order to let off steam.

The afternoon of 30 May was quiet and Captain White walked around the ship, chatting and joking with the sailors. He was in the main passage when he heard the 3in rockets start firing.

Principal Warfare Officer, Lieutenant Richard Simmonds' first reaction during air attacks was to fire chaff delta (tin foil to confuse the radars on the attacking aircraft) before hitting the 'Action Stations' buzzer. Everyone started the desperate rush to close up when they heard the whoosh of the chaff – even before they heard the buzzer. Captain White ran up to the ops room to assess the situation.

The raid consisted of two Super Etendards and four A-4 Skyhawks. They had reached their turn-round point south of the Task Force and had banked north to head for home. One Super Etendard went to the east in a last effort to locate the fleet. He turned on his radar and got a blip – it was Avenger. They all turned right and attacked.

HMS Exeter picked up the first sweep of the Super Etendard radar and reported, 'Super Etendard radar bearing two zero zero.' Avenger was 10 miles south of *Exeter*. But the reported bearing was misheard on *Avenger* as 'Bearing "something" zero zero' and was assumed to be three zero zero because of the location of *Exeter*. Chief GI Taylor (Chief Petty Officer Gunnery Instructor) fired chaff very fast to his own tactical pattern – but for an attack from the north. PWO Richard Simmonds quickly swerved the ship away from this attack bearing.

When Captain White reached the ops room he realised that the bearing was wrong, and that now he had no time in which to present the stern of the ship to the incoming missiles. This manoeuvre is normally carried out to aid the process of decoy by chaff and to cover the attack with Sea Cat missiles. In the circumstances, White slowed the ship right down to present a slim bow target and minimum radar echo to what they thought were two Super Etendards.

The next pipe was horrifying: 'Impact imminent 12 seconds. Brace! Brace! Brace!'

From the bridge, three smoke trails could be seen – whisps on the horizon coming towards the ship. I was in the wardroom with the surgical team, listening to the terse piped reports from the bridge: 'We have just detected the signature of a Super Etendard doing a single sweep on his radar.'

The ship was swinging from side to side while the rockets overhead were pumping out chaff. In the ops room they heard the change of mode on ESM which

indicated missile release and assumed that there were two Exocets on the way. The radar picked up some small blips that were thought to be Exocets, but were probably Skyhawks. They watched the Super Etendards peel away and set off for Argentina.

The attack was coming in – in fact, one Exocet and four Skyhawks. *Avenger* fired chaff, which just had time to bloom. This time it was a full pattern all around the ship because, by now, Captain White 'had got over any feeling of a need to economise'. The situation was further complicated by a Wessex helicopter approaching the flight deck.

Avenger waited for what was still considered to be two Exocets to come within gun range. In fact, the guns were probably locked onto the two Skyhawks. Then, late into the attack, they saw three or four more contacts coming in – more than just the two Exocets they thought they had identified. The Wessex helicopter quickly left *Avenger*, flying out through a cloud of chaff.

The First Lieutenant kept the company informed over the tannoy:

'We have detected an Exocet launch, range 28 miles – on a bearing directly for us... the bearing is confirmed.'

At Mach 0.9 it doesn't take long to travel 28 miles. In the wardroom we were lying face down on the carpet. The next pipe was horrifying: 'Impact imminent 12 seconds. Brace! Brace!' We closely examined the weave of the wardroom carpet, trying very hard not to think of *Sheffield* and of the point just along the corridor which the missile was programmed to hit – amidships, nine feet above the waterline.

The bridge reported a fireball on the horizon and three aircraft coming in low. The gunners had been told to shift from the Super Etendard onto the Exocet and then fire when the targets came in range. They, therefore, assumed that they had shot down the Exocet. When the fireball was reported, the contact under fire had faded from the screen. In fact, *Exeter* had fired a Sea Dart over the top of *Avenger* and hit one of the Skyhawks, although it was assumed in *Avenger* that her gun – which was firing every couple of seconds – had splashed the second Exocet.

By *Avenger's* reckoning, this left one Exocet and three Skyhawks still coming in. Captain White continued to pore over his radar screen, trying to cover all the alternatives. On the green screens they watched as the Exocet blip homed in and, very slowly – 'so slowly that it seemed like an age' - it bore to the left, passed through a chaff cloud beside the ship, and then ran out of fuel and hit the sea.

In the ops room Able Seaman 'Buster' Brown was on the Missile Gun Director Blind's Display, keeping the radar locked onto the incoming aircraft and tracking the missile. The tracking of a target has to be dead accurate in order to get a good radar lock so the gun can hit it. *Avenger's* gun was now pumping out airburst HE shells to explode 4500yds from the ship, creating a flak barrage through which the A-4s would have to fly. *Avenger* was moving very slowly, trying to stay within the pattern of the chaff. She was

Bottom: A view from the bridge of an incoming A-4 Skyhawk attack. The Argentinian pilots came in fast and low and had to fly through a barrage of anti-aircraft fire on their way in to the target ship. During the air attack on *Avenger* on 30 May, the frigate succeeded in splashing one of the four enemy A-4s with her 4.5in gun.

HMS *Exeter*

Track of Sea Dart missile

④

Two A-4s get through and make a low-level attack on *Avenger* with bombs. The bombs miss the ship, and explode harmlessly on either side of the bow.

swathed in gunsmoke. The sea was calm and there was good visibility.

Meanwhile, the Skyhawk raid was getting closer. Then the gun stopped – a minor fault. The incoming aircraft now appeared very big and very close. The gun started firing again. The First Lieutenant was worried that the Skyhawks would open fire with cannon and kill everyone on the bridge. He piped: 'Brace! Brace! Brace!' and fell to the deck. Action Officer of the Watch Lieutenant Simon Wall remained on his feet throughout.

There was a tremendous *whoosh* as two aircraft went either side of the bridge – at the same height – flashing across the width of the ship. The third plane was hit by the 4.5in gun and cartwheeled into the sea off the starboard bridge, 100yds away from the ship.

As the men on the bridge leapt to their feet, fountains of spray shot into the air on either side of *Avenger* as the bombs went off, straddling the bow. The two surviving Skyhawks wheeled hard left for Argentina. With the passing of the aircraft, there was a huge sigh of relief on *Avenger's* bridge. Tony Bolingbroke recalled:

'The whole thing took about two minutes, but it seemed like ages with lots of time in which to get frightened. I could see the enemy pilot's face and had the sudden feeling that one could never

Below: HMS *Avenger* (right) stands by the damaged Modified Type 12 Frigate HMS *Plymouth*, close to the shoreline. *Plymouth* was hit by four bombs which started a serious fire and it took 50 minutes to bring the situation under control.

Below left: *Avenger's* First Lieutenant during the Falklands conflict, Lieutenant Commander Tony Bolingbroke. Right: Captain Hugo White.

survive such a close contact' Captain White's pipe broke the unbearable tension being suffered by those of us not directly involved with the defence of the ship. He quickly reported what had happened and added:

'I told you when I left "Guzz" (Plymouth) that I was lucky. Well, here's proof of it. Well done to you all for a very cool and professional effort.'

Debris was spotted off the starboard bow so the sea boat was launched to investigate. A 'Lox bottle' (aircrew oxygen cylinder) was found, and what looked like a sheepskin pilot's seat cover. In fact it was a human lung turned inside out.

The 'shooting down' of the Exocet became very important for the crew of *Avenger*. After the loss of *Sheffield*, the Exocet had become the great scourge of the campaign, and *Avenger* had defeated it. The incident reinforced Hugo White's claim to good fortune and that nothing would hit *Avenger* – his luck was a talisman that seemed to protect the whole ship. Hugo White is a 'pirate' captain, quiet with a wicked sense of humour, always amused, always amusing, and absolutely cool. His very sharp brain instantly absorbed information and his unerringly rapid reactions to events gave his crew the confidence to do instantly what he said. His First Lieutenant recalled:

'He had an aura and was much admired. It was not hard to convince people that this ship was going to be alright.'

At last light on the 30th *Avenger* was released from the *Hermes*/*Invincible* group and steamed south to insert our team. One hundred and twenty five HE shells were fired onto suspected Argentinian positions on Mount Brisbane and the insertion went smoothly.

On 12 June, the night HMS *Glamorgan* was hit by a

CAPTAIN H. M. WHITE, CBE

Captain Hugo White joined the Royal Navy in 1958, and after cadet training at the Britannia Royal Navy College Dartmouth and an initial commission in an anti-submarine frigate, spent the majority of his early career at sea in submarines. Before joining the nuclear attack submarine HMS *Warspite* as navigator in 1966, he served in a number of diesel boats. In 1970, after a tour as First Lieutenant of HMS *Osiris*, he commanded HMS *Oracle*, an Oberon class diesel-electric with which he escorted nuclear-powered boat HMS *Dreadnought* to the North Pole and carried out ice trials.

In 1971 he returned to Dartmouth to teach cadets and was promoted to Commander. In 1973 he became the first Commander Submarine Training at HMS *Neptune* at Faslane in Scotland. As Captain of HMS *Salisbury* (an air-defence frigate) he patrolled the northern fishing grounds during the so-called second 'Cod War' of 1975.

From 1976 to 1980 White worked at the Ministry of Defence, where he planned the careers of Seaman officers, and on promotion to Captain – as the Assistant Director of Naval Plans – was responsible for the future size and shape of the fleet.

In 1980 he was appointed to command the general-purpose frigate *Avenger* as Captain of the 4th Frigate Squadron of Type 21s. In December 1982, after commanding *Avenger* in the Falklands conflict, White became Principal Staff Officer to the Chief of Defence Staff in the appointment of Commodore. He now commands HMS *Bristol*, the only Type 82 destroyer, which has been made flagship of the Second Flotilla.

---

land-launched Exocet, *Avenger* had the opportunity to see the effect of this weapon at close hand. Late on 11 June, she sailed from San Carlos to the gunline south of Stanley where she joined *Glamorgan* and *Yarmouth*, firing in support of 45 Commando's attack on Two Sisters and Tumbledown. *Glamorgan* and *Yarmouth* finished firing first. *Avenger* was having problems with her gun and stayed on to finish her firing. *Yarmouth* and *Glamorgan* departed southwards. *Glamorgan* then turned east, towards the Task Force, while *Yarmouth* continued south.

Captain Nigel Bedford of 148 Battery, located on Mount Harriet, saw an SSM launch from the shore and attempted to warn the ships by radio.

Action Officer of the Watch on *Avenger*, Lieutenant Simon Wall, reported a fast, bright, white light from the north of Stanley. Looks like a missile.' The missile was streaking south, a bip on the ops room radar, stepping remorselessly down the screen towards *Glamorgan*, with every sweep of the dish.

Glamorgan saw the missile coming and fired a Sea Cat. The two missiles sped towards each other and, as the echoes merged on the screen, everyone prayed that they had a hit. Then the Exocet emerged from the bip, carried on south and thumped into *Glamorgan*.

Hugo White watched grimly:

'I had a sudden cold feeling in my heart. *Glamorgan* was in deep trouble. Moreover, I knew that I would have to risk my ship inside Exocet range and help.'

This time the Argentinians had got their Exocet launch drills correct. The whole episode took no more than 30 seconds.

Captain Bob Harmes of 148 Commando Forward Observation Battery, who was to become the 'Jonah' of the fleet – he was 'sunk' three times while on gunships as a liaison officer – was on *Glamorgan* when she was hit. He had been in the ops room, drafting a signal with the Captain's Secretary, Lieutenant David Tinker. Tinker was also the Flight Deck Officer and so, having completed the signal, he

Below: HMS *Avenger* at Portland in the summer of 1986, preparing to embark on the 'Thursday War' – the weekly battle-training exercise. Since her return from the South Atlantic, *Avenger* has again seen service in the Caribbean as the Belize guardship, visiting ports throughout the area.

went aft to the flight deck. A few minutes later, he was killed. Bob Harmes left the ops room five minutes after Tinker. As he was opening the slide hatch from the ops room he heard a loud crash – just a noise – no shudder or vibration. He had an overwhelming desire to see daylight and smell fresh air. When he emerged on deck there was a scramble of people. A petty officer shouted, 'We've been hit by an artillery shell!'

There were fires on the port side aft. Avgas was burning and the Lynx helicopter had burned out. Harmes went aft and started to work with the fire-fighters. When the flames looked like they were getting close to the Sea Cat missiles, it was decided to fire them – but those aft were not told. Harmes remembered that 'the sudden launch of the Sea Cats was the most terrifying bit of it all. *Glamorgan* continued to steam flat out so the flames and fire went aft and did not spread'

There was a poignant ceremony of Last Post at the memorial to her sister ships *Ardent* and *Antelope*

With *Glamorgan* alight, *Avenger* raced south and, with *Yarmouth*, joined *Glamorgan* to escort her out to the Task Force. Bob Harmes commented:

'It was a very gallant effort to keep *Glamorgan* going. The fires could easily have got completely out of control and the ship been lost there and then that night.'

HMS *Avenger* took part in many different operations during the Falklands conflict – from escorting the diesel submarine *Onyx* safely through the crowded and dangerous traffic of San Carlos Water at night, to accepting the surrender of 1000 Argentinian troops at Fox Bay.

The ceasefire was followed by nine weeks of guardship duties. There was also a poignant ceremony of Last Post at the memorial to her sister ships *Ardent* and *Antelope* on a hill overlooking San Carlos.

Finally, on 23 August 1982, *Avenger* sailed north for home. She had fired over 1000 4.5in shells in support of the troops ashore and had sailed thousands of miles through waters that were often hostile – and she was unscathed.

Avenger and the other gunships, many of which had been fighting the war for longer than her, had by coming close inshore night after night to fire, put themselves at constant risk. Outsider Captain Bob Harmes summed up their contribution:

'At sea you can't run away from it like you can on land. I got to know a lot about the weave of gunship wardroom carpets as the tannoy gave blow-by-blow accounts that I would have preferred not to have heard.

'I reckon that there were more men killed on gunships, firing in support of the ground battle, than anywhere else – certainly more than in any one major unit in action. They were pretty gallant little ships.'

THE AUTHOR Major Hugh McManners, as a captain, was one of the Naval Gunfire Forward Observers of 148 Commando Forward Observation Battery during the Falklands campaign of 1982. The author and publishers would like to thank Captain Hugo White, Captain Chris Craig – *Avenger's* current commander – the officers and crew of HMS *Avenger*, without whose generous assistance the publication of this article would not have been possible.

THE KRONSTADT MISSION

On the night of 17/18 August 1919, eight Royal Navy Coastal Motor Boats launched a bold torpedo attack on key elements of the Russian Red Banner Fleet, berthed in Kronstadt Harbour

ALLIED INTERVENTION IN RUSSIA

In November 1917 the republican government of Russia (which had replaced the Tsar's autocracy the previous March) was overthrown by the Petrograd Soviet of Workers' Deputies. The predominantly Bolshevik government which now came to power was committed to end Russia's involvement in World War I. This policy was welcomed by the Germans, who had a large army on the Eastern Front that could be shifted west. Accordingly, the Treaty of Brest-Litovsk was signed on 3 March 1918. The western Allies – Britain, France, Italy and the United States – were concerned that this would tilt the balance of forces on the Western Front against them. While Lenin struggled to consolidate the new Soviet state, the Allies sought to add to the general insecurity by sending military supplies to any force opposed to Bolshevik power. They followed this up with troops and naval vessels to assist the anti-Bolshevik effort. By the time Germany had been defeated on the Western Front, in November 1918, the Allies were inextricably involved in several concurrent attempts to overthrow the Bolsheviks. These interventions continued until 1920, when the anti-Bolshevik forces were finally driven from the Soviet Union.

Previous page: Full speed ahead for a Coastal Motor Boat (CMB), one of the vessels used to devastating effect on the Kronstadt raid. Above left: Pamyat Azova lists helplessly after being struck by a torpedo from CMB No.79. The raid was inspired by Augustus Agar (above right), whose daring attack on the Bolshevik cruiser Oleg earned him the Victoria Cross.

AT MIDNIGHT, on 17 June 1919, a 40ft motor boat stole out of a small harbour in Finland. It was dark, but the crew knew that the sun would soon begin to rise in this far northern latitude. In command was Lieutenant Augustus Agar, RN, and with him were Midshipman John Hampsheir, RNR, and Chief Motor Mechanic Hugh Beeley, RNVR. All three were on secondment to the Secret Service, and were engaged in the task of ferrying agents into and out of Petrograd (Leningrad). However, they were now engaged in a task which had only the tacit authorisation of the British Senior Naval Officer, Baltic, Rear Admiral Walter Cowan – they were out to sink the Bolshevik cruiser Oleg.

The Oleg was engaged in the bombardment of the Krasnaya Gorka fortress whose garrison had mutinied. The British, currently involved in several intervention operations aimed at the overthrow of the Bolshevik government in Moscow, were inclined to support the mutineers. Lieutenant Agar was aware of the desperate situation the mutineers faced – bombarded from the sea and besieged by land – and decided to use the small naval force at his disposal to strike a blow on their behalf. He was confident that Rear Admiral Cowan would support this action. An initial attempt on the previous night had been foiled when one of the two boats under Agar's command shed its propeller; now he was making a second attempt. Agar's Coastal Motor Boat (CMB) No.4 set out from its base at Terriokki and headed across the Gulf of Finland.

In order to reach the Oleg, moored at Kronstadt Roadstead, it was necessary to pass through a screen of four destroyers stationed off Tolboukin Lighthouse. Agar brought his boat around to the southwest of the Oleg and then proceeded northeast along the coast of Ingermanland. Agar slowed No.4 to reduce the noise of its engines and the spray from its bow, seeking to lessen the chance of detection. Suddenly, the boat shuddered as if it had struck something.

Hampsheir came up from below and informed his commander that the firing mechanism for the torpedo had gone off prematurely, though fortunately its locking system was still engaged – preventing the torpedo from being fired. There was now a 10-minute wait while Beeley and Hampsheir repaired the mechanism. The first streaks of dawn appeared at 0100 and Agar nervously watched the Bolshevik destroyers only 250yds away. Once the mechanism had been restored to working order, the relieved Agar set course full speed ahead for the Oleg, and the CMB quickly covered the few thousand yards that separated Agar from his target.

The Oleg went down in 12 minutes, with the surprisingly small loss of only five men

At 500yds range the torpedo was fired and Agar quickly turned No.4 around 180 degrees. Looking back he saw 'a large flash abreast the cruiser's foremost funnel, followed almost immediately by a huge column of black smoke reaching up to the top of her mast.' The destroyers in the area shelled No.4 as it retreated, but its small size, combined with the poor light, made it an impossible target to hit and the shells exploded harmlessly in the water. The Oleg went down in 12 minutes, with the surprisingly small loss of only five men. In recognition of this courageous exploit, Agar received the Victoria Cross, Hampsheir the Distinguished Service Order and Beeley the Conspicuous Gallantry Medal.

The sinking of the Oleg was the prelude to another attack by CMBs that was even bolder in its conception, and even more daring in its execution. Both operations are part of a nearly forgotten campaign conducted by the Royal Navy in the immediate aftermath of World War I.

In 1919 the situation in the Baltic states of Finland, Estonia, Latvia and Lithuania was extremely com-

Above: An icy grave for the *Oleg*, as she submerges beneath the waters of the Baltic. Left: Hoisting a CMB aboard for a re-fit.

plex, with four factions embroiled in a bitter struggle over the control of these new states. In each, the contest centred around two rival governments vying for political control – an anti-Russian grouping, and a pro-Bolshevik one. The British (with their French, US and Italian allies) supported the anti-Russian nationalists, while the Soviet government took the side of the pro-Bolshevik socialists. Complicating the situation, the wealthiest people in the Baltic states tended to be ethnically German and their ambition was to establish a single Baltic state with close ties to Germany. Furthermore, anti-Bolshevik Russian forces – known as 'Whites' – were also active in the area. They sought a restored Russian Empire that would incorporate the four Baltic states.

At the end of 1918 the only strong military presence in the area was a German force occupying the Baltic states as defined by the terms of the peace treaty, signed the previous March, with the Soviet government. The armistice which ended World War I, in November, required these troops to remain in place until nationalist governments were strong enough to assert their authority. The Soviet government felt threatened by this concentration of force, which was known to be sympathetic to the anti-Bolshevik cause, and it rightly suspected the Germans of having designs of their own on the Baltic states. The socialist claimants to power in the Baltic provided a useful pretext for intervention, and Red Army troops marched into Estonia to support the authority of the pro-Bolshevik faction. This brought Britain into the conflict. Already engaged in military intervention on several fronts against the Bolsheviks, the Cabinet decided that the Baltic nationalist regimes would provide a useful focus for anti-Soviet action in the region, as well as hampering the efforts of the Germans to establish a puppet regime. Accordingly, a British fleet of cruisers and destroyers was sent into the Baltic to assist the Estonian National

The success of Agar's attack on the *Oleg*, using a 40ft CMB (above), prompted the British Navy to use these craft in a bold strike at the heart of Kronstadt Harbour: the CMB's shallow draught and high speed would be able to penetrate the harbour's formidable defences, which included an extensive minefield. Operation 'RK', as the attack was codenamed, utilised seven 55ft craft, each armed with two torpedoes. Right: The engine-room of one of these enlarged CMB's, capable of generating a top speed of 42 knots. Top left: Primary target of the raid, the Bolshevik battleship *Andrei Pervozvanni*.

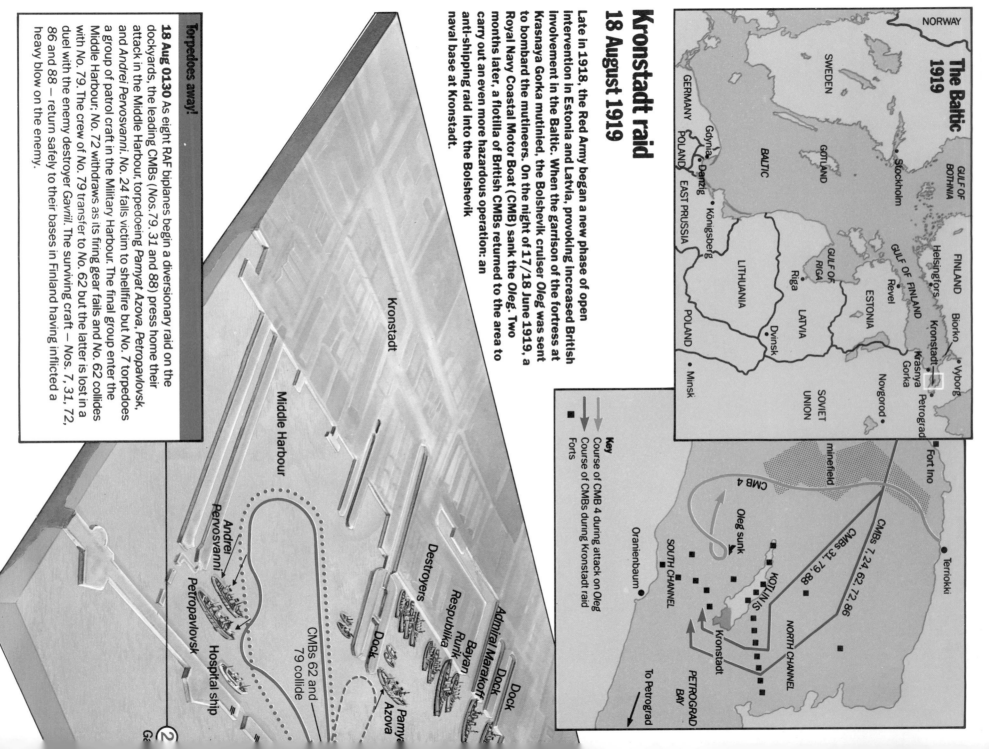

The Baltic 1919

NORWAY

SWEDEN

GULF OF BOTHNIA

BALTIC

GOTLAND

• Stockholm

FINLAND

Helsingfors • Biorko

GERMANY

Gdynia • • Danzig

POLAND

EAST PRUSSIA

• Königsberg

GULF OF FINLAND

Revel

Kronstadt
Krasnya
Gorka • Petrograd

Wyborg

LITHUANIA

GULF OF RIGA

Riga

ESTONIA

LATVIA

POLAND

• Dvinsk

Novgorod •

SOVIET UNION

• Minsk

Key
- Course of CMB 4 during attack on Oleg
- Course of CMBs during Kronstadt raid
- Forts

Fort Ino

minefield

• Terriokki

Oranienbaum •

CMB 4

Oleg sunk

SOUTH CHANNEL

KOTLIN'S

NORTH CHANNEL

CMBs 7, 24, 62, 72, 86

CMBs 31, 79, 88

Kronstadt

PETROGRAD BAY

To Petrograd

Kronstadt raid
18 August 1919

Late in 1918, the Red Army began a new phase of open intervention in Estonia and Latvia, provoking increased British involvement in the Baltic. When the garrison of the fortress at Krasnaya Gorka mutinied, the Bolshevik cruiser Oleg was sent to bombard the mutineers. On the night of 17/18 June 1919, a Royal Navy Coastal Motor Boat (CMB) sank the Oleg. Two months later, a flotilla of British CMBs returned to the area to carry out an even more hazardous operation: an anti-shipping raid into the Bolshevik naval base at Kronstadt.

Kronstadt

Middle Harbour

Andrei
Pervosvanni

Petropavlovsk

Hospital ship

CMBs 62 and 79 collide

Destroyers

Bayan
Rurik
Respublika

Dock

Admiral Marakoff

Dock

Dock

Pamyat Azova

Torpedoes away!

18 Aug 0130 As eight RAF biplanes begin a diversionary raid on the dockyards, the leading CMBs (Nos. 79, 31 and 88) press home their attack in the Middle Harbour, torpedoeing Pamyat Azova, Petropavlovsk, and Andrei Pervosvanni; No. 24 falls victim to shellfire but No. 7 torpedoes a group of patrol craft in the Military Harbour. The final group enter the Middle Harbour; No. 72 withdraws as its firing gear fails and No. 62 collides with No. 79. The crew of No. 79 transfer to No. 62 but the latter is lost in a duel with the enemy destroyer Gavriil. The surviving craft — Nos. 7, 31, 72, 86 and 88 — return safely to their bases in Finland having inflicted a heavy blow on the enemy.

Council against the Red forces.

The original squadron was relieved in January 1919 by a force under the command of Rear Admiral Cowan, a man with a reputation for aggressive action. When, in spring, the ice around the Red Banner Baltic Fleet's base of Kronstadt began to melt, Bolshevik ships began manoeuvres in support of Red troops now openly engaged against Estonian, Latvian and 'White' forces. Cowan's orders afforded him a good deal of leeway in his operations, and his forces engaged in constant skirmishes with any Bolshevik forces they encountered.

The sinking of the *Oleg* gave Cowan the idea for a new operation. The 'White' forces based in Finland and Latvia, under the command of General Nikolai Yudenitch, were planning an attack against Petrograd through Estonia. This represented a much greater threat to the Bolshevik government than the Estonians and Latvians, and it was obvious to Cowan that the Red Banner Baltic Fleet would be deployed in much greater strength than might be used against the miniscule navies of the Baltic states. However, Cowan's temptation to launch a direct intervention in

Her engines overhauled, after a 2000-mile tow from England, *CMB No.24* (below) sets sail for the Royal Navy base at Biorko.

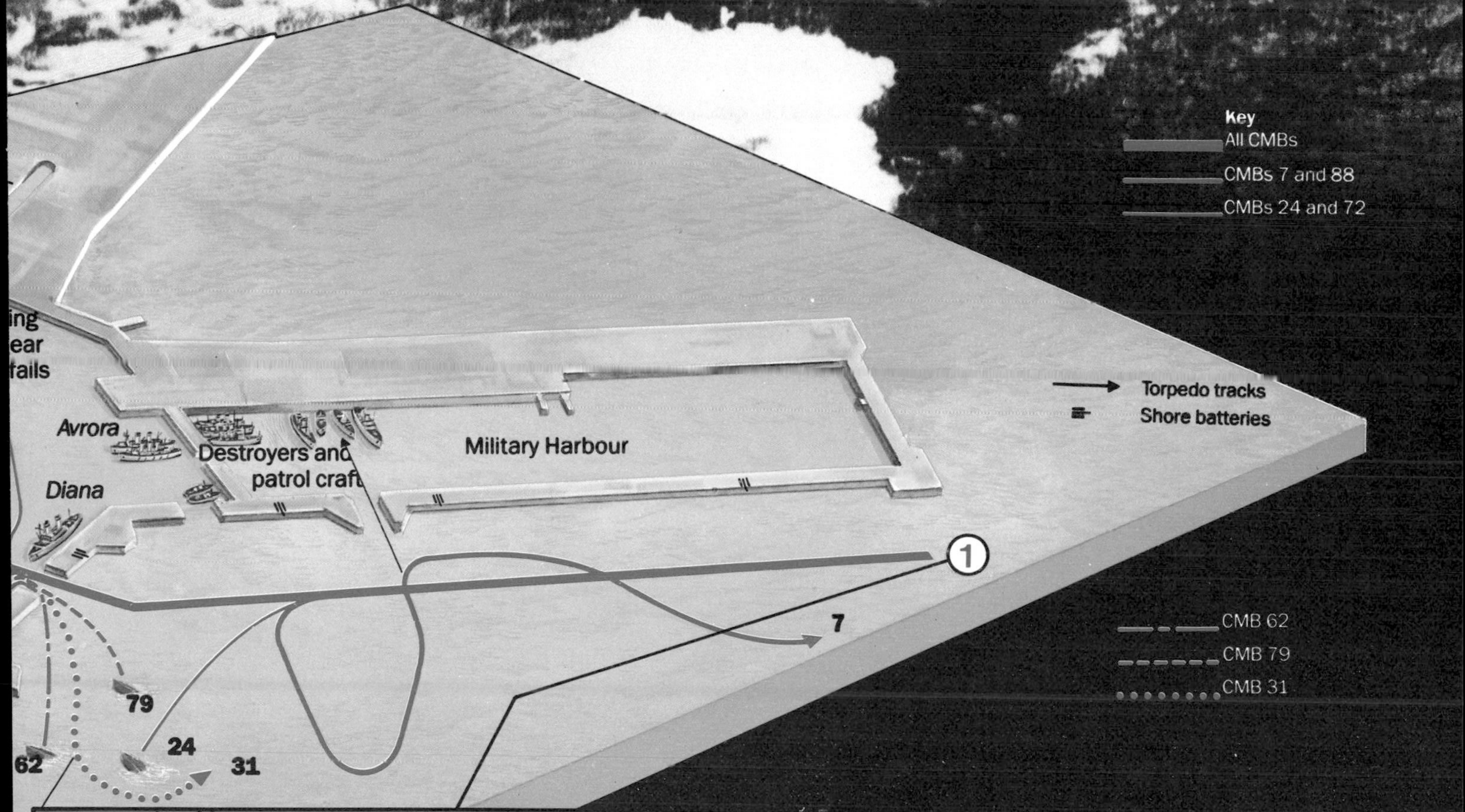

Kronstadt raiders

17 Aug 2200 Seven Coastal Motor Boats (CMBs) under the command of Commander C.C. Dobson leave the Royal Navy's base at Biorko in Finland and set course for a rendezvous near Terriokki with Lieutenant Augustus Agar in CMB *No. 7*. Agar, the hero of the *Oleg* exploit, guides the flotilla through the chain of Bolshevik forts defending the naval base at Kronstadt. Passing through the defensive chain at two points, the CMBs alert the garrisons and come under sporadic and ineffective fire. Wheeling round towards Kotlin Island and Kronstadt, the flotilla begins its final run in. CMB *No. 86* develops engine trouble and is unable to proceed.

favour of the 'Whites' was tempered by the formidable nature of the opposition facing him. Major Soviet battleships, such as the dreadnought *Petropavlovsk* and the pre-dreadnought *Andrei Pervozvanni*, would, in open sea, greatly outclass the cruisers and destroyers under his command. Therefore, Cowan opted to use a force of CMBs, operating under the cover of darkness, to raid Kronstadt Harbour itself. He selected five targets, and ranked them in order of priority: the *Andrei Pervozvanni*, the *Petropavlovsk*, the *Pamyat Azova* (a submarine depot ship), the *Rurik* (an obsolescent cruiser adapted for mine-laying) and a drydock in the corner of the Middle Harbour.

key

All CMBs	
CMBs 7 and 88	
CMBs 24 and 72	

→ Torpedo tracks
Shore batteries

CMB 62 — · —
CMB 79 – – –
CMB 31 · · · · ·

Military Harbour

Avrora

Destroyers and patrol craft

Diana

7

1

79
24
31
62

A flotilla of seven CMBs arrived from Britain at the beginning of August. Cowan left the detailed planning of the operation to Commander C. C. Dobson, who would lead the flotilla. Lieutenant Agar, who knew the area quite well from his night-time trips to Petrograd, would guide the flotilla through the chain of forts that protected Kronstadt against naval attack. Dobson divided his seven boats into three groups for the raid. *No.24*, under the command of Lieutenant L. E. S. Napier, would deal with the destroyer guardship at the entrance to the Middle Harbour. The harbour itself would be attacked by two groups, each comprising three boats. Lieutenant W. H. Bremner, on board *No.79*, would lead this first group into the harbour after using guncotton charges to destroy the boom, normally placed across the entrance. *No.31*, captained by Lieutenant R. Macbean, with Dobson on board, and *No.88*, under Lieutenant A. Dayrell-Reed, would follow Bremner and attack the *Andrei Pervozanni* and the *Petropavlovsk* respectively. The remaining three boats – *No.62*, commanded by Lieutenant Commander J. T. Brade, *No.72* under Sub-Lieutenant E. R. Bodley, and *No.86* under Sub-Lieutenant F. Howard – would launch a second attack on the battleships if Dobson and Dayrell-Reed failed in their task, or else would strike at the *Rurik* and the drydock. Between the entrance of the first group into the Middle Harbour and the arrival of the second, there would be a 15-minute interval – to lessen the chance of any of the boats colliding while racing about the harbour.

No.31 fired its two torpedoes, which struck their target amidships on the port side

The seven CMBs departed from Biorko, the main Royal Navy base in the Gulf of Finland, at 2200 on 17 August 1919. Rendezvousing with Lieutenant Agar's boat at midnight off Inonni Point, the eight craft then set off for the base at Kronstadt. It proved impossible to maintain visual contact in the darkness and the eight boats split into two groups on their approach to the line of nine forts guarding the North Channel. Lieutenant Gordon Steele on *No.88* later recalled:

'The seconds seemed like hours; it appeared outside all possibility that they would not see us I stood by the Lewis gun pointing it at the fort as we passed – not that it would be of much use, but it gave one confidence.'

They passed through the chain at two points and the noise of the boats' engines did in fact alert the garrisons. However, the searchlights of the fortresses were not switched on and the Bolshevik garrisons were unable to damage the CMBs with the sporadic rifle fire that echoed through the darkness.

The CMBs now began to turn in a wide circle, with the glittering lights of Petrograd situated to port and the dark mass of the island of Kotlin, with Kronstadt at its southeastern tip, to starboard. One boat, *No.86*, developed engine trouble just inside the fortress chain and was unable to proceed any further; it would be subjected to a hail of bullets from the forts while the other boats pressed home their attacks.

At this stage, about 0130 on 18 August, a diversionary operation by the RAF began. Cowan had eight biplanes at his disposal and he deployed them to bomb Kronstadt dockyard just before the CMBs were due to attack. They diverted the enemy's attention by diving again and again, dropping 112lb bombs on the naval installations, and strafing searchlights and shore batteries. 'The Kronstadt

garrison turned its searchlights skywards and opened fire with machine guns and 47mm quickfire (QF) guns. Neither the RAF, nor the Bolsheviks were experienced in night-time aerial operations and, judged purely as an air raid, the attack caused minimal damage. However, it had compelled the garrison to remain under cover while the CMBs made their final approach.

As the three lead CMBs neared the entrance to the Middle Harbour, they cut their speed to reduce engine noise and bow wave visibility. Managing to crawl past the destroyer guardship *Gavrill*, without being spotted, Lieutenant Bremner kept a watchful eye for the defensive boom at the harbour entrance. To the surprise of the raiders, the boom was missing! The fortunate CMB crews opened up full throttle and roared into Kronstadt Naval Base.

CMB No.79 headed straight for the *Pamyat Azova*, which was berthed alongside the central jetty. As the assault craft began to make a tight turn out of the harbour, it fired one torpedo. This struck the depot ship and detonated. The *Pamyat Azova* listed almost immediately and rolled over onto its starboard side before sinking to the bottom of Kronstadt's shallow harbour. *CMB No.31* followed *No.79* into the harbour and began a long turn to port to set up its shot on the *Andrei Pervozanni*. *No.31* fired its two torpedoes which struck their target amidships on the port side and erupted in what were later described as 'two terrific explosions'.

The attack on the *Pamyat Azova* and the *Andrei Pervozanni* alerted the garrison to the presence of the CMBs. The searchlights, which had previously focused on the aerial attack, now turned their attention to the harbour, sweeping across it wildly, probing for the raiders' frail craft. Machine and 47mm QF guns also concentrated their efforts on the harbour and the slow, staccato rhythm of Putilov-manufactured Maxims mingled with the rattle of British Lewis guns as shore batteries and CMBs exchanged fire.

Taking prompt action, Steele shifted his dying comrade, and turned the wheel hard over

CMB No.88 began its sharp turn in the wake of *No.31*. It had a difficult shot to make since the *Andrei Pervozanni* and only 150ft of the target's hull was visible. As Dayrell-Reed aligned his boat with the bows of the *Petropavlovsk* onshore batteries unleashed a burst of fire and he was struck in the head by a bullet. With its commander slumped over the wheel, *No.88* continued to turn to port swinging past its target. Lieutenant Steele, manning the Lewis gun at the rear, instantly realized that something was wrong. He turned and saw the mortally wounded Dayrell-Reed. Taking prompt action, Steele shifted his dying comrade, and turned the wheel hard over. Course corrected, *No.88* fired two torpedoes before stopping one engine to help the boat turn quickly and then speeding towards the harbour entrance. Steele heard, first, the two explosions of *No.31*'s torpedoes, and then, quickly following, a third explosion. This had struck the *Petropavlovsk* directly under its bow turret, and *No.88* was so close that the picric powder from the explosive charge showered the stern of the CMB. As Steele throttled back, he took a last look over his shoulder; the explosion produced a high column of flame that illuminated the whole basin

The attack on Kronstadt Harbour was planned down to the last detail by Commander Claude Dobson (above). Drawing upon the invaluable knowledge of Lieutenant Agar (right), Dobson also made several reconnaissance flights to pinpoint the targets. Below: Midshipman John Hampsher (left); and (right) Lieutenant Gordon Steele, whose quick thinking ensured that *No.88*'s torpedoes found their mark, earning him the Victoria Cross.

Before World War I the firm of Thornycroft had designed a few hydroplane craft on an experimental basis. In January 1916 the Admiralty ordered 12 craft based on these designs for use in 'tip-and-run' raids across the North Sea. These craft were 40ft long, displacing a mere five tons and with a draught of only two and a half feet. Powered by a petrol engine providing 250bhp, they had a top speed of 24.8 knots, and carried a crew of three. Armament comprised two or four .303in Lewis guns in twin mountings and a single 18in torpedo in the stern. Thirty-seven of this type were built.

Enlarged models were ordered after the first 12 had entered service. These were each 55ft long, with a draught of three feet, and weighed 11 tons. They had two propeller shafts, compared to the single one of the 40ft boats. Eleven different types of engine were used in the 80 boats built, giving top speeds of between 34 and 42 knots. Some were equipped with a single torpedo, while others had two. They all had four Lewis guns and could carry up to four depth charges. They were crewed by three to five men.

Both types had two drawbacks when operational: no reverse gear was fitted, preventing them from travelling astern. Berthing them rather resembled landing an aircraft: speed was steadily reduced as the boat neared its mooring place, until finally the engine was switched off. The other disadvantage was the large amount of room the CMBs required to manoeuvre due to their high speed. This luxury was not available in the restricted area of the Kronstadt Dockyard.

Augustus Agar's No.4 is preserved at the Imperial War Museum at Duxford.

Meanwhile, outside the entrance to the Middle Harbour, the second group of attackers had arrived. No.24 lined up for an easy shot on the Gavriil but Lieutenant Napier was mortified when his torpedo passed under the destroyer's hull. The Gavriil opened fire immediately and shore batteries, now fully alerted to the danger, brought the full brunt of their guns to bear against the tiny CMBs. Bolshevik retaliation was brutal, and a small shell struck No.24, splitting the frail craft in half. Agar's boat, No.7, manoeuvred to a position in front of the entrance to the Military Harbour, adjacent to the Middle Harbour. Inside were an assortment of tugs and small patrol craft at their berths. Agar's torpedo smashed into a group of these, berthed just inside the entrance, and detonated, effectively sealing it up. No.7 then retired to a waiting position in the South Channel.

The last two boats, No.72 and 62, were by now entering the Middle Harbour. No.72 lined up for a run on the large drydock in the northeastern corner. However, a shell from a QF gun had shot away part of the torpedo firing gear, and it proved impossible to launch the torpedo. No.72 abandoned its mission and returned to the fortress chain in the North Channel to rescue the stranded No.86 from its uncomfortable position under fire from machine guns. No. 62, commanded by Lieutenant-Commander Brade, was entering the harbour when disaster struck.

Brade responded in the spirit of Nelson by attacking the Gavriil with his two torpedoes

Blinded by the searchlights, Brade made a sharp turn, instead of heading straight on, and ploughed into No.79 as the latter was effecting its escape from the harbour. The two CMBs remained locked together and displaying great presence of mind Brade kept going and carried the wreckage out of the harbour. This gave Lieutenant Bremner the opportunity to transfer his crew onto No.62 and destroy No.79 with guncotton charges, having first clambered to safety himself. All this commotion took place under the guns of the Gavriil, and the crew of the Bolshevik destroyer opened fire on the heavily laden CMB. Shells splashed all around the small craft. Brade responded in the spirit of Nelson by attacking the Gavriil with his two torpedoes. But, like those of No. 24, both missed. When a shell from the destroyer struck the engines of No.62, the gallant crew and their boat remained stopped in the water – until sunk by gunfire. CMBs No.7, 31, 72, 86 and 88 all made it safely back to their bases in Finland.

The operation was a complete success and no large units of the Red Banner Baltic Fleet emerged from Kronstadt for the rest of 1919. Dobson and Steele were both awarded the Victoria Cross, and four DSOs, eight DSCs and 15 CGMs were also awarded. That the Bolsheviks also recognised the gallantry of this action – an act of state-sponsored piracy that ranks with the deeds of Drake and Hawkins – is demonstrated by the fact that the 11 bodies they recovered were buried with full military honours.

THE AUTHOR P.M. Szuscikiewicz is an American writer, based in London, who has published several articles on naval and military affairs.

The origins of the Buckley class of destroyer escorts (DEs) lay in the Royal Navy's need for convoy protection ships in the Battle of the Atlantic. An initial order for 300 units was placed between November 1941 and December 1942. When America entered the war, the country's naval planners were confronted with the need for a large number of cheap escorts and, in consequence, the production run of the DEs was increased.

Some 560 escorts were built during the war, of which 425 left the construction yards between April 1943 and April 1944. The output of the DEs was divided between several classes, depending on the type of powerplant fitted. Equipped with two turbo-electric steam turbines, the USS *England* was of the Buckley class. Great emphasis was placed on armament. Typical of its sister ships, the *England* displaced 1740 tons fully loaded and was 306ft long. The power generated by the two steam turbines could propel the ship through the water at speeds of up 24 knots.

The *England's* surprisingly large crew of 220 men lived in cramped conditions and, among their other duties, had charge of the ship's armaments: three single 3in guns, six single 40mm guns, and two twin and four single 20mm anti-aircraft guns. The vessel's anti-submarine equipment consisted of the Hedgehog bomb system and a number of depth charge chutes and throwers. The ship also carried three 21in torpedo tubes.

The DEs enjoyed a remarkable wartime record and many remained in service as either fast transports or radar pickets in the post-war period. Above: The US Navy officer's cap badge.

DESTROYER ESCORT

In May 1944, USS *England*, armed with the devastating Hedgehog spigot mortar, accounted for six Japanese submarines in a single patrol

THERE'LL ALWAYS be an *England* – in the US Navy.' This message of congratulation, sent at the height of the titanic battle for naval supremacy in the Pacific during World War II by Admiral Ernest J. King, Chief of Naval Operations, had a certain irony, for the autocratic Irish-American was a noted Anglophobe. However 'Ernie' King could hardly withhold his praise on this occasion, as the vessel in question, destroyer escort USS *England* (DE-635), had just sunk six Japanese submarines in quick succession, a feat without parallel in two world wars.

The 1400-ton Buckley-class destroyer escort's remarkable cruise began on 18 May 1944, when the ship's captain, Lieutenant-Commander William B. Pendleton, took his vessel out of Purvis Bay in the southern Solomons. His orders were to operate with two other DEs, the USS *George* and the USS *Raby*, in a search for Japanese submarines carrying vital supplies to the troops defending Bougainville, one of the northern Solomon islands. The crew of the USS *England* had a lot to live up to: their ship was named after a reserve ensign killed aboard the battleship USS *Oklahoma* during the attack on Pearl Harbor in December 1941. The men were also acutely aware that the *England* had been in commission for only eight months and had yet to be proved in battle.

On the next afternoon, as the three-ship hunter-killer group steamed in line abreast, the *England's* ever-watchful sonarman reported a contact, a large submarine running below the surface. Without hesitation, Pendleton ordered an attacking run and fired the ship's Hedgehog spigot mortar. Moments later, the device's 24 contact-fuzed bombs arced over the bow of the *England*, seeking out a target. A second salvo, close on the heels of the first, produced tangible results: the unmistakable sound of two direct hits. However, lacking clear confirmation of a kill, Pendleton ordered three more salvoes. The last volley of bombs was followed almost immediately by a further three underwater explosions. While trying

Below: Destroyer escort DE-635, the USS *England*, on duty in the northern Solomons, a few months after her lethal foray in the Philippine Sea, which had such devastating effect on the Japanese submarine fleet.

to regain contact with the target following this last attack, the *England* was rocked by a massive explosion that marked the end of the Japanese submarine *I-16*, a 3655-ton monster that, at 356ft, was some 50ft longer than the *England*.

Following this early success, the three escorts turned north, heading for what their captains had been told was a 'picket line' of enemy submarines trying to detect and sink US surface vessels. The Japanese operation, part of the 'A-Go' naval offensive in the Philippine Sea, aimed to lure major US naval units to the waters north of the Admiralty Islands, 1500 miles north of Purvis Bay, where some 25 submarines would be waiting to spring a potentially devastating trap. So thorough were the enemy's plans, that some of the boats had been waiting in the area for over a month.

Before first light on 22 May, at about 0350 hours, the three DEs were about 300 miles to the northeast of Manus Island when the sound of diesel engines was detected on sonar – from the signature, the vessel, a submarine, was on the surface and probably recharging its batteries under cover of darkness. The hunter-killer group swung into action. Bearing down on the prey, the *George* caught the submarine with its searchlight as the enemy captain ordered his crew to crash-dive and fired off its Hedgehog. There appeared to be no result but the *England*, coming up fast, soon changed all that. Unleashing a salvo from its own Hedgehog, the *England* was rewarded with a direct hit. Only oil and twisted wreckage marked the watery grave of *RO-106* and its 38-man crew.

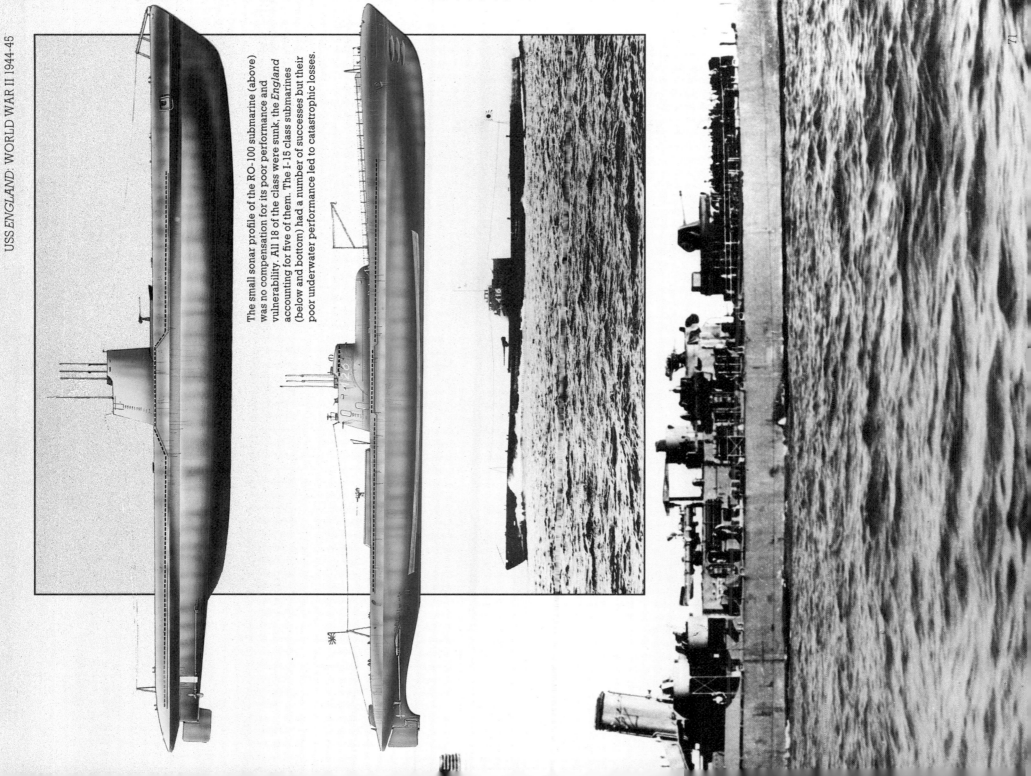

The small sonar profile of the RO-100 submarine (above) was no compensation for its poor performance and vulnerability. All 18 of the class were sunk, the *England* accounting for five of them. The I-15 class submarines (below and bottom) had a number of successes but their poor underwater performance led to catastrophic losses.

ENGLAND'S VICTIMS

The six enemy submarines accounted for by the England during May 1944 came from two distinct classes: five were of the small RO-100 type, the sixth was a unit from the I-15 group of much larger ocean-going boats.

The RO-100 boats were first intended to serve in the shallow home waters around Japan, and as such the series had serious disadvantages in the deeper waters of the Pacific. Their surface range, 4040 miles at 12 knots, and diving depth, a safe maximum of 200ft, made them of little use in the deep-water naval campaign against the US Navy. The submarines carried only seven torpedoes, too few to make any lengthy tour of duty worthwhile, and a 3in gun, mounted forward of the boat's conning-tower.

Although the short length of the boats (200ft) gave them a small sonar profile, their overall lack of performance made the RO-100s extremely vulnerable. Eighteen saw service in the war; all were sunk.

In contrast to the RO-100s, the I-16 had been built for long-duration, deep-water operations. A remarkable 356ft in length, the submarine displaced 2590 tons on the surface and 3655 tons submerged, and was capable of travelling at a top speed of 23½ knots.

Designed to strike at will, the class had a surface range of up to 16,155 miles. The boats also carried a wide array of armaments: a single 5.5in gun, two small-calibre anti-aircraft guns and six 21in torpedo tubes.

The running of each submarine rested with a crew of 100 men.

The I-15 class did score some successes, but their poor underwater performance and limited torpedo-carrying capacity limited their effectiveness. Only one of the 20 built by the Japanese survived the war.

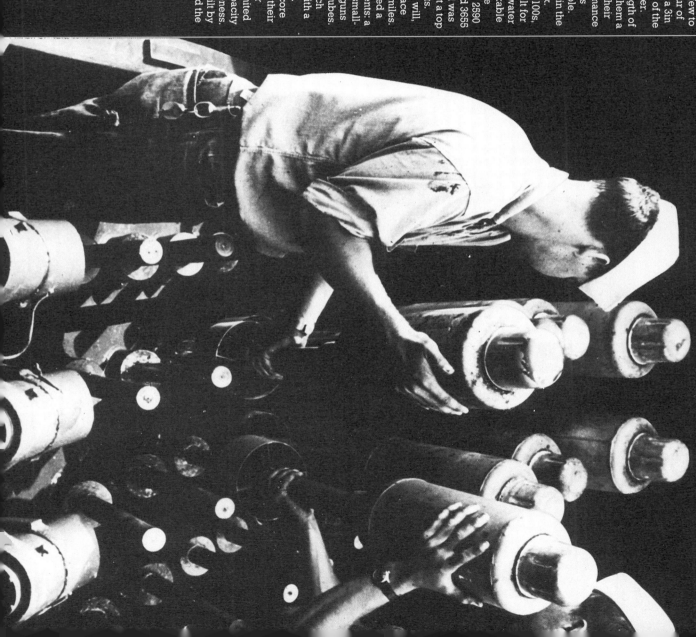

Working on available intelligence, seemingly confirmed by the England's two kills, the hunter-killer group's 'tactical commander, Commander Hamilton Hains, estimated the likely position of the enemy's patrol line and then shaped a southwesterly course that would take the three DEs down the line. It was a canny decision that was to add to the England's tally of victories over the Imperial Japanese Navy.

On the morning of the 23rd, well before the crews were able to sit down to breakfast, the ships ran into the RO-104 as the submarine was diving. Both the George and the Raby attacked in quick succession, but no avail. Again it was left to the England to deal with the enemy – the vessel's third kill in five days.

After despatching the RO-104, the group continued along the enemy's patrol line, moving further southwestwards. Early on the morning of the 24th, less than a week after the England had sailed from Purvis Bay, the DEs made contact with another enemy submarine, later identified as the RO-116. The initial contact was made by the George, just as the target was submerging to avoid the escort group.

In a desperate attempt to shake off his pursuers, the Japanese captain took his boat down to 168ft, where the sonar conditions were later described as 'feeble'. His manoeuvres were to no avail; the England charged up to the enemy's estimated position and its Hedgehog crew, firing their last few bombs, scored a direct, killing hit. A muffled explosion, welling up from the deep, signalled the end of the RO-116.

With the group's supply of Hedgehog bombs all but exhausted, Hains ordered the DEs to break contact and head for Seeadler Harbour on the north side of Manus Island. On the way to the rendezvous, on the 26th, the Raby made sonar contact with an enemy submarine but failed to score a hit. The England, picking up the contact, then raced in to unleash a lethal salvo against the RO-108 lying some 250ft below the surface. Again, a succession of explosions, clearly audible on the surface, heralded the end of another A-Go raider. It was the England's fifth kill in eight days, but not the end of the ship's remarkable sub-killing exploits.

After completing a speedy replenishment from a

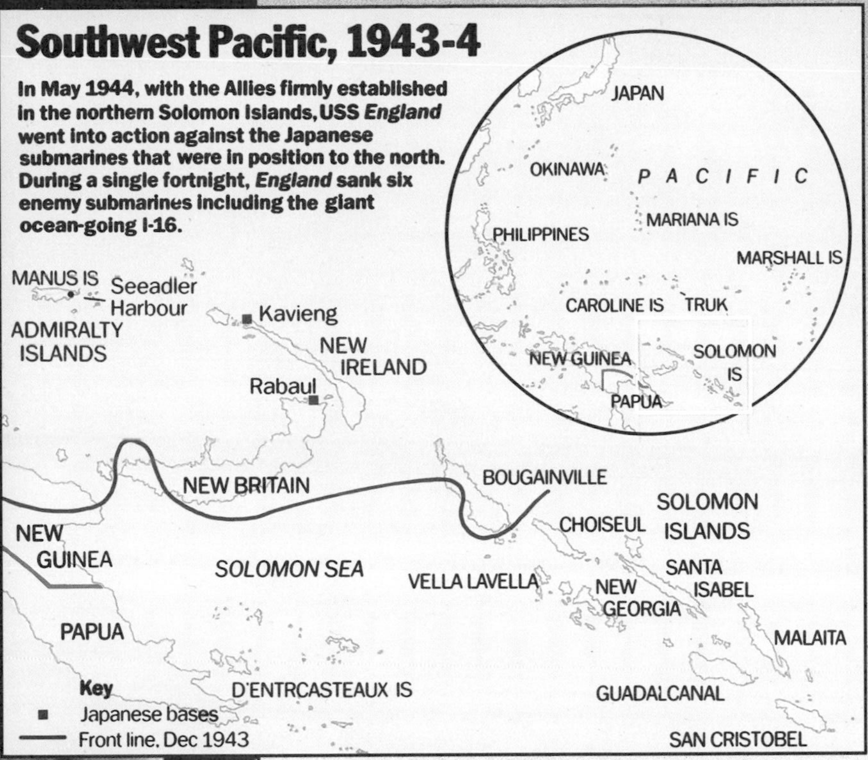

Early on 31 May, one of the ASW group's destroyers tracked down an enemy submarine, but unable to put in an attack, the ship reported the coordinates to the DEs. The *Raby* and *George* set off in pursuit and remained in sonar contact with the target throughout the hours of darkness. Although the two ships carried out a series of attacks, they failed to sink the submarine, the *RO-105*, even when it was on the surface. Next, the *George*, *Raby* and *Spangler* attacked in turn; again the Japanese boat survived their attentions. It was time for the *England* to make an appearance. At 0735 hours, the ship launched a single Hedgehog salvo – it was enough. The *RO-105* was the *England's* sixth and final victim in a patrol which had lasted only 12 days.

The performance of the *England* during the ship's 12-day cruise in May 1944 was outstanding by any standards: many sub-hunters never gained any kills against enemy submarines; those that were successful were the exception rather than the rule. The quality and eagerness of the ship's crew undoubtedly played a key role in the *England's* achievement, and there was also an element of good luck involved.

They failed to decipher messages indicating that at least seven enemy submarines had sailed from Truk

In the run up to the *England's* patrol, cryptanalysts at the Fleet Radio Unit Pacific Fleet (FRUPac) based at Pearl Harbor had been working on a new Japanese five-digit code. However, they failed to decipher messages indicating that at least seven enemy subs had sailed from Truk, part of the Caroline Islands, to form a picket line between Manus and the northeastern end of the Admiralty Islands. The Americans might never have discovered the enemy's intention except that a patrol aircraft sighted *RO-104* running on the surface to her assigned station. It was a lucky break that would lead to the *England's* six victories.

The Japanese submarine fleet commander, Vice-Admiral Takagi, was informed by his own radio monitoring service that the Americans had detected

Southwest Pacific, 1943-4

In May 1944, with the Allies firmly established in the northern Solomon Islands, USS *England* went into action against the Japanese submarines that were in position to the north. During a single fortnight, *England* sank six enemy submarines including the giant ocean-going I-16.

MANUS IS – Seeadler Harbour
ADMIRALTY ISLANDS

Kavieng
NEW IRELAND
Rabaul
NEW BRITAIN
BOUGAINVILLE
SOLOMON SEA
CHOISEUL
SOLOMON ISLANDS
SANTA ISABEL
NEW GEORGIA
VELLA LAVELLA
GUADALCANAL
MALAITA
SAN CRISTOBEL

NEW GUINEA
PAPUA
DENTRCASTEAUX IS

Key
■ Japanese bases
— Front line, Dec 1943

JAPAN
OKINAWA
PACIFIC
MARIANA IS
MARSHALL IS
PHILIPPINES
CAROLINE IS
TRUK
SOLOMON IS
NEW GUINEA
PAPUA

All of the *England's* kills were accomplished with the Hedgehog spigot mortar. Twenty-four small bombs are loaded (left) in four rows of six each. The contact-fuzed anti-submarine missiles drop some 200yds ahead of their launch vessel (right) in a pattern around the target with a diameter of about 140ft.

destroyer escort at Seeadler Harbour, the three ships immediately put out to sea, heading for a US anti-submarine warfare (ASW) group based around an escort carrier. Joined by a fourth DE, the USS *Spangler*, the reinforced group was divided in two, with the *England* and *Spangler* operating together under Commander Thorwald.

the *RO-104*, his response was to shift the patrol line some 60 miles to the southeast. It was a fatal mistake. Here, at last, was a message that FRUPac could decipher, at least in part. The decoders were able to produce a series of map coordinates that gave the rough dispositions of the submarines in the picket line. It was this vital information that sent the *England* and the other DEs steaming out of Purvis Bay on 18 May.

Two of the kamikazes were shot down but the third slipped through and made straight for the ship

The glaring success of the *England* could have alerted the Japanese to the fact that their codes had been broken. However, the US Pacific Fleet was able to give the ship full praise for its victories without alerting the enemy to the break in their ciphers. By suggesting that the DEs had 'just happened' to stumble on the line of submarines, they lulled the Japanese into thinking that the six boats had been lost through bad luck. It was to prove a costly misreading of the situation. The American ploy worked, and 17 of the estimated 25 enemy submarines in the area were sunk, including the six accounted for by the *England*.

These kills marked the high point of the *England's* career in World War II. Almost a year later, after long, fruitless months of routine anti-submarine patrols, the DE joined the mighty armada of transports and naval vessels lying off Okinawa. The initial assaults of Operation Iceberg, the US plan for the occupation of the island, went in on 1 April. On 9 May the *England* was 'bounced' by three Japanese kamikaze bombers. Two were shot down by a combat air patrol that was on the scene but the third slipped through the top cover and made straight for the ship. The DE scored several hits on the aircraft, setting it on fire, but the pilot steadied his dive and crashed into the vessel's starboard side, below the bridge. The devastating combination of fiercely burning

wreckage and the bombs slung underneath the kamikaze killed 37 members of the crew and wounded a further 25.

Despite the ship's terrible injuries, fire and damage-control parties managed to keep the *England* afloat, and she was able to limp back to the Philippines, where emergency repairs were carried out. The ship, however, needed considerable attention and was forced to sail home to the Philadelphia Navy Yard. On arrival, the *England* was immediately taken in hand for conversion to a high-speed transport. The work was never completed. With the Japanese surrender in September 1945, the US Navy no longer had any use for the vessel. The *England* was formally decommissioned in October and sold in the following year.

Despite the anti-climax of the *England's* performance in the closing stages of the war in the Pacific, the ship's efforts in May 1944 were without equal. Although other anti-submarine escorts sank a greater number of submarines in total, none was able to match the *England's* score of six boats destroyed in less than a fortnight. The *England* did have prior knowledge of the rough location of the enemy craft, thanks to the hard intelligence provided by the FRUPac in Pearl Harbor, but so did the other DEs in the group – yet they repeatedly failed to notch up even a single victory. Their repeated failure to sink a target suggests that for all the back-up facilities it was, in the end, the skill, training and efficiency of the *England's* crew that produced the outstanding record of May 1944. The ship's battle stars were well earned. Official recognition came when the ship was awarded a Presidential Unit Citation for its distinguished war record. As Pendleton summed up the affair. 'It does seem that practice does make perfect.'

Below: Shrouded in smoke, destroyer escort crew members bring forward ammunition during a kamikaze attack. It was this that effectively brought to an end the *England's* brief but illustrious service. In May 1945, the ship was attacked by three Japanese aircraft off Okinawa. Although hit by one of them managed to break through and dive into the starboard side of the *England* to cause major damage, including a huge fire, and claimed the lives of 37 crew, with a further 25 wounded. Damage-control parties laboured to contain the havoc and managed to keep the ship afloat. The wounded were transferred to other vessels and – still afire – the *England* was taken under tow, back to the Philippines. After emergency repairs, the ship returned to the US where she was to be converted to a high-speed transport. But the work was never completed. Within three months the war was over and the *England* was never again to see active service. But this sorry ending does not detract from the accomplishment of the USS *England* and her crew, and a record still unmatched by a US Navy warship.

THE AUTHOR Antony Preston is naval editor of the military magazine Jane's *Defence Weekly* and author of numerous publications including *Battleships, Aircraft Carriers and Submarines.*

HOMBRES OF THE DELTA

The US Navy SEALs were commissioned as a unit in January 1962 with the aim of greatly expanding the role and capabilities of the already-existing combat swimmer force, the Navy underwater demolition teams (UDTs). Most SEAL personnel are former UDT members but, once assigned to a SEAL Team, their training in unconventional warfare is considerably broadened. SEALs are instructed in the demolition of enemy shipping, harbour facilities, rail links, bridges and other riverine installations, and a wide range of counter-guerrilla and clandestine operational techniques.

These include jungle warfare, hand-to-hand and unarmed combat skills, escape and evasion techniques, survival, and extensive weapons training. They are also taught reconnaissance and surveillance, and how to organise and work with friendly military or paramilitary units. Finally, parachute training is provided, including high-altitude low-opening jump techniques.

The basic SEAL tactical unit is the Team, of which there are two, under the command of the Naval Special Warfare Groups. Each Team consists of 27 officers and 156 men, divided into five platoons, and like most special ops forces, the structure is streamlined so that each platoon is capable of mounting self-contained operations. SEALs were deployed extensively in Vietnam against the Viet Cong in the Mekong delta and saw action more recently in the October 1983 US invasion of Grenada. The SEAL cap-badge is shown above.

US Navy SEALs were rated the toughest fighting men battling against the communists in South Vietnam, in the swamp warfare of the Mekong delta

FOR THE AMERICAN soldier, the great delta where the Mekong river flows into the sea in the southernmost corner of South Vietnam was one of the deadliest and most treacherous areas of the whole Vietnam war zone. It was an area of open water, swamp and rice paddies, criss-crossed by some 6500km of waterways and canals, difficult to navigate and harder still to pacify. It was also one of the main strongholds of the Viet Cong (VC). For the VC, the delta provided a massive natural area of defence; they knew it like the backs of their hands, launching savage attacks and ambushes and then melting back into the swamps as silently as they had come. It was an unconventional war that required completely unconventional counter-measures.

With 80,000 VC operating in the area in 1966, the first elements of a new special ops group began to arrive in Vietnam and, although they were also to see plenty of action later throughout the war zone, their initial target was the delta. This new unit was the US Navy SEALs. They drew their name from the three elements they were trained to fight in, under and on - sea, air and land (although most SEALs in Vietnam would have substituted the word 'swamp' or 'mud' for land in their title).

All special ops personnel tend to be clannish and secretive about their unit and its work. The rigorous

selection such troops undergo before being accepted into the unit usually assures a strong sense of belonging to an elite brotherhood - a brotherhood that cannot be bettered. A large proportion of those who served in special ops in Vietnam (such as the Army Special Forces) will concede, however, that the SEALs were the foremost proponents of 'kicking ass and taking names' - the toughest hombres in the delta, and probably in the war. SEALs weren't numerous in Vietnam, but those who were there were formidable.

On arrival in Vietnam, the SEAL teams operated by setting up observation and listening posts along the countless waterways and trails used by the VC. Once bases or routes had been located and identified, the SEALs would then mount raids or set up ambushes to cut VC supply routes. So successful were these reconnaissance missions that within a year of the SEALs' arrival in Vietnam, listening posts were inserted for anything up to a week, during which the SEALs would continuously observe and monitor VC movements in their sector. It was not an easy task since it required immense stealth and self-discipline and any form of resupply was completely out of the question.

SEALs were also used on wider-ranging patrols, especially in the Rung Sat Special Zone south of Saigon. Rung Sat was an area of dense mangrove swamps and was heavily infested with VC. Small three-man detachments of SEALs would be inserted into 'Indian country' using 'Mike' boats (heavily armed riverine patrol craft), and then either walk or swim - usually a combination of the two - to a point where they could observe and perhaps ambush the enemy. During operations, the SEALs normally

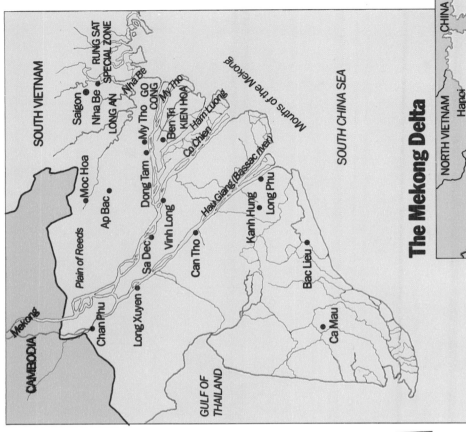

The Mekong Delta

SOUTH VIETNAM

Saigon
Nha Be
RUNG SAT SPECIAL ZONE
Nha Be GO CONG
LONG AN
Moc Hoa
My Tho
Ben Tri
KIEN HOA
Ap Bac
Dong Tam
Cai Luong
Ham Luong
Co Chien
Plain of Reeds
Sa Dec
Vinh Long
Hau Giang (Bassac river)
Kanh Hung
Long Phu
Chan Phu
Long Xuyen
Can Tho
Mouths of the Mekong
Mekong
CAMBODIA
Bac Lieu
Ca Mau
GULF OF THAILAND
SOUTH CHINA SEA

CHINA
NORTH VIETNAM
Hanoi
LAOS
Mekong
THAILAND
SOUTH CHINA SEA
SOUTH VIETNAM
Nha Trang
Saigon
CAMBODIA
GULF OF THAILAND

Page 75 : Cam cream liberally applied, a SEAL prepares for action in the della. Above left: Kitted out in 'tiger-stripe' fatigues, a member of a SEAL team waits in ambush. He is armed with a 5.56mm M63A1 Stoner light machine gun. The Stoner system was developed in the early 1960s as a multi-purpose weapon which could be quickly converted for a number of different roles including sub-machine gun, assault rifle, light machine gun and medium machine gun. In its LMG configuration it held a 150-round drum magazine and was highly regarded by SEAL teams operating in the Mekong delta.

maintained complete silence, communicating with hand signals or relying on the hours of operational experience with fellow team members which had taught each man how his colleagues worked, and how they would react when the going got rough. Fighting fire with fire, they often laid booby traps along known VC trails as well as setting up ambushes, and the two techniques were frequently used in conjunction with each other. Claymore mines, explosive devices with a directional blast that could knock a sizeable hole in a retreating VC column, were set along likely escape routes from a SEAL ambush. At the ambush site itself, demolition cord – a cord with a high-explosive core and protective outer sheath – might be strung out along the ditches on either side of the trail to catch any VC diving for cover when the SEALs opened up. The SEALs' missions were often quite simple and direct – to search out and destroy VC. *Sat Cong* (kill communists) was their primary goal and the SEALs were experts at it.

In dense swampland, choppers from Naval Light Helicopter Attack Squadrons were brought in

The SEALs are fundamentally a highly mobile force, trained to operate everywhere from the Arctic to the jungle, and although in action they are designed to be self-sufficient and able to fight without support, during the insertion and extraction phases of their missions considerable quantities of equipment are made available for their transportation. In early operations in the delta the SEALs were dropped from Mike boats, but later on in the war 'Boston

Whalers' were introduced for this purpose. These were 16ft glass-fibre craft with a very shallow draft which enabled the SEAL squads to be inserted in the narrowest of waterways where there was likeli-hood of detection. The Whalers were powered by 40hp or 85hp outboard engines and were capable of high speeds should the SEALs have to make a quick getaway. For insertions from submarines, or on other such clandestine ops, the light and silent-running IBS (inflatable boat, small) would be used. Originally designed as an emergency lifeboat for sea-going vessels, the IBS has proved extremely useful for the Navy's SEAL and underwater demolition units. It can carry seven men with up to 500kg of equipment, and can be rigged with a parachute for dropping from an aircraft; it can also be launched and recovered from the deck of a submerged submarine.

For larger operations where a whole SEAL team was being inserted or where fire-support was necessary, the medium SEAL support craft or fast, heavily-armed patrol craft was used. Whatever type was deployed, the boats would immediately move up or downstream so as not to give away the SEALs' position as they headed into the swamps.

For operations in dense swampland where the use of boats would be impossible, choppers from Naval Light Helicopter Attack Squadrons would be brought in, the SEALs normally abseiling into the water or onto the land, or diving directly into the water from the chopper. The key to all SEAL ops was versatility and the golden rule was to use the right equipment for the job.

In 1966 the SEALs, along with the US Army Special Forces, became involved in the ICEX (Intelligence and Exploitation) Program which was aimed at identifying and destroying the VC infrastructure within South Vietnam. Operating far inland, the SEALs' performance record was impressive. They killed and captured numerous VC, unearthed arms and supply caches, spearheaded other US and South Vietnamese units on search and destroy missions, and provided regular and accurate intelligence on enemy troop and supply movements. At the same time, SEALs were also being used for intelligence missions over the border inside North Vietnam. Haiphong harbour, the main port of entry for Soviet and Chinese arms and equipment shipments, was visited by SEALs fairly frequently.

Later in the war, North Vietnamese harbours and

bridges would be sabotaged by SEAL teams, although these missions have never been publicly acknowledged. On at least one occasion, it is said, a SEAL infiltration team was captured within North Vietnam but managed to kill all its captors and make a getaway, despite having been disarmed.

On Tanh Dinh Island they blasted the VC bunkers out of existence

By 1967, as area commanders began to hear of the significant results achieved by SEAL exploits, requests were forwarded for the deployment of further SEAL teams in Vietnam and their numbers were increased. Operating from a base at Nha Be, as well as from mobile bases on barges, the SEALs continued to mount hunter-killer and intelligence missions throughout the Mekong delta. Occasionally they were deployed in their role as divers to clear wreckage, or carry out other underwater demolition tasks. They performed numerous blasting jobs to open up rivers to allow US vessels to penetrate deeper into the delta and were sometimes assigned the unenviable task of recovering the bodies of downed US aircrews, trapped in the sunken wreckage of their aircraft.

SEALs also acted as scouts and spearhead forces for larger riverine operations mounted in the delta.

Left: A SEAL M60 gunner blasts away from a Mike boat along a waterway in the Mekong delta. Right, top to bottom: SEALs prepare to come ashore from a river patrol boat; a SEAL sets demolition charges to blow up a VC bunker on Tanh Dinh island during operation Bold Dragon III; and SEALs watch their charges destroy VC bunkers from the safety of a Mike boat.

On a demolition raid against enemy installations, the tasks performed by each man are well defined.

Personnel include the officer-in-charge, known as the 'wheel', swimmer scouts, the 'powder train' who look after the explosives, and 'riggers' whose job it is to lead the powder train to and from the objective and supervise the laying of charges. Approaching the shore in inflatable boats, the raiding party waits beyond the surf line while the swimmer scouts are despatched to scout the area. If all is clear the main force is signalled in. On reaching the beach, a detachment of men sets up a defensive perimeter known as the BDP (Beach Defense Perimeter) to protect the party from surprise attack and to guard the extraction area. The demolition team then sets out for its objective, moving as quietly and invisibly as possible. When the SEALs arrive at the target the charges are set and the riggers and powder train withdraw, leaving the swimmer scouts behind. Covered by the BDP, the explosives men put to sea and when all men have been accounted for, the scouts receive a radio command to pull the fuses. The scouts then withdraw and head back to the beach. On a properly executed raid, the charges will detonate when all the personnel are well out to sea.

US Navy SEAL, Vietnam 1960s

Wearing locally-made 'tiger stripe' fatigues this soldier's face and hands are camouflaged in distinctive SEAL style. Nylon and leather jungle boots, and an olive-drab towelling headscarf complete his outfit. He is armed with an M16A1 rifle (fitted with an M203 grenade launcher) and, attached to his belt, is a USMC Ka-bar fighting knife and fragmentation grenade.

In Operation Crimson Tide in September 1967, and Operation Bold Dragon III in March 1968, for example, they scouted and blew up a number of enemy installations, and during Bold Dragon did especially heavy damage on Tanh Dinh Island where they blasted numerous VC bunkers out of existence. Acting on intelligence from a VC defector, they also succeeded in destroying a VC weapons factory during this op. Despite their small numbers, the SEALs' targets were many and widespread. In Operation Charleston, for example, captured VC documents revealed that the VC were using a number of fresh water wells in the southern part of the Rung Sat Special Zone, and the SEALs were called upon to put a stop to this valuable source of supply. A series of carefully co-ordinated demolition raids were launched and their success was such that the VC logistics were severely disrupted.

Late in 1967 the US initiated the Phoenix Program, a combination of in-depth intelligence gathering and a programme of counter-terror ops. On this project, the SEALs worked very closely with the 'prews' (PRU – Provincial Reconnaissance Units) in the Mekong delta. The PRUs were drawn from a variety of sources including Special-Force trained local MIKE forces (elite mobile strike units) and 'Chieu Hoi' communist turncoats. The PRUs were well-paid professionals and were among the most effective indigenous troops used in Vietnam.

Both Army Special Forces and Navy SEALs acted as advisers and trainers to the PRUs. As the Phoenix Program's action arm, the PRUs operated in 10 to 20-man teams under Special Forces and SEAL tutelage and carried out reconnaissance and intelligence-gathering missions and ambushes and raids against VC tax collectors and political cadres in the villages. They were also used for 'snatch' operations

IBS (inflatable boat, small)

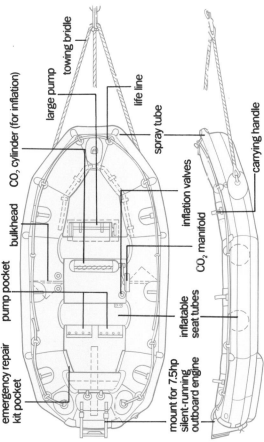

towing bridle
large pump
CO_2 cylinder (for inflation)
bulkhead
pump pocket
life line
spray tube
emergency repair kit pocket
inflation valves
CO_2 manifold
carrying handle
inflatable seat tubes
mount for 7.5hp silent-running outboard engine

to kidnap certain VC officials likely to be able to provide valuable intelligence, or in selected 'wet' ops when assassination or counter-assassination was called for. The Phoenix Program was especially effective in the delta due to the presence of the SEALs and the PRUs they worked with, and overall, between 1967 and 1971, the VC infrastructure within Vietnam was cut from a strength of between 80,000 and 100,000 to less than 2000 (some reports indicate less than 1000).

15 SEALs with 19 Vietnamese militiamen smashed into the camp and fought a running gun battle

In their advisory and training capacity, the SEALs also helped to select and train the Vietnamese version of the SEALs, the LDNN (Lin Dei Nugel Nghai). The US SEALs conducted numerous operations alongside the LDNN during the latter stages of the US involvement in Vietnam, including many raids into VC POW camps in the delta to free prisoners. On 22 November 1970, 15 SEALs with 19 Vietnamese militiamen smashed into a VC POW camp and fought a running gun battle with the guards who were forced to flee under the savage onslaught. A few SEALs were also assigned to special operations which reportedly included landings by submarine in North Vietnam.

In a few cases, SEALs were involved in the setting up of security cordons around US port facilities and in underwater patrolling to prevent the infiltration of enemy frogmen. For the most part, however, such security was carried out by attack-trained dolphins, although at the Cam Ranh Bay facility and elsewhere, SEALs may have worked in conjunction with the killer dolphins. Up to 60 enemy combat frogmen may have been killed by these dolphins.

Above: The IBS (inflatable boat, small) was utilised by the SEALs in Vietnam for a variety of missions. **Below:** SEALs leap from a river patrol boat beached on a canal in the delta 100km from Saigon during a raid on a Viet Cong base in January 1968. **Above left:** a US Navy SEAL takes aim in the surf with his shotgun. The Ithaca 12-gauge shotgun is a pump-action weapon with a five-round magazine.

Despite this impressive operational record, only one Navy SEAL won the Congressional Medal of Honor for service in Vietnam. Lieutenant Joseph Kerrey won his award for a mission launched on 14 March 1969 in Nha Trang Bay. Kerrey was leading an operation to capture VC political cadre members on an island. He and his team scaled a 350ft cliff to get above the enemy but as they descended for the attack they came under heavy fire. Kerrey was badly wounded by a grenade, but he still managed to direct his team's fire effectively into the enemy position. He remained conscious and in command while his men secured an extraction site and laid down covering fire as the chopper came in to pull

them out. After Vietnam, Kerrey remained in the SEALs and was training with the British Special Boat Squadron shortly before the outbreak of the Falklands conflict in 1982.

For the execution of their missions, the SEALs were equipped with some highly sophisticated weapons and equipment, and, as with most of the world's special ops groups, a wide range of armament could be drawn on to suit the requirements of the task in hand. For small-unit ops, such as ambushes and close-quarters fighting, firepower was crucial. A typical three-man SEAL fire element would normally be armed with an Ithaca M37 12-gauge fighting shotgun (reports suggest that SEALs used special 12-gauge flechette rounds in their Ithacas), a 5.56mm Stoner M63A1 light machine gun and an M16 assault rifle with an M203 grenade launcher attached. The five-round pump action Ithaca could stop a man dead in his tracks while the Stoner, normally equipped with a 150-round drum magazine, provided sustained firepower. The US Navy SEALs are the only unit to use the Stoner, since in less experienced hands, the weapon has a tendency to malfunction and go onto full auto without notice.

The SEALs, however, took a great deal of care of the weapons on which their lives depended and found the Stoner a very satisfactory weapon in action. With the high-velocity M16 and the extra firepower of its grenade launcher, the SEAL fire element packed a hefty punch and was a formidable opponent in close-quarters combat.

On more clandestine ops, the SEALs carried the 9mm Smith and Wesson Mark 22 Model O silenced pistol, known as the 'hush puppy' since it was originally designed for use in neutralising enemy guard dogs. In Vietnam it proved a very effective silent killer for taking out VC guards and the weapon was fitted with a slide lock to keep the action closed when firing, thus eliminating any tell-tale clicks of the mechanism. The hush puppy utilised special subsonic ammunition and was made of stainless steel to prevent it rusting up in salt water. SEALs were also trained in the art of hand-to-hand combat and made good use on occasion of the Randall, Ka-bar, Gerber and various other fighting knives.

Other firearms in the SEAL arsenal included the XM177E2, a retracting-stock version of the Colt Commando carbine, the M14 rifle, the German

The XM177E2 version of the 5.56mm Colt Commando (top left) was possibly the most formidable close-action weapon of the Vietnam conflict. The 9mm M45 'Carl Gustav' sub-machine gun (above left) was popular due to its reliability and folding stock; also in use was the old .45in M3A1 SMG (above centre), a rugged if somewhat crude gun. More sophisticated was the West German 7.62mm Heckler and Koch G3 (above right). The Claymore mine (right inset) was a highly effective anti-personnel device. Background picture: Two SEALs armed with an M60 GPMG (left) and an M79 grenade launcher (right).

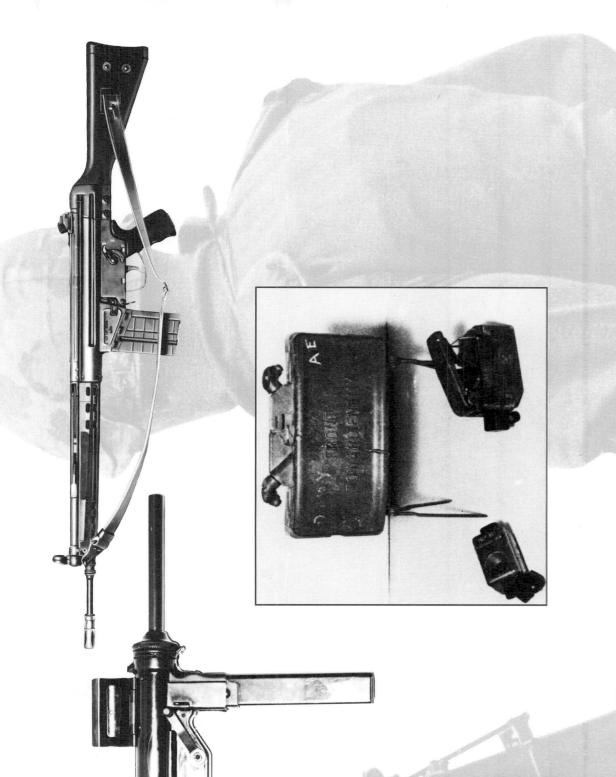

Heckler and Koch G3 assault rifle, the British Sterling L34A1 silenced sub-machine gun, the M3A1 'grease gun' and the Swedish 9mm 'K' sub-machine gun. Devices such as Claymore mines, M26A1 grenades, demolition cord and satchel charges were all favourites with the SEALs as well.

Also of interest is the special combat coat developed for use by the SEALs. Made of camouflage material, this coat was designed to carry everything the SEAL would need on a mission. It even had a built-in flotation bladder. There were three versions of the garment – for rifleman, grenadier and radio-man – with pockets and pouches to suit the wearer's particular assignment. Because of the highly secret nature of their missions and the tendency of SEALs to keep their mouths shut, many of their operations and exploits, such as those in North Vietnam, are still shrouded in secrecy. SEAL teams always operated quietly, except when they were detonating explosive or shooting things up. Most available information on the SEALs states that the last detachments, those acting as advisers to the LDNN, were out of Vietnam by 1971 or 1972; however, there is good reason to believe that a few SEALs remained and

carried out special ops almost to the fall of Saigon in April 1975.

I occasionally worked with the SEALs when assigned to special operations in Vietnam, and I remember them as tough professionals. Almost any other troops, having been extracted after a hazardous mission, were only too anxious to get a beer and some sleep, but, more often than not, a SEAL team would still be looking for a target on which to expend any remaining ordnance. SEAL after-action reports abound with instances of SEALs attacking and destroying enemy installations or ambushing enemy personnel on the way back from an already successful mission. During the war they accounted for some 580 VC killed in action and over 300 probable kills, but the SEALs didn't rest on their laurels. SEALs were tough with a capital 'T'; both their enemies and their friends agreed on that.

THE AUTHOR Leroy Thompson served in Vietnam as a member of the USAF Combat Security Police. He has published several books on anti-terrorist methods, and is the author of *Uniforms of the Elite Forces* and *Uniforms of the Indochina and Vietnam Wars*.

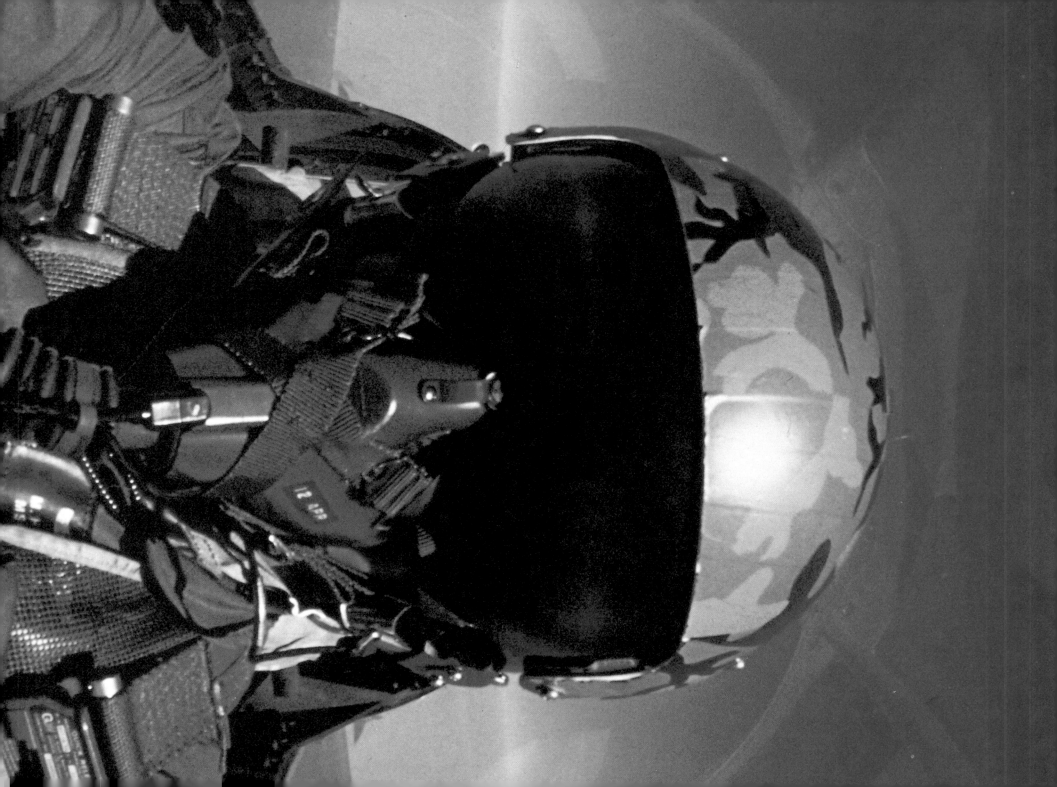

FALKLANDS
AIR STRIKE

The Sea Harriers of 800 Squadron fought to the finish against the Argentinian Air Force in the South Atlantic, and by the end of the conflict the Argentinian pilots had nicknamed them *La Muerte Negra* – the black death

FOLLOWING THE Argentinian seizure of the Falkland Islands on 2 April 1982, and the decision by the British government to repossess the territory, No. 800 Squadron was ordered to embark on HMS *Hermes* and make ready for sea. Under the command of Lieutenant Commander Andy Auld, the squadron was hastily expanded from its normal peacetime complement of five aircraft to 12, with additions of aircraft, instructors and trainee pilots from No. 899 Squadron. At the same time. No. 801 Squadron, No. 800's sister unit. was embarked on HMS *Invincible.* On 5 April *Hermes* and *Invincible*, carrying a total of 20 Sea Harriers, left Portsmouth for the South Atlantic. The squadrons immediately began a period of intensive training.

For many pilots it was the first time they had seen a carrier from an aircraft in flight. Some had only just started their training at Yeovilton; others had been hastily recalled before finishing their 're-fam' (re-familiarisation) courses. Training on board *Hermes* helped to iron out any problems and prepare the pilots for the difficult conditions of the South Atlantic. Landing on *Hermes* was a tense time for the Sea Harrier pilots. Cloud cover was often as low as 70m, and visibility was regularly reduced to 800m. The slightest error of judgement, all too easy when trying to compensate for the heaving of a flight-deck buffeted by high winds and drenched in spray, could have led to tragedy, and the loss of an almost irreplaceable pilot.

Fully armed Sea Harriers were held on deck alert throughout the day and night

By 21 April the carriers were well south of Ascension Island and the period of intensive training was declared at an end. From now on fully-armed Sea Harriers were held on deck alert throughout the day and night.

A quick response to enemy attacks was crucial. In the Total Exclusion Zone aircraft were kept at Alert Five: Sea Harriers were armed, manned and ready to launch within five minutes of a scramble. Pilots sat in a cramped cockpit for up to two hours at a time. There was little regard for personal comfort in a war zone. Damp got everywhere and control panels were usually dripping wet. Groundcrew ingenuity solved the major problem – clingfilm 'borrowed' from ship's stores and stretched over the aircraft's vitals kept out the worst of the weather. Although tired and cold, pilots usually got into action in under five minutes. If the Sea Harrier was ready for action, the groundcrew had to be top.

NO. 800 NAVAL AIR SQUADRON

The Insignia of No. 800 Naval Air Squadron shows a trident with two winged swords. In the Falklands campaign of 1982 the squadron's air-crews, waiting long hours at combat readiness in the Sea Harriers on the flight deck of HMS Hermes, may well have considered particularly apt their squadron motto, 'Numquam non paratus' – 'Never unprepared'.

The squadron was formed in 1933 with Hawker Nimrod fighter planes. It has achieved several notable firsts in Royal Navy aircraft-carrier operations. In 1938 it flew Blackburn Skua fighters from a carrier, making it the first operational unit to deploy monoplanes in that way; in 1951 it was the first operational unit to fly jet aircraft (Supermarine Attacker fighters) from a carrier. And in 1980, the unit was re-commissioned with Sea Harriers and began training aboard HMS Invincible. It was the first operational unit to fly jump-jets from a carrier.

The Falklands campaign was to present a stiff challenge to the stamina of the small Sea Harrier strikeforce. Once past Ascension Island a 24-hour alert was maintained and engineers, technicians and ground crew worked round the clock to keep a maximum complement of the Sea Harriers on Hermes at constant combat readiness. Pilots flew as many as four sorties in a day, remaining in the cockpit between flights. Yet what they achieved in support of the main operations was succinctly expressed by Admiral Sir Henry Leach, First Sea Lord: 'Without the Sea Harrier there could have been no Task Force'.

The change to a war footing was timely. That same day a pilot of No. 800 Squadron had the first encounter with an Argentinian Air Force plane. Lieutenant Simon Hargreaves was scrambled to investigate a radar contact 240km south of the warships, thought to be a commercial airliner. As he closed on the aircraft, a Boeing 707, he suddenly made out the Argentinian flag on the nose and tail, and the lettering Fuerza Aerea Argentina (Argentinian Air Force) along the fuselage. In fact the Boeing was on a reconnaissance flight from Buenos Aires, bent on establishing the southward progress of the British fleet. With strict orders to do nothing to exacerbate the already difficult situation between the two countries, Hargreaves could only close on the intruder and take photographs. He maintained contact with the Boeing until it broke away to the west and headed for home. During the days that followed there would be further meetings with reconnaissance Boeings, until the British government made it known that further Argentinian aircraft approaching the ships of the Task Force would meet a lethal reception.

Seeing no prospect of a peaceful solution to the Falklands crisis, on 30 April the British government

Page 85: Lieutenant Simon Hargreaves – at cockpit readiness in his Sea Harrier – awaits the order to go into action.
Left: Sea Harriers stand on deck as HMS *Hermes* leaves Portsmouth. The pre-war tail markings of 800 Squadron are clearly visible here. Left: Lieutenant Commander Blisset's Sea Harrier (with empty starboard missile rack) returns to the *Hermes* after shooting down an A-4 Skyhawk on 21 May. Below: Sea Harriers in the main hangar of *Hermes* are made ready as the Task Force sails south. Right: Flight Lieutenant Dave Morgan inspects the damage done to the fin of his Sea Harrier by a 20mm cannon following the raid on Port Stanley airfield.

The nine Sea Harriers bound for Port Stanley airfield made their landfall as briefed at Macbride Head, some 30km due north of the target. There Lieutenant Commander Tony Ogilvy and three other pilots split away from the main force, and moved into position to mount a toss-bombing attack on the target from the northeast. As Ogilvy pulled away, Auld led the remaining five aircraft in a wide arc to give the necessary timing separation between the two attacking forces, then his Sea Harriers headed straight for the Port Stanley airfield.

Right on time the toss-bombers turned into their attack runs, and as they reached the previously-computed pull-up points each pilot raised the nose of his aircraft by the required amount and released his three 1000lb bombs. Each aircraft then turned sharply through a semicircle to avoid going closer to the defended area than was necessary. The salvo of bombs continued in the same formation, following a curved trajectory that took them up to about 900m before they began to descend on the target. At a pre-set altitude, radar airburst fuses detonated nine of the bombs, raining thousands of jagged bomb splinters on the Argentinian anti-aircraft gun positions to the west of the airfield. The other three bombs were fitted with delayed-action fuses; they thudded into the airfield to detonate at random intervals during the hours that followed.

While the defenders' attention was distracted by the bombs exploding over their heads, the five remaining Sea Harriers streaked towards the airfield from the north and northwest, hugging the ground to maintain the element of surprise.

Even so, the first pilot to run in on the target, Lieutenant Commander Mike Blissett, found himself entering a hail of anti-aircraft fire.

'There was a lot of fire from just off the western end of the runway, and more from the hills to the southwest, all coming towards me. I did a very hard six-to-seven O jink to the left, held it for a few seconds, did an equally hard jink to the right, then levelled out and ran in to bomb.'

Blissett's jinking had made things difficult for the enemy gunners and also for his wing-man, Flight Lieutenant Ted Ball.

'At the target I was not aware of anyone shooting at me. All I was aware of was Mike about 500 yards in front of me weaving from side to side. But because we were jinking, one moment we were quite far apart and the next we were close together. When we rolled out and eased the aircraft up for our bombing runs we were quite close.'

'Suddenly there was a bloody great explosion behind me and the rudder started vibrating like mad'

The two Sea Harrier pilots released their cluster bombs on the airfield buildings, then returned to ground level again jinking to avoid the enemy fire.

Last over the target was Flight Lieutenant Dave Morgan, and by the time he got there everything seemed to be happening:

'As I passed over the sand-dunes I pulled up to about 150 feet getting ready to drop my load of cluster bombs; then I saw some of the damage done to the airfield. One of the buildings was covered in flames, with billowing black smoke coming out the back. There was lots of anti-aircraft fire, and missiles going all over the place.

ordered Rear Admiral J. F. 'Sandy' Woodward to begin military operations on the following day to re-take the islands. In any such undertaking the most important facility to be denied the Argentinian forces was the airfield at Port Stanley. On May 1, under cover of the early morning darkness, a Royal Air Force Vulcan, on a marathon flight from Ascension Island, dropped a stick of twenty-one 1000lb bombs across the airfield. One of the bombs scored a direct hit on the centre of the runway, temporarily putting it out of action. The Falklands air war was beginning to get under way.

Shortly after dawn the pilots of No.800 Squadron began to board the 12 Sea Harriers drawn up on the deck; each aircraft was loaded with three bombs on its wing and fuselage racks. Nine of the aircraft were to make a follow-up attack on Port Stanley airfield, the other three were to make an initial attack on the airfield at Goose Green. As the men prepared to go into action for the first time, each nursed his own thoughts. Lieutenant Commander Neil Thomas remembered:

'My main worry was that I would find something wrong with the aeroplane which did not make it completely unserviceable. If that happened and I said I was not going to take the plane, people might have thought I was "chickening out". But fortunately there was nothing at all wrong with my Sea Harrier.'

First to take off was the squadron commander, Lieutenant Commander Andy Auld. One by one, at measured intervals, the other eleven Sea Harriers followed. After take-off the raiders circled the ship and assembled in attack formation, then descended to 15m and headed towards East Falkland. Just before the formation reached the north coast of the island, the Goose Green raiding force broke away and headed for its target.

WEAPONS OF THE SEA HARRIER FRS 1

The British Aerospace Sea Harrier FRS 1 is a single-seat short-take-off and vertical-landing multi-role naval aircraft designed for three main operational missions – air defence, reconnaissance and surface attack. To achieve this versatility it is capable of carrying a wide range of weaponry on its seven weapons stations including free-fall, retarded and cluster bombs, rockets, air-to-air missiles, 30mm cannon and anti-ship missiles. In the reconnaissance role the Sea Harrier is armed with two 30mm Aden guns in fuselage-mounted pods and carries two 455-litre drop tanks on the inboard stations. Radius of action for a reconnaissance sortie is some 450 nautical miles. For high-level combat air patrol the Sea Harrier carries two AIM-9L Sidewinder air-to-air missiles on its outboard stations in addition to cannon and drop tanks and is able to loiter for an hour and a half some 100 nautical miles from the carrier with reserves for three minutes of combat time. On surface-attack missions in the Falklands the Sea Harrier carried three Mk 83 1000lb bombs or two BL 755 cluster bombs, each containing 147 bomblets.

Ferranti Blue Fox radar in folding nose

pitot tube

head up display

Doppler radar

air intake

auxiliary power unit

Martin Baker Type 10H ejection seat

Rolls-Royce Pegasus 104 turbofan engine

twin 30mm Aden cannon

rotating thrust nozzles

digital navigation and weapon aiming computer

auto pilot

ventral airbrake

A Tigercat missile came along the runway and passed in front of my nose, probably aimed at the parked aircraft, but before he could return to low altitude his Sea Harrier was hit:

'Suddenly there was a bloody great explosion behind me and the rudder started vibrating like mad. At the time I was hit I was going pretty fast, 500 to 600 knots [925 to 1110 kph], with the throttle hard forward. The aircraft was still responding to the controls; I took a quick look inside the cockpit to see if the engine instruments were all right. They were.'

While the attack on Port Stanley airfield went into its closing stages, Lieutenant Commander 'Fred' Frederiksen was leading in the attack at Goose Green. The three Sea Harriers approached the airfield fast and very low, and had released their bombs before the enemy anti-aircraft gunners opened fire on them.

Of the 12 Sea Harriers that took part in the attacks only one, Dave Morgan's, was hit by return fire. Once out of range of the defences he slowed his aircraft, and the vibration markedly decreased. He tried the controls, and found that the only thing not working

Morgan aimed his cluster bombs at one of the parked aircraft, but before he could return to low altitude his Sea Harrier was hit:

properly was the rudder trim. On the way back to the carrier another Sea Harrier moved into close formation with his aircraft and reported that there was a hole through the fin. Morgan let the other aircraft land before him, then put his Sea Harrier down carefully on the deck. Afterwards it was found that a single 20mm round had penetrated the fin from the port side, exploded, and blown a hole the size of a man's fist out of the starboard side. The damage was soon repaired, however, and the aircraft returned to flying.

During the rest of the day British fighters had several skirmishes with Argentinian aircraft. The first two aerial victories for the Sea Harrier, a pair of Mirage fighters, fell to aircraft of No.801 Squadron. Then it was the turn of No. 800. Lieutenant Martin Hale and Flight Lieutenant Tony Penfold were on patrol when they came under attack from Daggers – Israeli-built Argentinian fighter aircraft. One of the enemy fighters fired a missile which began to home on Hale's aircraft, forcing him to dive steeply to avoid it. The evasive manoeuvre was successful, and the Sea Harrier pilot warily began climbing back to join his comrade. As he did so he watched Penfold launch his counter-attack.

'I kept my eyes pretty much glued to my 6 o'clock [the rear] to see if there were any of their guys trying to get in behind me. As I was in the climb I heard Tony call that he had fired a missile and it looked like a long shot. I looked up and saw a missile trail very high, then an explosion.'

The wreckage of the Dagger crashed into the sea to the north of West Falkland.

During the first day's fighting the Sea Harrier force had shot down two Mirages, a Dagger and a Canberra, incurring no loss to themselves. Following these losses the Argentinian Air Force began to treat the jump-jets with considerably more respect, and three weeks were to elapse before their aircraft were seen again over the Falklands in large numbers.

On 4 May No. 800 Squadron mounted a second attack on Goose Green airfield, and suffered its first loss during the conflict. One of the three Sea Harriers that took part was shot down by ground fire. The pilot, Lieutenant Nick Taylor, was killed.

'The squadron had little further contact with the enemy until 9 May, when Lieutenant Commander Gordon Batt and Flight Lieutenant Dave Morgan came upon the Argentinian intelligence-gathering

Left: A Sea Harrier is refuelled on the deck of HMS Hermes between CAPs (combat air patrols). In action the blue/white/red roundels were re-painted less conspicuously in blue and red, as shown in this photograph. Far left: Sidewinder air-to-air missiles are mounted on a Sea Harrier. The aircraft of 800 Squadron were armed with the AIM-9L version of the Sidewinder, a considerable advance over earlier infra-red homing missiles which could only lock-on to subsonic targets from the rear. The AIM-9L could home on a target from almost any angle, providing the Sea Harrier pilots with greatly increased tactical flexibility.

radar warning receivers

trawler *Narwal* patrolling to the southeast of the Falklands. Morgan reported the find to his control ship, and was immediately ordered to attack the vessel. Three strafing runs from each of the Sea Harriers inflicted severe damage on the engine room, leaving *Narwal* dead in the water. Later in the day a Royal Navy party was landed on the ship by helicopter, but in spite of attempts to save her the trawler sank the next day.

On 18 May No. 800 Squadron received welcome reinforcement with the arrival of four more Sea Harriers brought south on the deck of the container ship *Atlantic Conveyor*. Allowing for the one aircraft lost in action, the squadron now had 15 planes.

On 21 May both Sea Harrier squadrons were heavily committed to providing air cover for the British warships and transports that were landing troops on the shores of San Carlos Water. If anything was going to draw the Argentinian Air Force back into action it would be a target such as this, and during the day No. 800 Squadron's pilots were in action several times. The first to achieve kills were Lieutenant Commanders Mike Blissett and Neil Thomas, who shot down two Skyhawks from a formation of four and forced the others to jettison their bombs. Just over an hour later Lieutenant Commander 'Fred' Frederiksen shot down a Dagger, and 50 minutes after that Lieutenant Clive Morell and Flight Lieute-

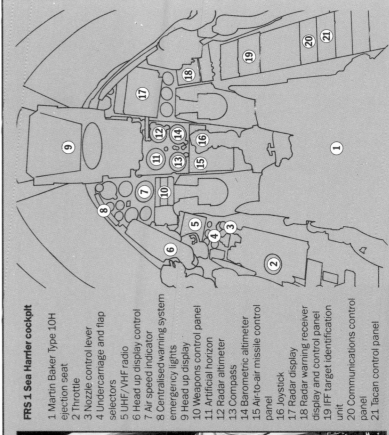

FRS 1 Sea Harrier cockpit

1 Martin Baker Type 10H ejection seat
2 Throttle
3 Nozzle control lever
4 Undercarriage and flap selectors
5 UHF/VHF radio
6 Head up display control
7 Air speed indicator
8 Centralised warning system emergency lights
9 Head up display
10 Weapons control panel
11 Artificial horizon
12 Radar altimeter
13 Compass
14 Barometric altimeter
15 Air-to-air missile control panel
16 Joystick
17 Radar display
18 Radar warning receiver display and control panel
19 IFF target identification unit
20 Communications control panel
21 Tacan control panel

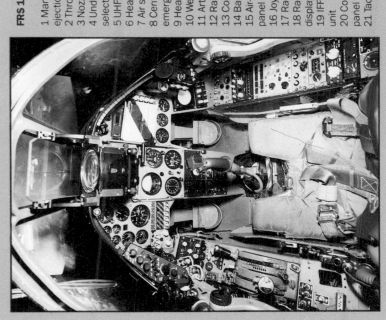

nant John Leeming caught three Skyhawks in the act of withdrawing down Falkland Sound, after bombing HMS *Ardent*, and shot down all of them.

Bad weather prevented the Argentinian Air Force from operating on the 22nd, but on the 23rd the attack resumed and Lieutenant Martin Hale shot down a Dagger. Flight Lieutenants Dave Morgan and John Leeming brought down two Argentinian helicopters and damaged another.

On the 24th Lieutenant Commander Andy Auld and Lieutenant Dave Smith had a remarkable suc-

BLISSETT

Action fought between 1304 and 1306 hours on 21 May 1982, by Lieutenant Commander Mike Blissett and his wing-man Lieutenant Commander Neil Thomas. Blissett begins his description at the point where the pair of Sea Harriers arrived over Goose Green to begin their patrol:

'We headed west-south-west at 300 feet – there were some patches of low cloud and we wanted to be beneath them. We were flying in defensive battle formation, in line abreast about 2000 yards apart with Neil to the north and me to the south. When we were three miles east of Chartres Settlement I caught sight of four Skyhawks in front of me about three and a half miles away, flying across my nose from left to right; they had just crossed the coast on their way in. With the very high closing speed there was no time for me to do anything but call to

cess when they shot down all three Daggers in a formation they intercepted coming in over West Falkland. Two of the raiders fell to Auld and one to Smith. Also on that day a pair of Sea Harriers of No.800 Squadron took part in a combined attack on Port Stanley airfield with some of the Royal Air Force Harriers that were also carried on *Hermes*.

Following the losses it had incurred during the hard battles around the San Carlos Water beach-head between 21 and 25 May, the Argentinian Air Force operations tapered off. The nickname that the Argentinians had given the Sea Harriers, *la muerte negra* (the black death), was a token of their effectiveness. There followed a period of poor weather that limited air operations by both sides. The Argentinian attack aircraft did not return to the Falklands until 8 June, when they made their devastating attack on the British assault ships *Sir Galahad* and *Sir Tristram* off Fitzroy. Two hours later a formation of

Neil "Break starboard!", because I really wanted him to come round hard. I pulled into a very hard turn to starboard. As we passed over the top of them they saw us, their nice arrow formation broke up and they began to jettison underwing tanks and bombs. Everything was happening very rapidly. They pulled round over some rising ground to the south-east of Chartres. By now I was in the lead with Neil to my left and about 400 yards astern, with all of us in a tight turn. The Skyhawks were in a long echelon, spread out over about a mile. I locked a Sidewinder on one of the guys in the middle and fired. My first impression was that the missile was going to strike the ground as it fell away - I was only about 200 feet above the ground. But suddenly it started to climb and rocketed towards the target. At that moment my attention was distracted somewhat as a Sidewinder came steaming past my left shoulder – Neil had fired past me, which I found very disconcerting at the time! I watched his 'winder chase after another of the Skyhawks, which started to climb for a patch of cloud above, then the aircraft disappeared into the cloud with the missile gaining fast.

'Then I glanced back to the right and saw my missile impact on the Skyhawk I had aimed at. Suddenly, about 800 yards in front of me, there was a huge fireball as the aircraft blew up in the air; there was debris flying everywhere. As I started to lock on my second missile I caught sight of something flickering to my left, out of the corner of my eye; it was the Skyhawk Neil's Sidewinder had hit, tumbling out of the clouds with the back end well ablaze. It came down cartwheeling slowly past my aircraft about 100 yards away, looking like a slow-motion replay.'

four Skyhawks arrived in the area to make another attack, but this time No.800 Squadron was ready for them. On their patrol line high above, Flight Lieutenant Dave Morgan and Lieutenant Dave Smith caught sight of the enemy aircraft, dived to engage, and quickly reached firing positions. Morgan later recounted:

'I wound across and got in behind with a massive overtaking speed. He was rapidly getting larger in my windscreen. I locked up my missile at about 1500 yards and fired at 1000 yards. My missile did

Below: A Sea Harrier of 800 Squadron takes off in a cloud of spray from the ski-jump on HMS *Hermes* to undertake a combat mission over the South Atlantic. The Sea Harrier was one of the great success stories of the Falklands conflict: well armed and highly manoeuvrable in combat it was also very reliable, and when used in conjunction with the ski-jump was a most effective CAP (combat air patrol) aircraft. A simple but highly effective device, the ski-jump was developed during the 1970s and allows the Sea Harrier a 65 per cent shorter take-off run or 30 per cent increased weapon and fuel loads. In addition there is no need for the ship to steam at high speed during the launch phase, thereby leading to a significant saving in the ship's fuel.

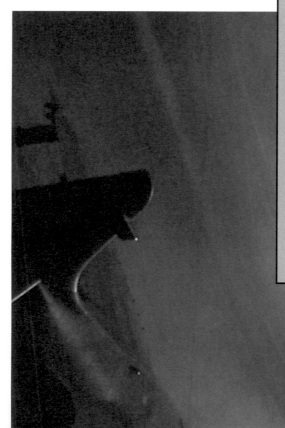

MORELL

Action fought between 1511 and 1514 hours on 21 May 1982, by Lieutenant Clive Morell and his wing-man Flight Lieutenant John Leeming. Morell begins the account when the pair of Sea Harriers were over Goose Green, passing 10,000 feet on their descent to take up a patrol position over Falkland Sound. Suddenly he saw bombs exploding in the water beside one of the Royal Navy frigates to the north of him:

'Having seen the bombs explode I deduced that the attackers would probably exit going southwest down the [Falkland] Sound. I looked to where I thought they would be and they appeared, lo and behold, below a hole in the clouds. They were easy to see from above, painted white. I said, "Christ, Leems, there they are!". We were in line abreast battle formation, I was on the left. I just rolled steeply down and he followed me. Once I had cleared the cloud I saw two of them and I slotted in behind the rear one. Leems went in behind the third man, who was back further still.

'I had some problems with my weapons system; by the time I fired my Sidewinder I was down at his altitude, about 100 feet, at a range of 800 to 1000 yards. The missile streaked after him and exploded within a foot or so of his jet pipe, virtually a direct hit. His aircraft went into the sea in a big ball of fire.

'Initially, my other missile refused to fire at the second guy. So I opened up with my guns but I didn't see any of the rounds hit. Having exhausted my ammunition I switched back to the missile, it was locked on to him and it fired on its own accord. At first it looked as if it was guiding nicely, then it just seemed to lose interest. It got to within a length or two behind him then stopped guiding and fell away into the sea.

'Now I had no more bullets or missiles, I looked round to see what was going on behind. To my left and behind I could see this large ball of fire going down into the sea. I thought, "I hope that's not my No.2." But then John called up and said, "Spag (my nickname), are you OK?" I said, "Yes, how about you?"'

On their return to *Hermes* Morell and Leeming each claimed one Skyhawk destroyed. However, examination of Argentinian records after the war showed that the second aircraft Morell fired at also went down. Some of his 30mm rounds had hit the aircraft and punctured the fuel tanks. Unable to regain his base in Argentina, the pilot flew to Port Stanley and ejected. All three Skyhawks in the formation had been destroyed.

a quick initial jink, then went off after him and exploded near his tail; there was a huge fireball and wreckage began to fall into the water. There was no reaction at all from the others, they were in a gaggle coming off the target with no attempt at mutual cover. They were running west up Choiseul Sound.

'I then pulled across after one of the others, who had seen either me or the explosion. He began a fairly gentle turn to port across my nose, almost as if he was looking to see what had happened to the man behind. My missile locked up, broke lock, then I locked it on again and this time the lock held. I fired at the second aircraft at about 1200 yards. I think he saw it coming, because he reversed his turn and broke away to starboard. The missile reversed its turn too, cut across my nose and went straight in and hit after he had turned through about 40 degrees. The explosion took off everything behind where the fin joined the fuselage, then the front end yawed violently and dropped into the water ...'

The fighting on the Falklands lasted a further week but, although the Sea Harriers mounted numerous patrols over the islands, there were no further encounters with Argentinian aircraft.

During the conflict No. 800 Squadron flew a total of 835 operational sorties, in the course of which it destroyed 15 enemy aircraft in air-to-air combat and at least three more on the ground, for the loss of one aircraft to ground fire and one in an operational accident. 800 Squadron had again proved itself the premier fighting unit of the Fleet Air Arm.

THE AUTHOR Alfred Price served as an aircrew officer in the RAF for 15 years, specialising in electronic warfare, aircraft weapons and air-fighting tactics. He has written extensively on aerial warfare and amongst his published works is *Air War South Atlantic*.

LT-COMMANDER PATRICK DALZEL-JOB

Patrick Dalzel-Job's association with Norway began prior to World War II. Between 1936 and 1939, anticipating that the Norwegian coast would be of great strategic significance in the event of war, he sailed his own schooner up the coast, charting the inlets and forwarding his work to the Admiralty.

At the outbreak of war in 1939, he left the schooner in Norway and returned to Britain. In April 1940, while still only a junior naval sub-lieutenant, Dalzel-Job went with the Allied Expeditionary Force to North Norway, where the Norwegians were fiercely resisting the German invaders. He was the first man ashore at Harstad on the island of Hinnöy. Using his knowledge of the coast and language, he organised the landing of about 6000 troops by large numbers of local fishing craft and some destroyers. Subsequently, he directed extensive troop movements along the coast near Narvik, using dispersed fishing fleets to reduce vulnerability from the air. In this way, he transported in all nearly 15,000 soldiers and about 4000 refugees, without loss. His caution was shown to be justified when the trooper Chrobry was used, against his advice, to take men south – she was sunk with serious losses, including the CO of the Irish Guards.

On 28 May the Allies seized Narvik. Dalzel-Job realised that the Luftwaffe would return to bomb and, without orders, he organised the evacuation of women and children to the port's neighbouring islands. The Luftwaffe inflicted considerable damage on Narvik, and Norway's King Haakon VII recognised Dalzel-Job's act with his thanks and the Cross of the Order of St Olav.

In 1942, MTBs began to cross the North Sea to plague German merchant convoys in the Norwegian Leads

FOLLOWING THE Allied withdrawals from Norway in May and June 1940, my thoughts turned often to finding a way of returning and striking back at the

cross the North Sea and work successfully against the enemy in Norwegian waters.

It was clear to me that the MTBs could not possibly hope to find a target, attack it, and return across the North Sea, all in one night. The boats would have to be kept on the Norwegian coast – if necessary for several days and nights – until a suitable target came in sight. The boats' range could be increased by carrying large quantities of high-octane fuel on deck, but even so, the distance from our base at Lerwick in the Shetlands to the Norwegian coast was about 200 nautical miles, and in the open sea the best

the MTBs could manage was about 15 knots.

Bad weather could also overtake the boats before their return to base. Our worst experience was when an MTB faced a northwesterly force nine gale all the way back across the North Sea. It suffered breaks in no less than 13 of its laminated frames, and conditions aboard were appalling. The bows crashed into the troughs of each wave until the hull shook like a hooked mackerel; men and movable objects parted company with the deck as it plunged, only to regain contact with a sickening shock as the bows surged upward in the next sea. Fortunately, however, the great skill of our meteorological officer, Special Branch Lieutenant George Westwater, made this kind of experience quite rare in the history of the flotilla.

The first MTB sorties went to Norway in November 1942. Lieutenant Prebensen with one group sank two small ships in Askvoll harbour, north of Sognefjord. More important still, the big MTBs found that they could penetrate into the Inner Leads with ease, and that they could lie hidden quite safely in the narrow inlets during the day. Lieutenant Ola Andresen took his two boats into Fröjsjöenand, being forced out of

German occupying forces. The best prospect seemed to be to operate Motor Torpedo Boats (MTBs) in the Norwegian Leads, using fuel dumps and hiding places in the rocky inlets. Although there were not many MTBs available in 1940, and their range was restricted by their size and fuel capacity, I still think it could have been done in those early days of German occupation. As it was, the idea was thought impractical by the British naval authorities, and the Norwegian flotilla in Dover had little hope of getting back to Norway.

For two frustrating years, therefore, I served on converted merchantmen in the Southern Atlantic, patrolling the ocean and watching in helpless pity as neighbours, in convoy fell one by one to U-boat torpedoes. Then, in January 1942, as my ship under went a refit in the Clyde for the Far East, I received a signal instructing me to report to the Admiralty in London. I felt like a man reprieved from the death cell. I was to be sent to a Fairmile Motor Launch working out of Kirkwall in Orkney, presumably to gain practical experience in Coastal Forces operating in northern waters. Then, late in June, I was appointed to the staff of Admiral Sir Lionel Wells, who was the Admiral Commanding Orkney and Shetland, and at Lyness I began at last to see what was expected of me. I had to collate all available

information about the west coast of Norway, a formidable undertaking which took me seven weeks, working up to 80 hours each week.

While in London in September, just after the costly Dieppe raid, I was summoned to see Lord Louis Mountbatten, who had recently been appointed Chief of Combined Operations. He told me that he had arranged for me to run special MTB operations in Norway – it was now up to me to make a success of them. Command-trained troops were to be carried in the eight big new D-class MTBs of the Norwegian flotilla. Although these boats were really small ships, powerful craft of over 100 tons with two 21in torpedo tubes and heavy deck armament, there were many problems to be overcome if they were to

his intended target ... a big German gunpost on the island of Bremanger in broad daylight at a range of about one and a half miles, flying the Norwegian ensign. The Germans took absolutely no notice at all; it can only be

FJORD RAIDERS

presumed that the idea of enemy torpedo boats being in those waters never entered their minds.

All the Norwegian boats came back safely; this was very encouraging to me. The darkest period of the year now being with us, the MTBs began to go to Norway whenever weather and moon were propitious. No two operations were the same, but the procedure in general was for the boats to slow their engines, and to fit external silencers, as they passed the outer rocks, then they went straight to their planned lurking places – narrow creeks, usually on islands, where they could lie two at a time alongside the rocks (there is very little range of tide on Norway's west coast). The boats were covered

Left: Although they sailed under escort, German convoys in Norway were under constant threat from the Fairmile D-class MTBs (below) of the Norwegian MTB flotilla. In addition to their four 18in torpedoes, the MTBs carried two 6-pounders, a twin 20mm cannon, and two twin 0.5in machine guns.

completely with camouflage nets after they had been secured, and a field telephone was run up to the nearest hill-top overlooking the shipping channels. The commando troops – about a dozen for each group of boats on normal operations – put out their guard pickets on the island, and the crews settled down to wait for sight or news of German ships.

It was not to be expected that every MTB patrol in Norway would be successful, and many of the Norwegian boats returned to Lerwick more or less damaged by the sea but with little else to report. Yet, one by one, the successes were achieved – German merchant ships and patrol craft sunk or raked by gunfire, watch-posts attacked suddenly out of the night, and bewildered German prisoners snatched for interrogation.

One of the most ambitious and successful of the early raids came in the third week of January 1943. It took place on the island of Stord, at the entrance to Hardangerfjord, where there was a copper pyrites mine of some value to the Germans. All available Norwegian MTBs were used, both for landing the men at Sagvaag and for making gun diversions elsewhere. The main diversions were at Marstein, a rocky offshore island with a lighthouse and gun battery, and at Lervik, lying on the southeastern side of Stord.

The Sagvaag raid was a credit to the spirit of co-operation between the Norwegian crews and the commando troops, who were commanded by a South African officer of the London Scottish, Major Ted

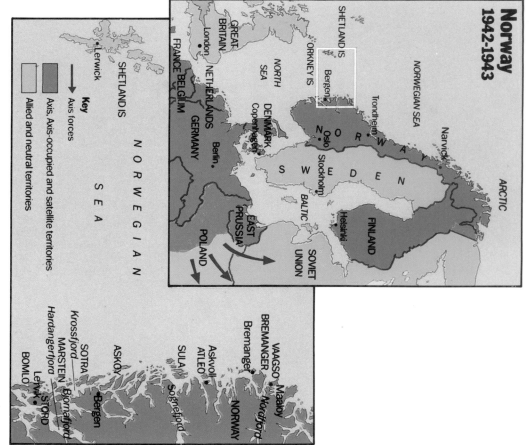

Norway 1942-1943

Key
→ Axis forces
Axis, Axis-occupied and satellite territories
Allied and neutral territories

ARCTIC

NORWEGIAN SEA

Narvik
Trondheim
Bergen
SHETLAND IS
ORKNEY IS
GREAT BRITAIN
London
NORTH SEA
NETHERLANDS
BELGIUM
FRANCE
DENMARK
Copenhagen
GERMANY
Berlin
EAST PRUSSIA
POLAND
BALTIC SEA
SWEDEN
Stockholm
Oslo
NORWAY
FINLAND
Helsinki
SOVIET UNION

NORWEGIAN SEA

SHETLAND IS
Lerwick

VAAGSO
Maaloy
BREMANGER
Bremanger
Nordfjord
Askvoll
ATLEO
SULA
ASKOY
Sognefjord
NORWAY
SOTRA
Krossfjord
MARSTEIN
Bjornafjord
Hardangerfjord
Lervik STORD
BOMLO
Bergen

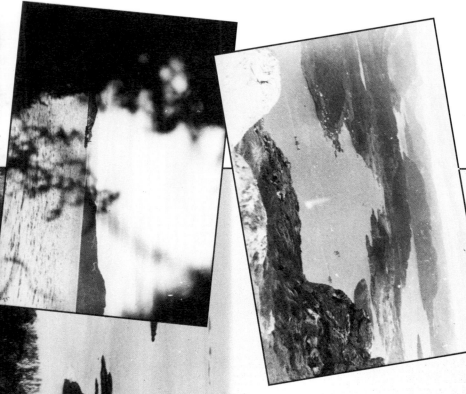

Fynn. The machinery at the copper mine was smashed with explosives, the quay was destroyed by torpedoes, one small enemy ship was sunk, and three German prisoners were brought back to the Shetlands. Only one of our men was killed, and no MTB was lost or seriously damaged.

Another very successful sortie from the Shetlands came very late in the season – during the first week of June, when in Latitude 60 degrees North there was scarcely any protective darkness, even at midnight. Lieutenant Tamber, Senior Officer of the Norwegian flotilla, took two of his MTBs (commanded by Lieutenants Prebensen and Bögeberg) into Krossfjord, the wide southern approach channel to Bergen. There the two boats lay hidden and camouflaged in a cove on the southwest side of a very small island called Traelsöy.

On the third night, a southbound German ship of 8132 tons, the *Altenfels*, came in sight with an M-class minesweeper following close astern as escort. Tamber's boats let go their lines from the rocks and moved to the southeastern end of the little island; when they entered the open fjord, the two forces came bow to bow at a range of about 700yds. *Altenfels* was hit by two MTB torpedoes, and sank in less than a minute, to the accompaniment of a brisk gun battle between the German escort ship and the Norwegian MTBs – a fight in which three German shore batteries and the guns of another German patrol boat soon joined.

With their task completed, the Norwegian boats slipped at speed through the islands and rocks to the open sea; and they came back to Lerwick with very little damage to show for a most courageous and successful operation. Total Norwegian casualties that night had been two killed and five wounded – including both Tamber and Prebensen. In the sinking of the *Altenfels*, 34 Germans lost their lives, and the German naval authorities were badly shaken by this unexpected MTB attack so near to mid-summer.

In the autumn of 1943 I was selected to participate in a slightly different kind of operation. It had been proposed that a British MTB should carry Chariot (manned torpedo) teams for strikes in the Norwegian Leads. Since random sweeps would be unlikely to find targets, the operational plan called for an observer to be planted above a major harbour with a wireless transmitter, while the MTB lay hidden and waiting at an offshore island.

The anchorage chosen was Askvoll, a harbour lying 60 miles north of Bergen on the main German shipping route. It was used frequently but irregularly by large enemy convoys. I was to be landed on the nearby island of Atleö, after which I would climb 2000ft to a vantage point over the fjord. Part of my task was to ascertain the nature of defences at Askvoll – our intelligence was that boom nets against submarines and at least one gun battery protected the area. I would be landed in uniform, and all contact with Norwegian civilians was to be avoided, for their sakes and for mine. Since the enemy convoy movements were unknown, I was given supplies for a stay of at least a week on the island.

On 14 October 1943, the British MTB set sail, carrying two torpedoes and their crews. Half an hour before midnight we came up to the low point of land that was Atleö's western extremity. I was landed by a small boat, and very soon both the boat and the MTB had gone. I was completely alone. It was hard going over boulders and furze with the heavy transmitter, and I did not reach my lookout post until 1700 hours the next day. I concealed the transmitter and checked my equipment for the long wait. If all was well, as I supposed it was, the MTB would now be lying among the rocks at Vaerö, about eight miles west of Atleö. At the pre-arranged time I signalled the single letter 'N', meaning 'nothing to report'. With dramatic suddenness, the answering 'dah-dit' came in my earphones. All was well.

That was to be my last contact with the MTB. When, in the evening of 16 October, I signalled that a convoy had anchored at Askvoll, I received no reply. Awaking at dawn on the 17th, I saw that the convoy was already heading southwards, making for the narrow gap of Krakhellesund before crossing the entrance of Sognefjord. No ships entered Askvoll that day, and my report that evening again elicited no response. With contact now lost for two days, I was expected to make an emergency rendezvous at Tevik cove at 2200 hours that evening. Although the rough country made this impossible, I fortunately had a sufficiently clear view of the sea during my descent to be able to check through binoculars that no MTB was in the vicinity.

The following days, 18 and 19 October, I spent holed up near the rendezvous, keeping out of sight and recording signs of enemy shipping. At about 1500 hours on the 19th, a harsh crescendo snarl shook me out of my thoughts, and a German fighter came suddenly over the hill behind me, to sweep low over the point where I lay hidden. Immediately afterwards, a second fighter came from the side, and swept so low that its shadow crossed in front of my hole. There was a moment of silence, then both fighters shrieked towards me – down, up, away and down again. This went on for a full half-hour, and then the first ships of a large and heavily escorted north-bound convoy came in sight in the channel. I decided that the fighters had been on a routine sweep ahead of the convoy.

At 2300 hours I resumed my watch. Two German patrol ships had been prowling off my point earlier in the evening, but they had now gone. Inside the islet of Skumsö, however, and about half a mile from where I sat on the rocks, there were two brightlights. The lights blinded me when I turned the binoculars on them, and I could not see what was under them.

About two hours later, I became aware of a faint

Left: Dalzel-Job had a clear view of Askvoll harbour and its merchant traffic from his observation point on Atleö island. Below left: In his hiding place near the emergency rendezvous at Tevik cove, he was able to photograph passing ships. Right: A German M-class patrol boat is observed from a hill top by a member of the MTB commando force as it searches the coast for Allied attack vessels. The second photograph (below), taken only minutes later, shows a Norwegian MTB 'lurking' out of sight in a rocky inlet. The Norwegian coast afforded many such hiding places and it was impossible for the Germans to investigate them all.

VP OPERATIONS

The neutrality of Norway in the early months of World War II was exploited by Germany in that her ships could sail in the Norwegian Inner Leads without threat from Allied forces. After the Germans occupied Norway in 1940 they did everything possible to defend the coast, and gun batteries, searchlights and minefields were installed at every entrance that could admit big ships. The Norwegian MTB flotilla, however, had details of at least 20 lesser entrance channels that were undefended save for the occasional watch-post. The minefields were usually too deep in the water to affect their craft.

The Germans had little or no radar on the coast, but for MTBs commencing VP operations (as the raids in the Inner Leads were known) it was essential to approach in darkness, so as not to be seen by shore observers or patrolling aircraft. Equally important, it was impossible to identify the intended entrance in darkness unless the moon was rising behind the land.

Approaching Norway against the moon, the mountains stood out in distinctive silhouette while the boats merged into the silvered sea behind them. If the moon was not in the right position, the favourable conditions were reversed and MTB operations became hazardous or even impossible.

and persistent humming noise which gradually became a definite, rhythmic throb. A shadowy shape appeared, grew and lengthened, then changed to a familiar silhouette. Four white spouts of water were gushing from its side; it was a D-class MTB. I showed my torch in a brief recognition signal and soon it was nosing gently into the abrupt rock slope where I stood waiting, until the high flare of her bow loomed above me. Whispering Norwegian voices asked my name, and a rope swung down towards me. While I was still scrambling over the bow with my pack, the MTB was backing into deep water, trembling to the throttled power of her four great engines. She was MTB 626, commanded by Lieutenant Bögeberg, an old friend, who was as surprised to see me as I was to see him. He asked me about the lights near Skumsö, but I could tell him nothing except that they had not been there the previous evening.

Conversation now ceased, and the two torpedoes left their tubes with sighs and shudders

The night was very still, and the only sound was the restrained murmur of our engines; but as we came closer to Skumsö we could see the outline of a large anchored merchantman under the lights. Conversation now ceased, and the two torpedoes left their tubes with sighs and shudders. After half a minute, a column of water began to rise against the night sky, and at the same instant a machine gun spattered viciously from a German escort near the shore.

Our many guns burst into joyous life, and the bright tracer bullets cut lines to and fro across the darkness. MTB 626 leapt beneath my feet to the deep roar of 4000hp as we turned towards the open North Sea beyond the islands. Astern, the shadow of the merchantman was already sinking slowly, our guns stopped reluctantly. One man on our stern had been very slightly wounded in the foot by a machine-gun bullet, but he was our only casualty. Lieutenant Bögeberg had not expected to find me

on Atleö for the MTB which had landed me had been unfortunate. At her lurking place a local man had appeared with urgent warnings about the frequency and thoroughness of German searches in the area. The British officers, on their first visit to Norway, had no way of ascertaining whether he spoke the truth and they had decided to leave Norway on the 16th. The MTB was spotted and attacked by German aircraft while at sea and it eventually reached a Scottish port after a fierce running battle in which a German fighter had been shot down.

My return from Atleö in MTB 626 was my last contact with the Norwegian flotilla. As it happened, little of importance was achieved by the MTBs in the year after I left the Shetlands, but the last winter of the war brought success to the Norwegian boats at the rate of three sinkings a month, culminating in the destruction of the German submarine U-637, two weeks before the end of fighting in Europe. By then, the Norwegian MTBs had made 152 crossings of the North Sea and had sunk 25 ships. Their success should not be measured only in ships sunk, for their presence in the Norwegian Leads had been a source of constant harassment and anxiety to the German authorities in Norway. In the two and a half years of patrolling, Norwegian casualties were 18 killed and 50 wounded. Sea and weather were seldom lesser perils than German guns: it was a fitting task for Norsemen.

THE AUTHOR Lieutenant-Commander Patrick Dalzel-Job directed the operations of the Norwegian MTB flotilla in the Norwegian Inner Leads from their commencement in November 1942 until October 1943. After the war, he served with the Royal Canadian Navy.

OPERATIONAL RESTRICTIONS

The involvement of the Special Operations Executive (SOE) and the Special Intelligence Service (SIS) in the Norwegian area was to be a cause of great frustration to the men involved in VP operations.

For example, in order to safeguard their arms-smuggling operations into Norway, SOE had powers to close sections of the coast to all other Allied forces for periods of several days. The Norwegian MTB flotilla would be poised for a promising operation, only to have its boats held in port by a ban imposed by SOE. The fact that SOE appeared to be achieving very little of military value in Norway served only to fuel the Norwegian force's resentment.

Also, hidden at different places along the coast were SIS agents with just one duty to perform – to report by wireless to London if they saw a German capital ship. These courageous spies were considered vital to Allied naval intelligence and no military action was permitted if there was the slightest chance that it would provoke a search to be made near a transmitter. SIS reports were thought by Naval Intelligence to be so sensitive that they were never passed to the MTB force, whose officers felt, understandably, that being the only Allied force actually fighting the Germans on the Norwegian coast they ought to be given all available information about the enemy.

Proudly flying the Norwegian ensign, MTB 626, captained by Lieutenant Bögeberg, bears Patrick Dalzel-Job homeward after the successful torpedo attack on a German merchantman near Skumsö island on 20 October 1943. The weapon shown is one of the twin 0.5in Vickers machine guns mounted on each side of the bridge.

CLASH ON THE KOLA RUN

Target: *Scharnhorst*
Range: 12 miles and closing
HMS *Belfast* opened up with a 12-gun
broadside, the first of many to be
fired in the epic and bitterly fought
Battle of the North Cape

HMS BELFAST

At the end of 1943, HMS *Belfast* was one of the most modern cruisers in the world. She had been built in 1938 with a standard displacement of 11,500 tons and a main armament of 12 6in guns in four triple turrets. She had been severely damaged by a German magnetic mine in November 1939, and the repairs had taken nearly two and a half years to complete.

Belfast emerged from her refit with improved underwater protection, in the shape of anti-torpedo bulges, and with more light anti-aircraft guns for close-range air defence. But the greatest improvement was the fitting of radar. *Belfast* carried the most modern equipment available to the Royal Navy, which meant that the ship's main armament (each 6in gun was capable of firing 12 112lb shells per minute) could be aimed and fired in all weathers.

Belfast was re-commissioned in November 1942 under the command of Captain Frederick Parham, a gunnery specialist whose previous appointment had been Deputy Director of Naval Ordnance. With Parham came nearly 900 men to work and fight the ship, many of whom had never been to sea before in their lives. Yet in a few months Parham and his executive officer, Commander P. Welby-Everard, had worked up the ship and her crew to a high state of readiness for operations at sea.

Above: The badge of HMS *Belfast*.

ON 26 DECEMBER 1943 HMS *Belfast*, in company with her sister ship HMS *Sheffield* and the older County-class cruiser HMS *Norfolk*, was spending an uncomfortable Christmas steaming through an Arctic gale. The three ships formed the 10th Cruiser Squadron of the Home Fleet (Force One) and were providing the heavy escort for Convoy JW55B, outward bound for Russia and consisting of 19 heavily laden merchant ships, and Convoy RA55A, homeward bound from Kola and consisting of 22 merchant ships. *Belfast* had made many of these trips before and her crew were no strangers to the 'Kola Run', as the route was known. Yet events were to prove that this escort duty was anything but routine.

For some time the Admiralty in London had been aware that the 34,000-ton German battle-cruiser *Scharnhorst* was under orders to attack a convoy going to Russia at the first favourable opportunity. *Belfast* and the other two cruisers were at sea to guard against such a threat, but as additional reinforcement the Commander-in-Chief Home Fleet, Admiral Sir Bruce Fraser, was also at sea in his flagship, the 35,000-ton battleship HMS *Duke of York*, with the cruiser HMS *Jamaica* and four other destroyers.

Scharnhorst was now alone and on a converging course with Burnett's cruisers

The British appreciation of the German Navy's intentions was correct. Convoy JW55B had been sighted by Luftwaffe reconnaissance aircraft, and on the evening of Christmas Day the *Scharnhorst* had sailed from Alte fjord with five destroyers. By 0400 hours on 26 December JW55B was 50 miles south of Bear Island, with the cruisers of Force One, led by Rear Admiral Robert 'Bullshit Bob' Burnett in *Belfast*, 150 miles to the southeast and Fraser's ships (Force Two) about 210 miles to the southwest. The Admiralty had already passed a general signal to the effect that they knew the *Scharnhorst* was at sea, and at 0628 Fraser ordered Force One to close on the convoy for mutual support. Half an hour later the *Scharnhorst* altered course to the southwest and the German destroyers spread out to search for the convoy. At 0820 *Scharnhorst* altered course again, this time to the northwest, but she failed to tell the destroyers and they played no further role in the action. *Scharnhorst* was now alone and on a converging course with Burnett's cruisers. At 0840, *Belfast's* radar picked up *Scharnhorst* at a range of 35,000yds, about 30 miles from the convoy and lying between the merchantmen and Burnett's cruiser escort. As the range fell to 13,000yds *Sheffield* came into visual contact and at 0924 *Belfast* opened fire with starshell to illuminate the target, but all the bursts fell short. Nevertheless, Burnett ordered his ships to open fire with their main armament while leading them around on a wide turn to port, to shorten the range and place the cruisers between the *Scharnhorst* and the convoy. But as this deployment took place, *Norfolk* fouled the range of the other two ships and they were temporarily unable to fire. Despite this set-back, *Norfolk* got in some accurate shooting and one of her shells destroyed the *Scharnhorst's* forward radar.

The *Scharnhorst* had been taken by surprise and she retired at high speed to the southeast, leaving

THE KOLA RUN

When Hitler invaded Russia in June 1941, the Allies prepared to divert Lend-Lease goods from Britain to the beleaguered nation. The first convoy sailed for Archangel in September, and in October large quantities of vital equipment were pledged, to include 400 aircraft, 500 tanks and thousands of tons of raw materials each month. Until March 1942 the convoys returned from their destinations, Archangel and Murmansk in the Kola Inlet, almost without casualty. However, Germany had realised the importance of the convoys to the logistics and morale of the Soviet forces, and in January 1942 Admiral Raeder stationed U-boats and surface vessels in the Trondheim fjords.

Together with the Luftwaffe they mounted an intense offensive on shipping passing round the North Cape in the Barents Sea. The convoys suffered heavy casualties, both of merchantmen and escorts, and in June 1942 the ill-fated Convoy PQ17, the seventeenth convoy to sail to Russia from Iceland, lost 22 of its 35 merchant ships. The disastrous fate of PQ17 resulted from a panicked Admiralty order to break formation, and in the following months there was a tightening of convoy discipline and a marked increase in escort ships, including aircraft carriers and anti-aircraft vessels. While each convoy was provided with an anti-submarine escort of destroyers and corvettes, capital ships such as HMS *Belfast* sailed to confront the big guns of the German Navy. The sinking of the *Scharnhorst* in December 1943 marked the end of that duty, for never again were the Arctic convoys menaced by a German capital ship.

Left: A side-view of HMS *Belfast*, one of the Royal Navy's most successful cruisers of World War II. Above: The 'A' and 'B' turrets of the *Belfast*, heavily encrusted with ice during a convoy run to Murmansk. The *Belfast* was armed with twelve 6in guns, mounted in four triple turrets, the maximum armament for a cruiser. Top: In readiness for action, Royal Marine gunners sleep by their guns; a shell lies in a loading cradle prior to ramming home in the breech.

The Battle of the North Cape
26 December 1943

The Battle of the North Cape, fought in the icy waters of the Barents Sea, was the last major capital ship action in European waters in World War II. By 19 December, Dönitz had decided to use Scharnhorst against the next Allied convoy on the run to Kola. On 20 December, Convoy JW55B sailed from Loch Ewe in northern Scotland; three days later RA55A set out from Kola in the opposite direction. The British cruisers Belfast, Norfolk and Sheffield were assigned to cover the convoys, while the battleship Duke of York and the cruiser Jamaica provided distant cover. Battle was joined on 26 December.

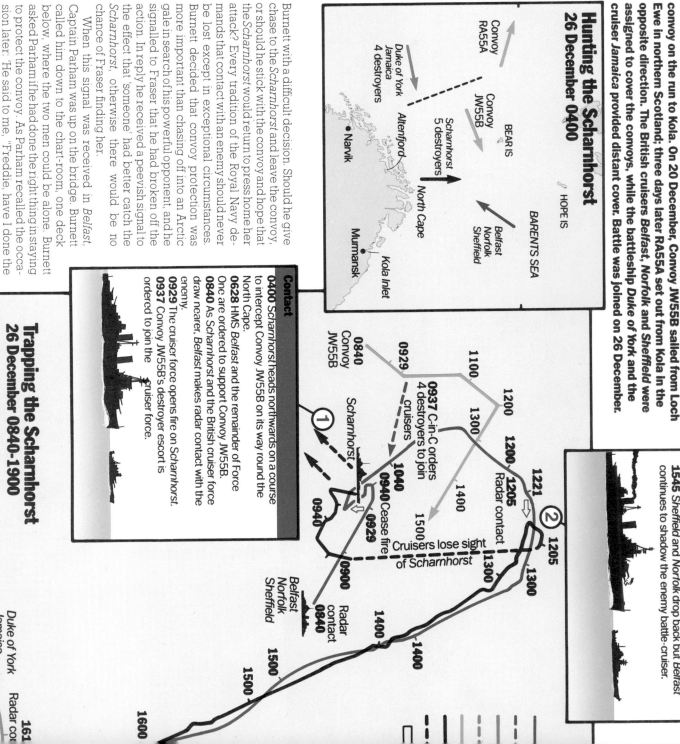

Hunting the Scharnhorst
26 December 0400

Contact

0400 Scharnhorst heads northwards on a course to intercept Convoy JW55B on its way round the North Cape.

0628 HMS Belfast and the remainder of Force One are ordered to support Convoy JW55B.

0840 As Scharnhorst and the British cruiser force draw nearer, Belfast makes radar contact with the enemy.

0929 The cruiser force opens fire on Scharnhorst.

0937 Convoy JW55B's destroyer escort is ordered to join the cruiser force.

Shadowing Scharnhorst

1211 After losing sight of Scharnhorst for some hours, the cruiser force re-establishes radar contact. As Admiral Fraser's Force Two approaches from the southwest, Force One shadows Scharnhorst as she heads southwestward.

1545 Sheffield and Norfolk drop back but Belfast continues to shadow the enemy battle-cruiser.

Trapping the Scharnhorst
26 December 0840-1900

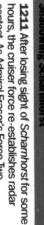

Burnett with a difficult decision. Should he give chase to the Scharnhorst and leave the convoy, or should he stick with the convoy and hope that the Scharnhorst would return to press home her attack? Every tradition of the Royal Navy demands that contact with an enemy should never be lost except in exceptional circumstances. Burnett decided that convoy protection was more important than chasing off into an Arctic gale in search of his powerful opponent, and he signalled to Fraser that he had broken off the action. In reply he received a peevish signal to the effect that 'someone' had better catch the Scharnhorst, otherwise there would be no chance of Fraser finding her.

When this signal was received in Belfast, Captain Parham was up on the bridge. Burnett called him down to the chart-room, one deck below, where the two men could be alone. Burnett asked Parham if he had done the right thing in staying to protect the convoy. As Parham recalled the occasion later: 'He said to me, "Freddie, have I done the right thing?" I said to him, "I'm absolutely certain you have." And afterwards, of course, his judgement was proved utterly correct, because the Scharnhorst turned up to look for the convoy. There is no question in my mind that Bob was right, absolutely right'.

Belfast was now joined by four destroyers, Musketeer, Matchless, Opportune and Virago, which Fraser had detached from the homeward-bound convoy. The destroyers' crews were keen for a fight but were having problems keeping up with the cruisers' speed of 24 knots in the heavy seas. The tension in the British ships was mounting: if Burnett was right it could not be long before the Scharnhorst

chase to the Scharnhorst and leave the convoy, reappeared. Both Norfolk and Opportune picked up radar contacts which proved to be false but which created great excitement aboard the ships.

Up in the Director Control Tower, the gunnery officer, Lieutenant Commander Mountfield, announced over the gunnery telephone system that there would be a break in the proceedings while the gunnery officer had his lunch. Ten minutes later came a call from X turret, manned by Royal Marines, to say that it was about time the gunnery officer finished his lunch and they got on with the action.

The unknown marine's wish was soon granted. At 1211 *Sheffield* got a radar contact, quickly confirmed by *Belfast* and *Norfolk*. The range was 12 miles and closing. By 1216 the contact was eight and a half miles to *Belfast's* starboard side, and this time there was no doubt – the *Scharnhorst* had returned.

Belfast opened fire with starshell from her 4in guns as Burnett took his three cruisers round to starboard at 20 knots to head the *Scharnhorst* off. The tactic worked and *Scharnhorst* hauled round to port at 1225 and settled on a southeasterly course away from the convoy. The gunnery duel was now in full swing.

Right: Rear Admiral Robert 'Bob' Burnett, commander of Force One, who directed the Battle of the North Cape from the *Belfast*. Right below: Captain Frederick Parham, commander of HMS *Belfast*.

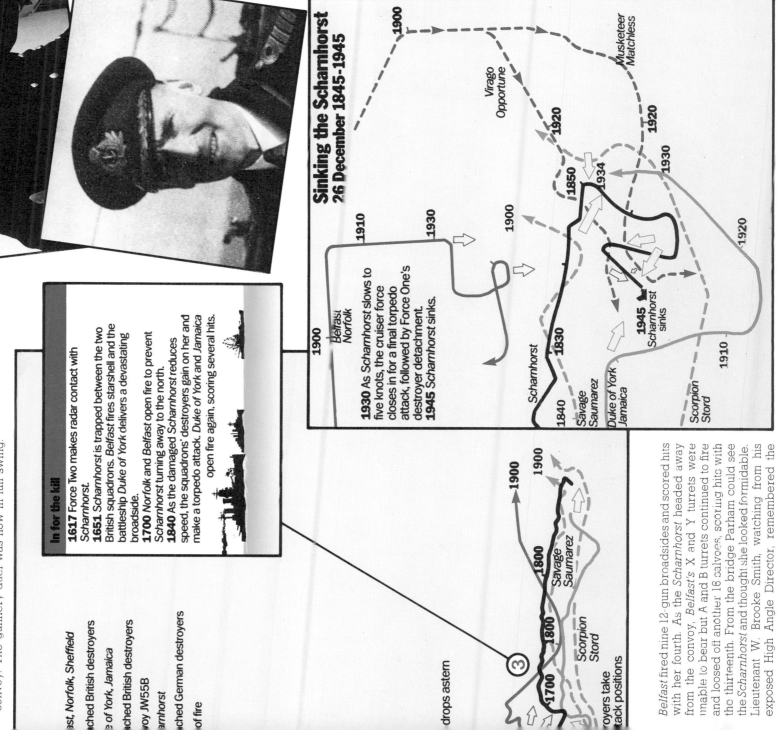

In for the kill

1617 Force Two makes radar contact with *Scharnhorst*.

1651 *Scharnhorst* is trapped between the two British squadrons. *Belfast* fires starshell and the battleship *Duke of York* delivers a devastating broadside.

1700 *Norfolk* and *Belfast* open fire to prevent *Scharnhorst* turning away to the north.

1840 As the damaged *Scharnhorst* reduces speed, the squadrons' destroyers gain on her and make a torpedo attack. *Duke of York* and *Jamaica* open fire again, scoring several hits.

Sinking the Scharnhorst
26 December 1845-1945

1930 As *Scharnhorst* slows to five knots, the cruiser force closes in for a final torpedo attack, followed by Force One's destroyer detachment.

1945 *Scharnhorst* sinks.

...ast, Norfolk, Sheffield
...ched British destroyers
...e of York, Jamaica
...ched British destroyers
...voy JW55B
...arnhorst
...ched German destroyers
...of fire

Belfast fired nine 12-gun broadsides and scored hits with her fourth. As the *Scharnhorst* headed away from the convoy, *Belfast's* X and Y turrets were unable to bear but A and B turrets continued to fire and loosed off another 16 salvoes, scoring hits with the thirteenth. From the bridge Parham could see the *Scharnhorst* and thought she looked formidable. Lieutenant W. Brooke Smith, watching from his exposed High Angle Director, remembered the descending flares of the starshell, the crash of main armament and wind screaming through the rigging.

Because Brooke Smith's director crew were not directly involved in the action he was able to pass a commentary on the action by telephone to the men in fire control centre, deep inside the ship. 'That last one landed astern,' he said, referring to the *Scharnhorst's* shells. 'There! She's fired again!' The petty officer in charge below took out his watch and began counting off the seconds. 'If she's made the right corrections she should hit us... now!' But the German gunnery was not as good as it should have been and the shells landed astern.

By 1300 Burnett had decided that *Scharnhorst* had given up her attempt to attack the convoy and was heading for home. He therefore felt no qualms about leaving the merchant ships, and his cruisers took station on *Scharnhorst's* port quarter at a range of seven and a half miles. *Belfast's* role in the action had now changed; the immediate task of protecting the convoy had been accomplished but *Scharnhorst* now had to be shadowed and her position, course and speed reported to Admiral Fraser, who was coming up with Force Two from the southwest to cut off *Scharnhorst's* retreat. With this object in mind, Burnett made no attempt to engage the *Scharnhorst*, as he was anxious to avoid scaring her into drastic alterations of course. On board *Duke of York*, Fraser and his staff could see by looking at the plot that *Scharnhorst* was headed straight for them. As one of Fraser's staff said, 'It was money for old rope.'

The trap was sprung – *Scharnhorst* was caught between Force One in the north and Force Two to the southwest

At 1545 *Norfolk* had to reduce speed in order to put out fires which had sprung up after hits from *Scharnhorst's* shells. The *Norfolk* had not been using flashless cordite and had become *Scharnhorst's* main target. As *Norfolk* fell away Burnett noticed the *Sheffield* was also dropping back. 'Come on!' he signalled to her – but no sooner had this signal been sent than a message arrived from *Sheffield* saying that the gearbox on the port inner turbine had failed and speed would have to be reduced to five knots. *Belfast* was now chasing the *Scharnhorst* through the gale on her own, keeping Fraser supplied with the vital information of *Scharnhorst's* position.

In contrast to *Sheffield*, *Belfast's* machinery was working superbly. Speeds of 28, 29 and 30 knots were achieved and maintained, despite the fact that the ship was 14 months out of dock. But this very efficiency now placed her in danger. The *Scharnhorst's* after radar was still working and the Germans must have known something of their pursuers. Parham was amazed and relieved that the *Scharnhorst* did not turn and fight for 'she could have blown us clean out of the water.' Despite the risk, *Belfast* kept up with the *Scharnhorst* and at long last *Duke of York* came into radar contact with the German battle-cruiser. By 1637 hours, *Belfast* and *Duke of York* were in touch

Top right: A gunnery officer yells orders as HMS *Duke of York* prepares to fire a broadside from her 14in guns. Bottom left: Dejected survivors of *Scharnhorst* are brought ashore. Bottom right: The victors. Admiral Sir Bruce Fraser with commanders and officers of the ships that sank *Scharnhorst*. Main picture: HMS *Belfast* went on to play a key role in the naval bombardment in support of the Allied landings in Normandy in 1944.

with each other and the trap was sprung – *Scharnhorst* was caught between Force One to the north and Force Two to the southwest. At 1645 *Belfast* illuminated the target with starshell, and as the flares burst everyone who saw the *Scharnhorst* noticed that her turrets were trained fore and aft: she had been taken by surprise. At 1651 the first broadside of 10 14in guns from *Duke of York* straddled the *Scharnhorst*, and the third and final part of the action had begun.

Belfast remained to the north of the *Scharnhorst* and fired two 12-gun broadsides and five salvoes from A and B turrets to prevent her from breaking away to the north. At 1700 *Norfolk* arrived, her fires put out, and announced her arrival with a broadside from her 8in guns, which took everyone on *Belfast's* bridge by surprise.

The *Scharnhorst* was a blazing shambles, dead in the water and listing to starboard

From *Belfast* the *Scharnhorst* could just be seen as a long grey shape, when it suddenly lit up as the *Duke of York's* shell struck home. But when *Duke of York* ceased fire to allow Fraser's four destroyers to make a torpedo attack, the *Scharnhorst* seemed to brighten as her main armament came into action in a desperate attempt to keep the destroyers away. The sky seemed full of flying tracer and those on *Belfast's* bridge could only marvel at the courage of the destroyer crews, some of whom came to within 1800yds of the *Scharnhorst* to fire their torpedoes. A total of 38 torpedoes was fired and four hits were claimed, one of which fractured a propeller shaft, causing the *Scharnhorst's* speed to fall off.

At 1901 *Duke of York* opened fire again, followed by broadsides from *Belfast* and *Norfolk* at 1915. *Belfast* fired five 12-gun broadsides, scoring hits with the third. With all her turrets out of action, the *Scharnhorst* was a blazing shambles, dead in the water and listing to starboard. Fraser ordered *Belfast* to sink her with torpedoes, and at 1927 *Belfast* fired three torpedoes from her starboard tubes. One hit was claimed, though it was not observed by any other ship and Fraser considered it 'unlikely'. Nevertheless, Burnett always believed that his ship had administered the coup de grâce. After Burnett's four destroyers had made another torpedo attack there was a massive underwater explosion and the blip on the radar which had been *Scharnhorst* slowly faded. When *Belfast* came round at 1948 to fire another three torpedoes there was only wreckage lying in the oily water. In the end, only 36 of *Scharnhorst's* crew of 1968 were rescued.

The Battle of the North Cape was the last capital ship action in European waters in World War II. HMS *Belfast*, and the other cruisers of Force One, brilliantly handled by Burnett, who received the KBE for his part in the battle while Parham received the DSO, had played a vital role in the destruction of the *Scharnhorst*. The Arctic convoys were now safe and, even more important, there was now no chance of the *Scharnhorst* breaking out into the Atlantic to threaten the vital convoys bringing troops and supplies for D-day and the Second Front in Normandy.

THE AUTHOR Paul Kemp is a photographic researcher at the Imperial War Museum and is author of several articles on naval subjects. For three years he was closely associated with HMS *Belfast*, which is now under the administration of the museum.

BIG JOHN

On patrol in the Mediterranean, USS *John F. Kennedy* provides the operational base for one of the US Navy's formidable air wings. Day or night, the *JFK* stands ready to launch its aircraft into combat

Below: With its wings deployed for maximum lift, a Tomcat F-14 from the 'Swordsmen' squadron is cleared for take-off. Above, far left: USS *John F. Kennedy*. Above: Two Grumman A-6s stand ready on the forward cats of 'Big John'. Above centre: The 'Island' of the *JFK* bristles with communications and radar equipment. It is from here, in the Primary Flying Position control room, that launches and recoveries are co-ordinated.

BEWARE OF ROTORS

PROPS & JET BLAST

USS JOHN F. KENNEDY

USS *John F. Kennedy* was commissioned in 1968 and is due to remain in service until well after the year 2010. It is certain to be the last fossil-fuelled aircraft carrier in service with the US Navy. 'Big John' measures 1052ft long and 252ft across the flight deck, and has a displacement of 82,000 tons when fully loaded. The flight deck covers 4.56 acres and is served by four elevators that transport aircraft to and from the hangar deck.

Each of the two electronically-powered anchors weigh 30 tons and, if they were operated without proper warning while the ship was connected to a power source onshore, the subsequent surge in electricity could black out a small city.

The *JFK* is capable of carrying over 2150 tons of aviation ordnance, stored in over 30 magazines with a combined capacity of over 500,000 square feet. Even for a standard patrol, 'Big John' carries 1,922,024 gallons of JP-5 aviation fuel, 25,312 gallons of Avgas and 2,274,896 gallons of DFM for the carrier's four-shaft geared steam turbines.

The ship's complement is 150 officers and 2750 ratings, while that of the air wing is approximately 2500.

It is not surprising, therefore, that the total wage bill is in excess of two million dollars. On average, the *JFK* can launch an aircraft every 30 seconds. On their return to the flight deck, the aircraft land at a speed of 150mph and are brought to a complete halt in the space of one second. Each arrestor cable has a tensile strength of 176,000lb and, after a very short working life, it is thrown over the side of the ship so that it can never be used again.

John F. Kennedy is armed with three octuple Sea Sparrow surface-to-air missile launchers, and three 20mm Phalanx cannon. It also has the OE-82 satellite communications system.

WITH A MIGHTY ROAR, a brace of F-14 Tomcat air-defence fighters are propelled into the air from the forward 'cats' of USS *John F. Kennedy* (*JFK*). Within seconds, the groundcrew go to work again as the arresting hook of a Grumman E-2 Hawkeye brings the aircraft safely to a halt after a bone-jarring landing on the aircraft carrier. Day and night, this scene will be repeated, with as many as 20 aircraft patrolling the Mediterranean skies at any one time.

Operating as the ocean-going home of Carrier Air Wing Three (CVW 3), the *JFK* has the capability to launch air strikes deep into the heart of enemy territory. This is peacetime, however, and the *JFK* is simply fulfilling her commitment to NATO as part of the formidable US Sixth Fleet.

USS *John F Kennedy* (designated CV67) is the last conventionally-powered multi-role aircraft carrier to have been brought into service with the US Navy. Nevertheless, she is capable of a turn of speed that is comparable to that of her nuclear-powered sisters, and can deliver more than 10 times the firepower that any of the US carriers possessed during the Battle of Midway in World War II. More than this, she provides the home and working environment for 90 aircraft and over 5000 officers and men.

The fighting arm of the *JFK* is provided by CVW 3, commanded by Commander Robert E. Houser. The wing comprises nine squadrons, each of which is equipped to perform a specialised role. The 'Swordsmen' and 'Top Hatters' of VF-32 and VF-14 Squadrons provide the *JFK* with its outer defence zone. Flying their F-14s, these squadrons can engage multiple enemy aircraft from over 100 miles away with the Tomcat's AIM-54C Phoenix missiles.

They can also fire medium range AIM-7M Sparrows or the shorter range AIM-9M Sidewinders. The Grumman A-6E Intruders of VA-75 and VMA-533 comprise the attack capability of the air wing. The Intruders are equipped with a Target Recognition Attack Multi-sensor (TRAM) system, and can deliver a typical payload of thirty 500lb bombs in clusters of six. They can also fire Harpoon anti-ship missiles.

During any foray into enemy airspace, the Intruders would be preceded, or accompanied, by EA-6B Prowlers flown by VAQ-140. The complex electronic counter-measures (ECM) equipment of the Prowler, including the ALQ-99 active jamming system, is capable of blanketing enemy radar cover. The US Navy has recently given authorisation for the EA-6B to carry Harm anti-radar missiles. Another squadron on board the *JFK* flies the Grumman KA-6D inflight-refuelling tanker, allowing the fighter and attack aircraft to operate hundreds of miles from the carrier itself.

The Grumman E-2C Hawkeyes, flown by the 'Seahawks' of VAW-126, constitute the air wing's Airborne Early Warning (AEW) capability. The Hawkeyes are able to track more than 250 targets simultaneously, and their AN/APS-138 radars can detect a missile from a range of 115 miles. The highly automated APA-171 antennae of the Hawkeye can also locate aircraft up to 300 miles away. These sensors are housed inside a distinctive discus-shaped radome, designed to drop by 18in when the aircraft is being stored onboard the aircraft carrier.

For anti-submarine warfare (ASW), Carrier Air Wing Three relies on the Lockheed S-3 Vikings of VS-22. In 1975, the *JFK* became the first carrier to operate the S-3 at long distances from the Task Force. The squadron normally operates 10 Vikings and is proud of the role it is called upon to perform. Below deck, over a bulkhead in one of the passageways that lead to VS-22's ops room, there is a small sign that reads, 'You are now entering Viking Country BOW down.' A further anti-submarine screen is provided by the Sikorsky SH-3A helicopters of HS-7 – the 'Hero' squadron. This unit also performs an air-sea rescue role for the Grumman and Lockheed aircrews of the *JFK*.

With air ops continuing day and night while the carrier is at sea, the task of seeing to the crew's needs and maintaining the aircraft in operational order requires the striking of a delicate balance. Aircrews average a 12-hour day, and when the pilot and navigator of a Tomcat are eating, relaxing or sleeping in their tiny staterooms, many of their colleagues are being briefed or debriefed concerning yet another mission. On the hangar deck, the mechanics will be working on major repairs. There is not enough space to store all of the aircraft in the hangar itself, and many are kept on the flight deck. Indeed, space is a luxury that is in relatively short supply on board the *JFK*. Three-tiered bunk beds are closely packed together in the crew quarters, and the lights are permanently switched on. The only time that the men can enjoy complete privacy is when, after a long watch, they finally retire behind the thin curtain of their bunk. Listening to their Sony Walkmans, for a few hours they can shut out the world.

Newcomers to the *JFK* are escorted around the carrier for the first few days of their posting, enabling

Far left, above: Before the steam catapults can go into action, every spare man takes part in the ritual FOD Walkdown. Minutes later, an E-2C Hawkeye is ready for launch (far left). Flight ops continue day and night, and a wide range of flight-deck personnel is required to keep the air wing at combat status. While technicians perform routine maintenance (above centre), a 'purple jacket' drags a fuel hose towards a waiting aircraft (top left). Left: In dry dock, the huge size of the *JFK* is revealed to the camera. Each of the carrier's two rudders weighs an incredible 24 tons.

CAPTAIN JOHN A. MORIARTY

Born in Providence, Rhode Island, John Moriarty (above) graduated from the Massachusetts Maritime Academy in 1960, and was commissioned into the navy as an ensign.

His first tour of duty was with VA-65, operating from USS *Enterprise*. Moriarty was then assigned to VA-45 at Cecil Field, Florida, and later attended the US Naval Test Pilot School at Patuxent River, Maryland. Following graduation he was assigned as a test pilot to the Service Test Division at the Naval Air Test Center.

In 1968 Moriarty joined VA-113 and completed two tours of duty on USS *Ranger*. His next assignment was with VA-122, stationed at Lemoore, California. Following this, Moriarty was posted to VA-94 onboard USS *Coral Sea*, first as the squadron's executive officer, and later as commanding officer. In August 1980 he became executive officer onboard USS *Coral Sea*, and three years later he was promoted to commanding officer of USS *Mars*. He held this post until January 1985, when he was transferred to the Office of the Chief of Naval Operations. Later that year he took up command of USS *John F. Kennedy*.

Captain Moriarty's decorations include two Meritorious Service Medals, two Air medals, 15 Flight/Strike Medals, the Vietnam Cross of Gallantry with Bronze Star and nine Navy Commendation Medals.

If fire breaks out, his actions will be governed by a simple rule – get the men out first

The officer in charge of moving and parking the aircraft around the *JFK* is known as the 'Handler' or 'Mangler'. It is the responsibility of the Handler and his staff to know the exact position of every aircraft on board the carrier. Nothing moves without his authority, and each move is carefully plotted on a miniature model of the ship. The Handler and his staff cannot see the flight deck or hangar deck, but they keep in contact with the handling crews by using two-way radio headphones. These are known in the trade as a 'mouse', because of the silhouette they provide when worn over the ubiquitous protective helmets.

During flight ops, the deck of the *JFK* is saturated with a mass of men that service, fuel, arm and move the aircraft. Before operations can even begin,

them to adjust to the carrier's complex layout. Passageways are so narrow that there is scarcely enough room for two men to pass without turning sideways. The extent to which the corridors twist and turn makes it impossible (except on the flight deck) to walk the length of the carrier in a straight line. As a result of this labyrinthine layout, a small group of men aboard 'Big John' rarely get the opportunity to go 'up top' for some fresh air. These are the engineers, and they are a breed apart. Commonly nicknamed 'snipes', they are responsible for the massive steam turbines that push the *JFK* through the water at a speed of 33 knots. Very occasionally, a crewman might catch a glimpse of an engineer as the latter climbs up to 'Vultures Row' to see what the world looks like.

The ship's complement is 2900 officers and men, while that of the air wing is 2500. With such a massive concentration of personnel, the *JFK* resembles a small town – it is equipped with a hospital that can deal with over 80 patients, a library, shops, and even a radio and television station. At any time of the day or night, the crew can find a hearty meal, either in the mess hall or in the ship's fast food shop, known as the 'Gedunk'.

however, the 1000ft flight deck is meticulously combed for foreign objects. In a daily ritual known as the 'FOD Walkdown', the men form a single line across the deck and move from bow to aft. This ensures that there is nothing left lying around that could be sucked up by the Grumman's powerful jet engines.

There is a clear hierarchy within the deck crew, and at the top of the tree are the yellow-jacketed flight-deck chiefs. They receive their orders from the Handler, and nothing moves without their blessing. The fuel teams wear purple jackets. Using huge pipes that run from 26 fuelling points along the deck edge, these teams can force feed the wing's aircraft within a matter of minutes. The 'red shirts' can arm the aircraft with everything from Sidewinder air-to-air missiles and Smart bombs to the various nuclear weapons that are at the disposal of each Task Force Admiral within the US Sixth Fleet.

When the day's operations begin in earnest, the 'green shirts' are by far the largest element on the flight deck. These men are responsible for guiding the aircraft around the deck and hooking them up to the cat launchers. Again, colour plays an important part in the launch ritual, with each type of aircraft using a specially coloured bobbin, or 'holdback'. These connect the aircraft to the steam catapult and have a break strength that differs according to the type of aircraft being launched. For the F-14 Tomcat, weighing in at 33,725kg combat-loaded, the minimum catapult length required is 76 to 91m.

In the control tower, 16m above the flight deck, the 'Air Boss' and his assistant, 'Miniboss', co-ordinate flight operations during the take-offs and recoveries. As the complex pattern of launches unfolds, the Primary Flying Position (Pri-Fly) control room echoes with the sound of disembodied voices from the multitude of radios that link the Air Boss with the deck. Both the Air Boss and Miniboss have been

Below: Undoubtedly the most potent interceptor in the US Navy's inventory, an F-14 Tomcat waits to be connected to the catapult that will send it roaring down the flight deck (top right). Far right: A Lockheed S-3 Viking from VS-2 gets an 'okay three wire' on its return to the flight deck of the *JFK*.

carrier pilots themselves, and both understand the enormous pressure that pilots are under during both the launch and recovery phases. Their main role is therefore to launch and recover their aircraft quickly and safely. The *JFK* is capable of launching an aircraft every 30 seconds, but precise co-ordination and attention to safety factors are essential if this ratio is to be achieved. Once the nose wheel has been hooked onto the catapult and the jet's after-burners have been ignited, the Air Boss gives the order to 'Fire the cats.' Within two seconds, the aircraft will have reached 150 miles per hour – only now can the pilot resume control of his aircraft.

The Air Boss is also faced with the task of directing aircraft back onto the flight deck while others are taking off. He has to be certain that if the pilot misses the arresting cables he has a clear run to 'Touch and Go' – throttle forward, fly back around the carrier and attempt another landing.

Sitting in one of the crew pits on the flight deck is a man clad in silver fire-proof clothing. In the event of an accident, it is his job to rescue any aircrew who get trapped in the aircraft. If fire breaks out, his actions will be governed by one simple rule – get the men out first, then worry about the plane.

Once all the aircraft are safely in the air, control passes several decks down to the Carrier Air Traffic Control Center (CATCC). It is here that the aircraft are co-ordinated during flight ops. As the aircraft all proceed on their different missions, the Tomcats, Intruders, Prowlers and Hawkeyes will all report in to the CATCC. The combined power of the *JFK's* and other Task Force radar screens will then give the Task Force Admiral a clear picture of the overall situation. Battle commands are filtered through the Combat Information Center (CIC). This operates separately from the CATCC, thereby lessening the chances of flight ops conflicting with the overall pattern of combat ops.

At the end of each flight mission, the returning aircraft come under the control of the Landing Signal Officer (LSO), who, along with his staff, stands on a small platform at the aft of the ship. Like all the senior staff on the *JFK*, the LSO is a veteran pilot, and he is in direct contact with both the Air Boss and the CATCC. It is his job to make sure that each approaching aircraft is on the correct flight path and is coming in at the right height and speed. Once the pilot has sighted the Light Landing Device, known as the 'meatball', the LSO calls all the shots. Using a device known as the 'pickle switch', he operates a series of red lights that indicate to the approaching pilot whether or not the deck is clear. If the approach path is satisfactory, the LSO will drop his arm and call the pilot in to land.

'You're trying to land on something that looks like a pinball machine at the end of a football field'

As the aircraft touches down on the rubberised steel flight deck, the LSO and his staff drop low – the engines of an F-14 Tomcat, even when idling, can blow a man clean off the deck. The LSO then turns to see if the aircraft has made a successful 'catch'. The pilot is aiming for the third arresting cable out of four. The first and second are considered to be too close to the end of the deck and, if the pilot catches the fourth wire, his approach is considered to have been too high. The pilots are given marks by the LSO for every landing, and he has the power to break aircrews if their performance does not match up to his stringent requirements. One pilot described the ordeal of landing at night:

'It never gets to be fun. Every ounce of energy is funnelled into that last 10 seconds of the approach. All you can think about is grabbing the wire without hitting anything, and you don't want to go around again because it's so dark out there. You're trying to land on something that looks like a pinball machine at the end of a football field.'

Operating from the *JKF*, the aircraft of Carrier Air Wing Three roam the skies of the Mediterranean and possess a range in excess of 2000 miles. There is only

Above: The insignia of VF-14 – 'The Top Hatters'. Below: Wearing brown shirts, the 'plane captains' supervise the weapons handlers as they arm a flight of A-6 Intruders. The Intruder has one underfuselage and four underwing weapons attachments, and can carry a wide range of nuclear and conventional armament. Nuclear ordnance, however, can only be armed and used on the authority of the American President. The *John F. Kennedy* was scheduled to return to Norfolk, Virginia, in the spring of 1987, after a six-month tour of duty. In early 1987, however, her tour was extended when a series of kidnappings in the Lebanon resulted in the US Sixth Fleet being deployed off the Lebanese coast.

one land-based air mission that aircraft from the carrier cannot perform, and that is fleet replenishment. This role is carried out by the Grumman C-2A Greyhounds from Fleet Logistics Support Squadron 24 (VR-24), based at the US Naval Air Station at Sigonella, Sicily. These aircraft deliver cargo and personnel to the aircraft carriers of the US Sixth Fleet while it is on station in the Mediterranean. There are no women based on the *JFK*, but Patty Jedry, a Greyhound pilot, regularly calls in. Ask Jedry what is the most satisfying part of her job, and she will reply without hesitation: 'Getting an okay three wire at the ship.' This sentiment is echoed by most of the pilots on board the *JFK*, but if you ask them whether combat would worry them, they just shrug and grin before replying 'heck no!' These pilots, with an average age of 29, will have normally completed two years and 400 hours of training before they are attached to a fleet squadron.

During the *JFK's* most recent tour of duty, in the winter of 1986/87, the aircraft carrier conducted exercises in the Atlantic, made a number of visits to European ports and also visited Haifa in Israel. It carried out patrols off the Lebanese coast, and operated in the southwest region of the Mediterranean. In early 1987, as a result of the hostage crisis in the Lebanon, 'Big John' stayed on station with the US Sixth Fleet in the Mediterranean. Carrier Air Wing Three and the personnel of USS *John F. Kennedy* stand for the signal that could send them into action. Seconds after the water-cooled steel deflectors are raised to absorb the blast of jet engines, highly trained aircrews will be catapulted into the skies – prepared to tackle any task that the US Navy asks of them.

THE AUTHOR Michael Roberts runs a major picture library that deals with military subjects, and visited USS *John F. Kennedy* in December 1986. He would like to thank the officers and crew of the *JFK* and Carrier Air Wing Three for their help in the preparation of this article.

Inset left: Admiral Günther Lütjens, the squadron commander who took the *Bismarck* into the Atlantic. Below: The awe-inspiring bulk of the *Bismarck*, the finest warship of the German Navy. Bottom: The launching of the *Bismarck* at Hamburg in 1939 was declared a state occasion by the Nazi Party leadership.

MEN OF THE BISMARCK

In May 1941 the giant battleship *Bismarck*, pride of the German Navy, sailed for the Atlantic and a duel to the death with the Royal Navy

WHEN SHE put to sea on her fateful mission of May 1941, the *Bismarck* was the most powerful, most beautiful battleship ever built: 50,000 tons fully laden, a sixth of a mile long and 120ft wide, she carried eight 15in guns, six aircraft and a crew of 2200. It was the intention of the German Naval Staff that she and the heavy cruiser *Prinz Eugen* should link up in mid-Atlantic with the battle-cruisers *Scharnhorst* and *Gneisenau* (then in Brest) and, supplied by tankers and storeships, roam the seas for months in search of Allied convoys. It was these convoys with their cargoes of food, fuel and weapons that enabled Great Britain to sustain the fight against Germany. Already the convoys had been badly mauled by U-boats; and if the lifeline to America were ever cut, Britain would find it increasingly difficult, if not

impossible, to continue the war.

Fortunately for the Atlantic convoys, repairs to the *Scharnhorst's* boilers and air-raid damage to *Gneisenau* prevented their sailing; but on the evening of 18 May 1941 *Bismarck* and *Prinz Eugen* put out from the Polish port of Gdynia in the Baltic and headed west. Among the crew were meteorologists, bandsmen, prize crews for captured ships, a hundred midshipmen for training, half a dozen reporters and cameramen. In command of the operation was the dour Admiral Günther Lütjens who had recently taken *Scharnhorst* and *Gneisenau* on a foray, sinking 116,000 tons of Allied shipping.

At high speed the two ships passed through the narrow waters between Denmark and Sweden, rounded the southern tip of Norway and on the morning of 21 May entered Bergen harbour. They stayed there all day while the *Prinz Eugen* topped up with fuel and the crews wrote last letters home and lazed in the summer sunshine. On the night of the 22nd they sailed again, heading for the Denmark Strait that lies between Greenland and Iceland.

The British Admiralty had received intelligence reports of the break-out, and alerted Admiral Sir John Tovey, commanding the Home Fleet at its Orkney base of Scapa Flow. He at once ordered the cruisers *Norfolk* and *Suffolk*, patrolling the Denmark Strait under Admiral Wake-Walker, to keep a sharp look-out, and for the new battleship *Prince of*

Wales (not yet fully worked up) and the old battle-cruiser *Hood*, the largest ship in the Royal Navy, to sail under Admiral Holland for the southwest corner of Iceland: there they would cover both the Denmark Strait and the Iceland-Faeroes passage. He remained with his flagship, *King George V*, in Scapa until air reconnaissance revealed that Bergen harbour was empty, then, signalling the carrier *Victorious* and the old battle-cruiser *Repulse* to join him, followed Admiral Holland to the west.

Two days went by with both sides knowing the other was at sea, but ignorant of where and when they would meet. Anticipation ended on the evening of 23 May when Able Seaman Newell, one of the *Suffolk's* look-outs in the Denmark Strait, saw a giant warship swim into his binoculars. 'Ship bearing Green Four Oh!' he shouted out, then, as *Prinz Eugen* appeared, 'Two ships bearing Green Four Oh!' *Suffolk*, with helm hard over, scuttled into the fog, sending out a stream of reports of the sighting, then, when the German ships had taken up shadowing position by radar some 12 miles astern. Presently *Norfolk* joined her. Through the night the four ships bucketed southwards at 30 knots along the edge of the Greenland ice-pack, Lütjens desperate to reach the open Atlantic before enemy battleships could reach him.

But it was not to be. When Admiral Holland received the first sighting reports he realised he was well placed to intercept. Guided by Wake-Walker's signals of *Bismarck's* position, course and speed, he drove on to the southwest. Before dawn *Hood* and *Prince of Wales* went to action stations and hoisted huge battle ensigns. At around 0520 hours the black topmasts, first of *Bismarck* and then *Prinz Eugen*, climbed above the horizon. For 20 minutes, while the range closed, the two squadrons converged. Then from each side came flashes and smoke.

East and west, like the sound of tearing linen, the huge shells passed to and fro. After only six minutes, came disaster for *Hood*. A high plunging shell from *Bismarck* sliced through her thin armour-plating, penetrated all decks and exploded in the after magazines. Silently, it seemed to those watching, almost as though in slow motion, the great ship split in two: bow and stern pointed vertically towards the sky, then disappeared beneath the waves. 'Poor devils, poor devils!' muttered the gunnery officer of the *Prinz Eugen*, for what *Hood* had suffered, *Prinz Eugen* could suffer too. An hour later destroyers picked up only three survivors from a crew of 1400.

Now it was two against one, but not for long because *Prince of Wales* had taken a terrible pounding too. Three hits below the waterline had let in 400 tons of sea water, her bridge and aircraft had been destroyed, and because of technical defects half her main armament was out of action. Reluctantly, Cap-

tain Leach felt he had no option but to disengage and join *Norfolk* and *Suffolk* shadowing astern. He knew that Admiral Tovey and his ships were also converging on the enemy, and when they attacked from the east, he would re-engage from the north.

In *Bismarck* and *Prinz Eugen* there were great rejoicings at the sinking of *Hood* and withdrawal of *Prince of Wales*. Yet *Bismarck* had not emerged unscathed. One of *Prince of Wales's* shells had penetrated an oil tank forward, which not only let precious oil fuel out and sea water in, but reduced the ship's maximum speed by several knots. Realising that he could not continue operations without dockyard repairs, Lütjens signalled Berlin that he would release the undamaged *Prinz Eugen* for independent cruiser warfare and order *Bismarck* to shape course for St Nazaire. In the afternoon *Bismarck* turned briefly to the west. Wake-Walker with his three ships followed her; and *Prinz Eugen*, continuing at speed on the old course, disappeared over the southern horizon. (Soon after, because of a damaged propeller, she entered Brest.)

Many of the young Swordfish pilots had never flown from a carrier before. But extreme times called for extreme measures

Tovey, meanwhile, continued to close from the east and, from Wake-Walker's reports, reckoned that his force would be in action the next morning. But what if *Bismarck* were to alter course drastically during the night or put on a sudden burst of speed? To try to slow her up Tovey ordered *Victorious* to prepare a torpedo attack on her that night, although at 120 miles distance the enemy was at maximum aircraft range: moreover, many of the young Swordfish pilots had never flown from a carrier before. But extreme times called for extreme measures. All the attacking aircraft reached their target and, miraculously in the darkness, all returned. One hit was observed, but it struck the armour plating just below the waterline and did little damage.

For Lütjens, though, the attack was an indication that other enemy forces were in the offing, and that he must somehow give his tenacious shadowers the slip. From his hydrophone operators he learnt that the British ships were zigzagging to and fro across his stern (in order to avoid U-boats). When they were at the farthest point away from him, he ordered the captain to increase speed and put the wheel over to starboard. The ship described a huge loop, crossed

Above: A signaller aboard Prinz Eugen communicates with the Bismarck during an exercise in the Baltic.
Below: Camouflage designed to disguise the great size of the Bismarck is applied before the voyage.

THE MEN OF THE *BISMARCK*

The complement of the *Bismarck* numbered 2200 men, including the staff of Admiral Günther Lütjens, the naval squadron commander. In common with the crews of all the great battleships of the German Navy, the crew of the *Bismarck* were all volunteers and regulars who had undergone a strict examination to qualify for the service. They signed for four years initially, with an option at the end of that period of a further 12 years. Admiral Lütjens was the most senior officer on the ship. He had played a prominent part in the Norwegian campaign of 1940, deputising for Admiral Marschall as fleet commander aboard the *Gneisenau*, and had won the Knight's Cross. Tall, lean and wholly dedicated to the naval life, Lütjens was a professional who refused to abandon naval tradition for Nazism: to Hitler he gave the naval, not the Nazi, salute and he carried not the Nazi dagger but the admiral's dirk of the old Imperial Navy. He knew, however, that Germany could not win the unequal war at sea, and predicted to a friend that he would lose his life in the struggle.

The captain of the *Bismarck* was Ernst Lindemann, clever and cool, and accomplished in gunnery and engineering. A chain-smoker with sleek blond hair, he brought with him an ex-waiter from his favourite Hamburg restaurant to serve as his steward. A well-known anecdote relates how he amiably agreed to lend his ship's band for the commissioning ceremony of U-boat *U-556* in return for the submarine's protection on the high seas.

Above: The German Navy High Seas Fleet badge.

BISMARCK'S FINAL HOUR

Lieutenant-Commander Gerhard Junack was *Bismarck's* turbine engineer and one of the two officers who survived: 'The lower decks were brilliantly lit up; a *peaceful* mood prevailed, such as that on a Sunday afternoon in port – the silence broken only by the explosion of our own demolition charges below. I myself saw the result of the battle on the battery-deck. There was no electric light, only the red glow from numerous fires... and men were running here and there, apparently aimlessly: it seemed highly unlikely that one would survive... men were collecting between the rear turrets, but amidships there was a smoke-screen which prevented us from seeing what was happening forward; only the combat mast stood out from the dense black smoke. The flag was still waving from the rear mast, and the barrels of the rear turrets stood out starkly against the sky; one barrel had been split by a tremendous explosion. Only occasionally did I see dead or wounded comrades.'

Sinking the Hood

24 May 0520 *Hood* and *Prince of Wales* establish visual contact with *Bismarck* and *Prinz Eugen*.
0550 *Hood* closes to within 13 miles and opens fire. *Prince of Wales* opens fire.
0556 A shell from *Bismarck* strikes *Hood* in one of her magazines. *Hood* blows up and sinks immediately, and soon afterwards *Prince of Wales* disengages.
0609 *Bismarck* and *Prinz Eugen* cease fire.

Bismarck
0609
0603
0553
Prinz Eugen

DENMARK STRAIT

Hood blows up **0556**
0603
0609
0550
0538
Hood
Prince of Wales
0530

The escape

Air strike from *Victorious*

Air search from *Victorious*
25 May 0800-1100

U-Boat screen

Suffolk

Prince of Wales

0600
25 May 0400

25 May 0001

26 May 0852

25 May 1047

Repulse detached

King George V

Norfolk **26 May**

Air search from *Victorious* **25 May 2100-2400**

Victorious

Repulse

25 May 1100

26 May

25 May 0306 British ships shadowing *Bismarck* lose contact. *Bismarck* turns hard to starboard and crosses her own wake. Air searches from *Victorious* during the day are unsuccessful.

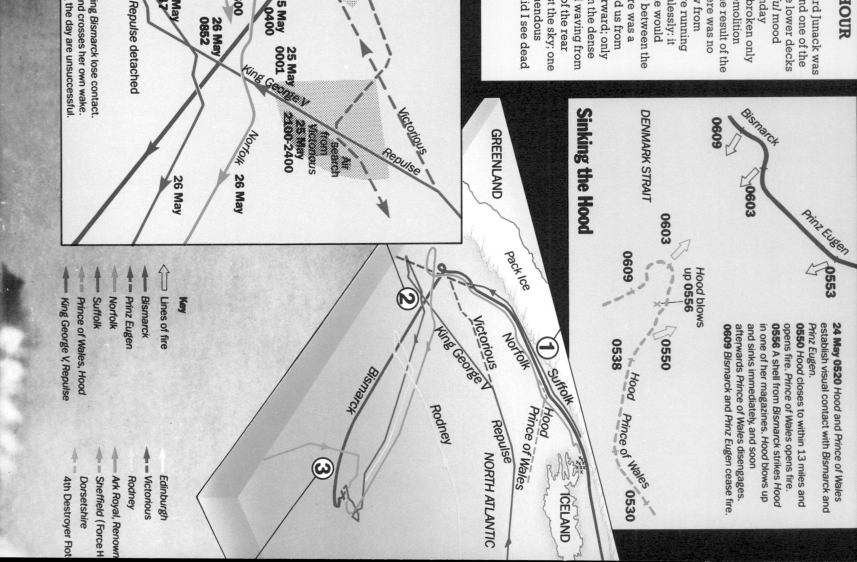

GREENLAND

Pack Ice

②

Norfolk
Victorious
Suffolk
Repulse
Prince of Wales
Hood

King George V

Bismarck

Rodney

③

NORTH ATLANTIC

ICELAND

Key

Lines of fire
Bismarck
Prinz Eugen
Norfolk
Suffolk
Prince of Wales, Hood
King George V, Repulse

Edinburgh
Victorious
Rodney
Ark Royal, Renown
Sheffield (Force H
Dorsetshire
4th Destroyer Flot

Hunting the Bismarck 18-27 May 1941

At 2130 hours on 18 May 1941 the German battleship Bismarck left the port of Gdynia in the Baltic accompanied by the heavy cruiser Prinz Eugen with orders to evade the Royal Navy and RAF patrols and make for the Atlantic. They were to link up with Scharnhorst and Gneisenau and prey on Allied convoys. With her primary armament of eight 15in guns, Bismarck represented a formidable threat — as soon as the British Admiralty received intelligence of the break-out, an epic naval hunt began.

Detaching their destroyer screen to Trondheim, the two ships made their way through the Denmark Strait, but on 24 May — having been spotted the previous day by British lookout ships — they were engaged by the Royal Navy battleship Prince of Wales and the old battle cruiser Hood. Within minutes Hood had been sunk by a shell from Bismarck. Prince of Wales disengaged and Bismarck was free to sail into the Atlantic. But her time was now short. On 27 May the hunt for the Bismarck reached its climax as two British battle squadrons closed in for the kill.

her own wake a long way astern, then set a new course for St Nazaire. The plan worked. The Suffolk's radar operators, exhausted by more than 36 hours continual operating, lost contact, and when dawn came the sea around the British was empty.

Where had the enemy gone? For a time the pursuers pressed on south, but in the morning Lütjens, unaware that he was no longer being followed, sent a long wireless message to Berlin. This was plotted wrongly in Tovey's flagship, to indicate that Bismarck had reversed course to the north and was returning to Germany the way she had come. Accordingly all the British ships reversed course to follow her. Now, and with every hour that passed, the gap between hunters and hunted widened.

Not until the late afternoon, by which time Bismarck had transmitted further signals which were correctly plotted, was the mistake discovered; and once again the British reversed course. But now Bismarck was 150 miles ahead of them, and it seemed that nothing could prevent her from reaching the safety of France. In Bismarck they realised it too, and for the first time in a week they stood down from action stations and relaxed; there was a special issue of chocolate and cigarettes in honour of Admiral Lütjens's 52nd birthday. Night closed on a turbulent sea, and when another dawn came, there was still no sign of the enemy.

But unknown to Lütjens, nemesis was at hand. Several Catalina aircraft from the RAF's Coastal Command were now sweeping the seas between Bismarck's last reported position and the Bay of Biscay, and at around 1015 the pilot of Catalina 209 sighted the battleship beneath him. He was Ensign Leonard Smith of the United States Navy, one of several American airmen secretly seconded to the RAF on President Roosevelt's orders.

Bismarck was only 100 miles away and his ships and aircraft stood between her and France

In the British Admiralty, Smith's report caused mixed feelings. Tovey in King George V (but without Victorious, Repulse, or Prince of Wales which had all gone to refuel) was still 135 miles to the north, and the old battleship Rodney which had come down from the Clyde was 125 miles to the northeast; both too far behind to catch up. But now, Britain's global seapower came to her aid. From Gibraltar another powerful force was heading northwards: under Admiral Sir James Somerville were the carrier Ark Royal, the battlecruiser Renown and the cruiser Sheffield. A glance at the chart told Somerville that Bismarck was only 100 miles away and that his ships and aircraft stood between her and France.

He made his dispositions: reconnaissance aircraft to relieve Smith's Catalina; Sheffield to find Bismarck and shadow from astern, and a squadron of Ark Royal's Swordfish to prepare for a torpedo attack. All went according to plan except that when the Swordfish pilots took off to attack Bismarck, they had not been warned that Sheffield would be in the vicinity, and they attacked her instead. Fortunately the magnetic pistols with which the torpedoes had been primed, failed to function as they should, and Sheffield escaped unharmed.

The day was now drawing to a close, and if Bismarck was to be stopped, it had to be before nightfall, for by next morning she would be only 150 miles from France and under the protection of the Luftwaffe. Feverishly the deck crews re-armed the

(Map labels)

BALTIC
Gdynia
Trondheim
NORWAY
Bergen
GERMANY
Prinz Eugen
GREAT BRITAIN
Brest
Lorient
St Nazaire
La Rochelle
FRANCE
Bismarck

The end of the Bismarck

Norfolk
Edinburgh
Rodney joins King George V
26 May 1800
Sheffield
Force H
4th Destroyer Flotilla
Ark Royal
Air search from Catalina Z/209
Sights Bismarck
27 May 1040 Bismarck sunk
Air strike from Ark Royal 26 May 2130
King George V 26 May
Dorsetshire

26 May 1020 RAF Coastal Command Catalina Z/209 sights Bismarck and the Royal Navy forces converge on her.
2130 1st air strike from Ark Royal cripples Bismarck's steering gear, forcing her to turn to port.
27 May 0848 Rodney and King George V open fire.
1040 Bismarck sinks.

Left: The end of the chase. Crippled by her broken steering gear the Bismarck flounders as the Royal Navy closes in. Shells from the Rodney are plunging down around her, and before long the torpedoes of the Dorsetshire will deliver the final blow.

THE BISMARCK

The Anglo-German Naval Treaty of June 1935 permitted Germany to build three 35,000 ton battleships, and the *Bismarck* was laid down at Hamburg in the same year. Her displacement was designed well in excess of the treaty's limits, 50,900 tons when fully stowed with fuel, a fact that was successfully concealed from the Allies. She was launched before an assembly of the German high command on 14 February 1939, and after her commission in August 1940 her crew of 2200 worked up to full operational readiness.

The pride of the German fleet, she was in every way superior to any ship Britain could throw against her.

The *Bismarck's* armour consisted of a wide belt of specially hardened 13in-thick steel around the water line, with similar steel on the turrets. Deck plating reached 5in thick. The German claim that she was unsinkable was founded in her construction: unusually strong bulkheads divided blast-resistant watertight compartments of flexible steel that were designed to channel the force of an explosion upwards, thus minimising damage caused to the interior of the ship. Her top speed of 30.8 knots was gained by three propellers driven by 12 high-pressure boilers linked to turbines.

The *Bismarck's* main armament, four turrets of paired 15in guns, was equal in destructive power to the 16in guns of older vessels. In addition, the warship bristled with 12 5.9in guns mounted in side turrets, one battery of 16 4.1in anti-aircraft guns and another of 16 20mm anti-aircraft guns, and 8 21in torpedo tubes. The ship also carried six Arado 196 float-planes, which were launched by a catapult running across the ship abaft the funnel. The *Bismarck* was also equipped with two direction-finding radio sets and one search radar installation.

Swordfish with torpedoes but, as a result of the *Sheffield* incident, with contact rather than magnetic pistols. At 1900, Somerville signalled the Admiralty that the new strike force had taken off. Now there was nothing to do but wait.

Within 30 minutes, the pilots were in sight of their target as she lumbered southeastwards through the heavy swell. The 15 planes divided into sub-groups of three to attack from both sides and so force *Bismarck* to divide her fire. As they levelled out at around 500ft all of *Bismarck's* guns that could bear (including the main armament) opened up at them.

But they pressed on gallantly and dropped their torpedoes at close range.

Miraculously, all fifteen planes got back to *Ark Royal*, although three had been so badly shot up they were complete write-offs. But what success had they had? Two hits were claimed, one on the starboard quarter, the other on the port beam. Anxiously the pilots waited for some sign of confirmation. Then it came: a signal from the shadowing *Sheffield*. 'Enemy steering 349 degrees,' followed soon after by a further signal. 'Enemy's course is north.' To those in the Admiralty, to Somerville in *Renown*, to Tovey in *King George V* now joined by *Rodney*, the news was incredible. *Bismarck* had reversed course and was now steering into the arms of the British fleet. Something very serious must have happened to her.

It had. The hit on the port side had done little damage, but that on the starboard quarter had penetrated and flooded the steering-gear compartment and jammed the ship's rudders at 15 degrees to port. On the bridge they tried to correct this by steering with the engines, but despite every combination of orders, the jammed rudders always brought the ship's head back into the wind – away from France and toward the the Royal Navy.

Nor was there any means of correcting the rudders, for the rise and fall of the stern in the heavy seas made it impossible for divers to work in the flooded steering-gear compartment, or to reach the rudders externally by going over the side. As the night wore on, the men of the *Bismarck* began to realise that nothing could save them. 'We were like meat on the butcher's block,' said Lieutenant-Commander von Mullenheim-Rechberg, 'waiting for the chopper.' Lütjens signalled Berlin that they would fight to the last shell. Berlin replied that U-boats and aircraft were on their way to help, and that all Germany was with them.

killed, and in which more than 50 major warships and some 300 aircraft had taken part. It was one of the great sea stories of all time, worthy to rank with Salamis and Tsushima, the Armada and Jutland.

Within a month, as a result of the breaking of the German Enigma ciphers, all *Bismarck's* tankers and supply ships were rounded up and sunk. Although for another two years the U-boats continued their campaign against the Atlantic convoys, the lifeline to America was never cut – but if *Bismarck* and *Prinz Eugen* had got away as they had intended, it might have been a very different story.

THE AUTHOR Ludovic Kennedy took part in the pursuit of the *Bismarck* while serving in the Royal Navy, and has since given accounts of the action in the film *Battleship Bismarck* and his book *Pursuit*. He is now well known as a television broadcaster.

Bottom left: Seen from the heavy cruiser *Prinz Eugen*, the mighty 15in guns of the *Bismarck* are unleashed on the *Hood* just before dawn on 24 May 1941. Within six minutes the *Hood* was blown out of the water. Bottom right: Only three days later the tables were turned. Survivors of the *Bismarck* are pulled from the oily sea aboard HMS *Devonshire*.

Tovey with his two battleships was now at hand. He could have attacked that night, but in the poor visibility there was a risk of mistaking friend for foe, and he decided to stand off until morning, to approach with all the advantages of sea and light. Soon after 0830 on 27 May, the great ship, which had filled the thoughts of the British for days, came into view, black and massive, wallowing helplessly in the foam-flecked sea. Outnumbered she might be, but they could take no chances; in six minutes she had sunk their beloved *Hood*.

Rodney opened fire first, then *King George V*, and soon both were observing hits. *Bismarck* returned the fire, at first accurately but later, her gun crews exhausted by the exertions of the last six days, increasingly raggedly. Now two cruisers joined in the battle, *Norfolk* in at the finish as she had been at the beginning and *Dorsetshire* just arrived from the south. All four ships pumped their shells into the stricken *Bismarck*, and slowly reduced what had once been a proud and beautiful ship to a burning shambles. She listed to port, her forward superstructure on fire, her big guns silent, one or two drooping like dead flowers or pointing drunkenly to the sky, smoke pouring from cracks in the deck. Soon a little trickle of men could be seen jumping into the sea; others were trapped at their posts.

Now *Dorsetshire* closed in to deliver the *coup de grâce*, firing two torpedoes into one side, one into the other. But one of the *Bismarck's* engineer officers had already given the order to open the seacocks and everywhere the water flooded in. At a little after 1000 hours, and still moving slowly ahead, the ship turned on her side until her funnel was level with the water, then turned until she was upside down. The stern went under first, then the main keel, lastly the bow. Europe's greatest battleship was no more.

Several hundred survivors were left swimming in the water. *Dorsetshire* and the destroyer *Maori* had picked up a hundred when a look-out sighted something on the water two miles away which could have been the periscope of a U-boat. In the circumstances, though with great reluctance, the two captains had no choice but to proceed at high speed out of the area, leaving the survivors to their fate.

So ended the *Bismarck's* first and last operational cruise, which in eight days had stretched from the Baltic to the Bay of Biscay, during which two admirals and 4000 sailors had been

SPECIAL OPERATIONS FORCES

On 1 January 1984 the United States set up the Joint Special Operations Agency (JSOA), an umbrella organisation designed to oversee the expansion of specialist warfare units or Special Operations Forces (SOFs) across three branches of the US armed forces. The SOFs include the Green Berets (US Army Special Forces), a psychological warfare (psyops) group, a civil affairs battalion, three Ranger battalions, US Navy SEAL Teams and various special air force units. Under the JSOA, the various skills of army, navy and air force personnel can be co-ordinated to maximum effect and are constantly at hand for rapid deployment.

The naval SOFs are controlled by two Naval Special Warfare Groups. Group 1 is based at the Naval Amphibious Base at Coronado, San Diego, California while Group 2 is based at Little Creek, Norfolk, Virginia. In July 1985 the two groups consisted of six Navy SEAL Teams, three Special Boat Squadrons, two SEAL Swimmer Delivery Vehicle Teams and several Special Boat Units. Of a combined total of 9100 SOF personnel on active duty, 1700 were US Navy men.

Between 1986 and 1990 substantial increases in the SOFs are planned and this will mean an increase in the number of SEAL Teams available for active operations and a further extension of SEAL facilities and specialised equipment. Above: An unofficial badge of SEAL Team 1.

As his Sea-Air-Land name suggests, the US Navy SEAL's training makes him equally capable of amphibious, airborne and land-based operations

THE TOUGHEST SPECIAL operations troops in the US armed forces are generally conceded to be the SEAL (Sea-Air-Land) Teams. My own first indication that SEAL personnel were exceptional came when I was in jump school at Fort Benning. Most of us, at the end of a hard day's training, were just glad to fall into our bunks. Not so the SEALs. They had already completed their own gruelling courses at the Basic Underwater Demolition School (BUD/S), and for them parachute training was something of a lark. The SEALs would often stay out celebrating into the small hours, and then still be ready to leap up at 0530 hours for PTs (physical training). Later, in Vietnam, I rarely worked with the SEALs since they were in the Mekong Delta and I was operating further north. But on the occasions I did run ops with them, the SEALs proved to be very hard men.

Before even applying for SEAL training, the applicant has to be in excellent physical condition and highly motivated to join a SEAL team. He has to be under 31 years old, with no history of claustrophobia or motion sickness, and be able to show a balanced attitude to explosives and being underwater. He must also have a good record of calm reactions under adverse conditions. These criteria fulfilled, he has to pass a series of physical tests. A 300yd swim has to be completed in under seven and a half minutes, followed within 10 minutes of finishing by 30 sit-ups within two minutes, 30 push-ups within two minutes, and six pull-ups within two minutes. Finally, a one-mile run in under seven and a half minutes completes the test. Individually, each of these tests may not seem difficult, but the cumulative fatigue causes 85 per cent of applicants to fail. Intelligence is also important in prospective SEALs, and an above-average intelligence rating is required of applicants. It goes without saying that the applicant comes under close scrutiny to determine his loyalty and integrity, and he must also be prepared for a minimum of two years' obligated service following the training.

Those who successfully face up to the screening are ready for BUD/S. Basic Underwater Demolition School is six months of the toughest military training in the world. The first six weeks stress the development of an outstanding physical condition and of the basic skills necessary for SEAL ops. Physical

Above: The SEAL (Sea-Air-Land) volunteer is rehearsed in every type of insertion and extraction from the combat zone. Here a trainee is plucked from the sea by an H-46 Sea Knight helicopter. Below: The IBS (Inflatable Boat, Small) is a key element in SEAL equipment, and muscle-straining IBS exercises are central to the SEAL training programme. Below right: The spirit of team endurance is fostered by log-carrying exercises.

training includes long runs in sand wearing combat boots, drills with the IBS (Inflatable Boat, Small), long-distance swims in the ocean, various team endurance tests carrying a huge log, and endless push-ups and other exercises. Double-timing everywhere is required of 'tadpoles' undergoing SEAL training. Along with the physical training comes instruction in first-aid and hydrographic reconnaissance. To get SEALs used to 'driving on' under adverse conditions, swims in icy water and periods spent immersed in treacherous sand or mud are stipulated during this first phase of training.

If the first few weeks seem terrible to the novices, it is only because they have not yet experienced 'Hell Week', the SEALs' equivalent of the SAS's Brecon Beacons endurance march, although the SEALs' course lasts much longer. Hell Week is intended to push the SEAL well past what he thought were his personal limits, to demonstrate just how much capability he possesses. In addition, one of the main purposes of Hell Week is to show the men how they can push themselves constantly onward in spite of little or no sleep. Thus, during Hell Week the SEAL is unlikely to be allowed more than a total of four hours of sleep. Not only does he become tired, but his clothes are kept soaking wet almost the entire time.

Divided into boat crews of seven men, the SEALs carry their 250lb inflatable boat everywhere they go during Hell Week, often over their heads in the shoulder-wrenching 'extended arm carry'. Throughout Hell Week, push-ups or other physical exercises are assigned over and over again. At night the SEALs have to carry out long paddles in their IBS, forcing themselves to overcome cold, fatigue, and the dispiriting effects of damp clothing. For 'fun', somersaults and headstands in foul-smelling mud are ordered after the SEALs' long paddles, just when their arms have become so tired it seems that they will never be lifted above the waist again. Night infiltration exercises are included, with additional push-ups in the surf being imposed as a penalty for being spotted by instructors. Occasionally, sandwiched between running, paddling, push-ups, and training exercises might come an opportunity for up to 30 minutes of numb, cold sleep, but only very occasionally. By the time it has finished, Hell Week has usually reduced the class of SEALs by half.

Push-ups are normally carried out wearing full diving gear, including twin oxygen and nitrogen cylinders

When, at last, Hell Week ends, those SEALs remaining move on to training in hydrographic reconnaissance, which includes day and night recons and submerged recons, the last designed for obtaining information on enemy-held beaches. High-speed deployment from the IBS is practised, and diving training begins.

At the start of the diving training, the prospective SEAL is introduced to the most elementary form of breathing equipment, the open circuit SCUBA unit. The open circuit type, so named because expended gas is released into the water rather than recycled, is the least economic breathing apparatus, since only five per cent of the compressed air is actually utilised. It is also unsuitable for clandestine SEAL operations because it leaves a trail of tell-tale bubbles, and its noise is sufficient to trigger off acoustically activated charges. However, the SCUBA is valuable for early training and for underwater searches and it allows diving to a depth of 130ft. It is also

used for exercises mounted to encourage the SEALs to regard the apparatus as part of themselves. Push-ups are normally carried out wearing full diving gear, including twin oxygen and nitrogen cylinders, a weight belt and so on. During this phase the student also learns the correct procedure for removing his diving equipment underwater, swimming around for a short while, then replacing the gear, often while instructors harass him to break his concentration.

These preliminaries over, the student begins underwater swims at San Diego Bay, near the Naval Amphibious Base at Coronado in California. Among other skills, these swims are intended to develop confident underwater navigation by compass. Soon the diver progresses to night swims and the solution of tactical problems, including mock attacks on ships.

As the SEAL's diving abilities develop, he moves on to more sophisticated equipment. The semi-closed circuit, which also utilises tanks of oxygen and nitrogen, is a very reliable and safe breathing unit, and the Mk IV SCUBA is generally used by the SEALs when operating their submersible Swimmer Delivery Vehicles (SDVs) as it allows an underwater time of 180 minutes. Although there is again a stream of bubbles produced by the semi-enclosed system, it is less obvious and may be disguised by a bubble-dispersing exhaust valve. The Emerson closed circuit system is also used on complicated manoeuvres in the bay, and mock attacks on ships are carried out with complex underwater navigation problems being built into each exercise. During this period, prospective SEALs make up to three dives a day and they soon feel completely at home in all kinds of underwater conditions. The final part of the SEALs' diving training involves controlled use of the Mk XV

While amphibious and underwater operations are the SEALs' speciality, each member has to prove himself an elite infantryman. Above: Prospective SEALs, armed with M-16 rifles, learn covert reconnaissance skills, while (above right and far right) others struggle to complete the gruelling routines that turn them into hard fighting men. Right and below right: SEALs throw themselves into an exhausting exercise in which buddies are carried through waist-deep glutinous mud.

In mid-June 1963, the US Navy accepted the Emerson Closed Circuit Oxygen Breathing Apparatus for service with naval divers. It replaced the German-manufactured Draeger LT Lund II, which had itself replaced the Italian-made Pirelli 901 and 701 models.

The Emerson apparatus consists, essentially, of a single cylinder of oxygen, linked with two breathing bags, a mask and mouthpiece assembly, and a carbon dioxide absorption canister. During the re-breathing cycle, oxygen from the cylinder passes into the right-hand breathing bag, which already contains an amount of nitrogen. On inhalation, gas is drawn from the bag through a one-way valve to the mouthpiece. On exhalation, gas passes through a second one-way valve, forcing gas collected in the left-hand breathing bag into the absorption canister, where granular Baralyme (barium hydroxide) removes the carbon dioxide. Gas that has previously been cleaned in the canister is displaced into the right-hand breathing bag where it mixes with oxygen from the cylinder for the next inhalation.

The movement of gas around the system thus ensures that the minimum of air 'unrefreshed' by oxygen is breathed by the diver.

The advantages of the Emerson system to SEAL teams are that all the gas may be used, prolonging the serviceable time of the cylinder, and that no bubbles are produced to betray the diver to the enemy. However, because oxygen is toxic at two atmospheres' pressure, the apparatus cannot be used below a certain depth. Excessive exertion must also be avoided, as the resultant build-up of carbon dioxide overloads the absorption canister and creates a danger of carbon dioxide poisoning

SCUBA rig, in which the mixture of oxygen and nitrogen required for various depths is governed by computerised circuitry.

Upon completion of this second phase, the SEAL receives training as an elite light infantryman and reconnaissance trooper. The development of such skills as weapons usage, small-unit tactics for raids and reconnaissance, demolitions and radio communication is included. Physical training during this phase is especially rigorous, but the SEALs who have got this far are now in top condition and they take the new challenges in their stride.

Firearms training is very thorough, as is the tactical training in quick-reaction drills, anti-ambush drills, silent elimination of sentries, prisoner snatches, and various types of infiltration. The finale of this phase takes place on San Clemente Island off the Californian coast, where demanding night tactical exercises are run, some on land and some in the water. Sophisticated demolition techniques are also taught, including those of underwater demolition, the speciality of the SEALs. Hydrographic reconnaissance of possible landing sites is combined with the use of explosives for clearing underwater obstacles, to give the SEALs the most realistic and practical training possible. Once the San Clemente Island

exercises are over, the recruit has completed BUD/S, but he is not yet a fully qualified SEAL.

The next step is parachute training at Fort Benning. This lasts three weeks, during which the SEAL will make five static-line jumps. Then, after the arduous weeks of para training, the SEAL undergoes tactical training with his team. This is the last step in the process of earning the trident of the fully qualified SEAL. As part of his team, he goes through tough physical training each morning. Along with the men who will be working with him in combat, he hones his small-unit tactical skills, his swimming techniques, and his shooting ability. Then, after successfully proving himself fit to serve on an operational SEAL team, he finally wins the coveted SEAL brevet. Incorporating a trident, an eagle, an anchor and a pistol, the brevet symbolises the range of highly developed skills possessed by the SEAL.

Upon completion of training, a SEAL will normally be assigned to one of the six operational SEAL teams, or to one of the two operational SDV teams. In actuality, the new SEAL is most likely to be assigned to one of the first five SEAL teams rather than the sixth. SEAL Teams 1, 3 and 5 are based on the West Coast of the USA, while SEAL Teams 2, 4 and 6 are based on the East Coast. SEAL Team 6, however, is a special anti-terrorist unit assigned to work with Delta and other US anti-terrorist forces and is not, there-

Left: Swim fins are worn on water jumps to enable the SEAL to deploy at maximum speed when he breaks the surface. Far left: A two-man Swimmer Delivery Vehicle on an exercise. During training, the maximum operating depth of the SDV is taken as 30ft. Below: SEALs practise diving from an IBS. Right: Using a life-support system, SEALs assist a novice's free ascent in the controlled conditions of a diving chamber.

Right: One of the less well-known duties of the SEALs has been the recovery of astronauts and their craft. Here, dwarfed by the looming bulk of a US Navy aircraft carrier, SEAL divers work on the capsule of an Apollo spacecraft which came down in 1971. Below: Looking on as the mighty US Marine Corps rumbles in from the sea, a lone SEAL stands sentinel on a beach at San Clemente Island, California. Coming ashore from the US Navy's amphibious ships are USMC LVTP-7s (Landing Vehicle Tracked Personnel Mark 7s), each armed with a turret-mounted 0.5in machine gun and capable of 40mph on land and 8.5mph in the water.

fore, likely to include personnel who have just completed training. Reportedly, members of SEAL-6 undergo training with men of the British SBS assigned to the Comacchio Company, the unit of the Royal Marines responsible for the security of the North Sea oil rigs. SEAL-6 reportedly carries out a form of anti-terrorist training as well.

The SEALs Swimmer Delivery Vehicle Teams, SDVT-1 (based on the West Coast) and SDVT-2 (based on the East Coast) operate one of the most interesting types of equipment in the SEAL organisation's arsenal. The Swimmer Delivery Vehicle is the modern descendent of the miniature submarines and human torpedoes developed during World War II. Its main purpose is to carry swimmers faster, further, and with less exertion than they could manage themselves, and it also transports their heavy equipment. Information about recent SDVs tends to be classified, but it is thought that some are equipped to deliver nuclear weapons. The SDVs are sometimes used by the SEALs to deliver conventional ordnance, but in most cases they are deployed solely for the transport of personnel.

There are several types of SDV described in the US Navy inventory. The SDV-EX-VIII is designed to carry six combat swimmers and their equipment. It is powered by electric motors supplied by batteries and is completely flooded when operational. The SEAL occupants are sustained by a vehicle life-support system supplemented by their own SCUBA equipment. The vehicle is fully pilotable in both the horizontal and the vertical planes, and the pilot is guided by a computerised Doppler navigation sub-system. Sonar is carried to provide advance warning of obstacles in the SDV's path, and all the electrical instruments are installed in airtight containers.

A smaller version is the SDV-EX-IX, which takes two swimmers. Unlike the SDV-EX-VIII, this type also functions as a surface boat, powered by a 55hp propane-fuelled engine; an electric powerplant is engaged when the SDV is submerged. Also in use are some older SDVs which are retained for specific purposes. The Mk VII Model 2, for example, is a four-man submersible constructed of fibre-glass and non-ferrous materials. Because its materials produce a low acoustic and magnetic signature on enemy electronic surveillance equipment, it is particularly suitable for infiltration missions into closely guarded areas.

Since the refit of Grayback, at least two nuclear submarines have been converted for special operations

SEALs assigned to the SDV teams tend to be very high calibre personnel. They must be able to maintain their vehicles as well as their other equipment, and they must be masters of the Mk XV mixed-gas computerised breathing apparatus, which has a long range and allows diving to depths considered unsafe with other forms of breathing gear.

When a large distance separates the SEAL teams from their objectives, they and their IBS and SDV craft are inserted by larger vessels, some of which are specially adapted for the purpose. The ASDV, for example, is a modified landing craft with the role of launching and recovering SDVs. Also, in 1967, the US Navy refitted a submarine – USS Grayback – for SEAL insertious. Hangars were built on deck to carry SDVs, and berths installed for 67 fully equipped SEALs (seven officers and 60 other ranks). The Grayback operates from Subic Bay in the Philippines, the primary overseas base of the SEALs and also the base of the US Navy's Naval Special Warfare Unit One. Since the refit of Grayback, it is reported that at least two nuclear submarines, probably of the Polaris class, have also been converted for special operations. For missions which do not require the transport of small craft, the SEALs operate infantry insertion and extraction vessels such as the Landing Craft (Personnel) Launch (LCPL) Mk 11, or the smaller, shallow-draught 'Boston Whaler' and 'Stab' boats for riverine operations.

Whether a new SEAL is assigned to an operational SEAL team or an SDV team, he can be sure that the has reached the apex of the US special forces. The SEALs are trained to operate in small units and every man has an important role to fulfil. Thus, should he eventually be assigned to instruct the recruits of the Underwater Demolition Teams (UDTs) at BUD/S, or posted for overseas duties at Subic Bay, at Holy Loch in Scotland, or afloat with naval task forces, he knows that what he has to offer is first-hand experience of the toughest all-round military training in the USA.

THE AUTHOR Leroy Thompson served in Vietnam as a member of the USAF Combat Security Police. He has published several books including *Uniforms of the Elite Forces* and *Uniforms of the Indochina and Vietnam Wars*.

Numbed by the cold, and with a potential gas bomb only feet above their heads, the Zeppelin crews set out to devastate London

IT WAS THE WORST conflagration to descend upon London since the Great Fire of 1666. The whole area to the north of St Paul's was in flames, separate fires, fanned by the wind, combined into a huge blaze that raged through textile warehouses, causing destruction amounting to more than half a million pounds. The firestorm had been started on the night of 8/9 September 1915 by the incendiary bombs of a single airship of the Imperial German Navy – Zeppelin L13 commanded by Kapitänleutnant Heinrich Mathy. In this one raid, Mathy caused one-sixth of the total damage inflicted on Britain during all the German air

attacks of World War I. One year later, on the night of 1/2 October 1916, Heinrich Mathy was once again en route to London, cruising high over the North Sea in one of the Navy's new 'super-Zeppelins', the L31.

The L31 was a far cry from earlier Zeppelin airships, such as the old L3, on which veteran commanders like Mathy had learned their trade. For the first two months of the war, the L3 had carried out the German Navy's airship operations single-handed, making a number of reconnaissance flights over coastal waters and the German Bight. By February 1915, the L3 had been joined by 10 more airships of the same class, built in record time by the Zeppelin company at their Friedrichshafen factory, and at two new construction sheds at Löwenthal and Potsdam.

The German Army was also desperate for new airships; of the five Zeppelins in army service at the outbreak of war, four had already been lost.

On 14 April 1915, in the wake of several abortive

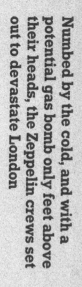

Above: May 1915 – the first Zeppelin raid on London. Right: The men who pioneered the development of the Zeppelin – Dr Hugo Eckener (left) and Count Zeppelin (centre), pictured with Peter Strasser, head of the Naval Airship Division. Far right: The giant L53, which raided England in 1917 but was shot down off the coast of Holland in August 1918.

missions by other Zeppelins, the Navy airship *L9*, commanded by Heinrich Mathy, set out to attack England. Armed with ten 110lb bombs and 40 incendiaries. *L9* had originally been engaged in a reconnaissance flight off the Friesian Islands but, after flying all day without sighting any British warships, Mathy obtained permission to carry out a raid on a British coastal target before returning to base. The objective Mathy selected was the shipyard complex at Tynemouth. However, landfall was made at Blyth, some miles further north on the Northumberland coast, and the *L9*'s commander mistook the River Wansbeck for the Tyne. Although most of his bombs fell harmlessly in open country, Mathy was convinced that the had inflicted considerable damage on the Tyne's shipyards and steered for home.

In May 1916 the navy received the *L10*, the first of 10 new and improved Zeppelins. They were 536ft long, powered by four 210hp Maybach engines and could fly as far as the west coast of England with two tons of bombs on board. Henceforth, while the older types were relegated to fleet support duties, the new Zeppelins would take on the task of raiding England. Their arrival, however,

ZEPPELIN TACTICS

Such was the weight of propaganda surrounding the airship raids on Britain, that it is for this type of operation that the Zeppelin is best remembered.

However, throughout the war, the primary task of the Naval Airship Division (whose insignia is shown above) was reconnaissance.

Far more could undoubtedly have been achieved if the German Navy had exploited its airships to the full. Capable of remaining airborne for 100 hours, with a maximum range of 3000 miles, the airships might have wrought havoc on Allied convoys in the North Atlantic had they been used in conjunction with submarines.

The techniques required for this type of operation had been demonstrated on 19 August 1916, when naval airships carried out long-range reconnaissance in support of German warships operating in the North Sea (left top).

Zeppelin tactics over the British Isles usually involved climbing to a height where the airship could exploit favourable easterly winds as it crossed the coastline. The Zeppelins could only fly in good weather and at night, providing there was little or no moonlight. The engines would be switched off as the airship approached the target area, making it virtually impossible to detect from the ground unless illuminated by searchlight. During the early stages of the Zeppelin campaign, Britain's air defences were so minimal that the airships were allowed free reign. However, the establishment of anti-aircraft batteries and the assignment of several squadrons of the Royal Flying Corps and Royal Naval Air Service to night flying made the German airships extremely vulnerable.

Above: News of another Zeppelin raid.

ZEPPELIN

came too late to enable the navy to strike Germany's first blow against London. The German Army also began to receive the new airships (army airships were designated with the prefix LZ, and carried out a series of probing attacks on Southend, Ramsgate and Bury St Edmunds. Then, on the night of 31 May, the army airship Luftschiff Zeppelin (LZ) 38, flew to London and dropped 3000lb of bombs on the northeast sector of the capital, killing seven people and inflicting damage amounting to over £18,000. On the night of 6/7 June, Hull was raided by Heinrich Mathy in the L9. Ten explosive and 50 incendiary bombs were unleashed on the town, starting numerous fires and causing damage amounting to £45,000. It was the most destructive attack carried out on England so far.

While Mathy ran for home after his successful raid, the LZ37 had run into trouble. Cruising over Ostend, in Belgium, after failing to reach London, she was sighted by Flight Sub-Lieutenant R.A.J. Warneford, flying a Morane Parasol. Warneford stalked the LZ37 and positioned himself directly above the airship. Taking careful aim he released his bombs, sending them cascading through the Zeppelin's envelope. She burst into flames and crashed near Ghent, killing all her crew with the exception of one man. The helmsman had jumped clear of the burning wreck 200ft above the ground and crashed through the roof

of a convent.

Because of the limited period of darkness during the summer, no major Zeppelin raids were made on British targets until 9 August, when the L9's bombs killed 16 people at Goole, in Yorkshire. Four other airships – the L10, L11, L12 and L13 – also set out that night to raid London, but all failed to reach their objective. Four more airships set out on 17 August; two turned back with mechanical trouble, and a third – the L11 – dropped her load on Ashford and Faversham. The fourth airship, however, succeeded in reaching London and dropped her bombs on the northeast suburbs, causing considerable damage and killing 10 people. The ship was the L10, and her commander, Oberleutnant zur See Friedrich Wenke, became the first naval officer to bomb the British capital. The L10 was normally commanded by

Below: As the commander shouts orders from above, a hoard of groundcrew manhandle the gondola of a Zeppelin at a German airfield.

of 12,795ft they could operate to a range of 1336 miles. The Type P Zeppelins were 536ft 5in in length, 64ft 4in in diameter, and the envelope contained some 1,126,540 cubic feet of explosive gas. Armament consisted of two 7.92mm Maxim machine guns, mounted above the forward hull, and bombs.

company with the L16 from Hage, and the L11, L14 and L15 from Nordholz. The L11 dropped her bombs soon after crossing the coast and did little damage, but the others went on to bomb London and its docks, killing 71 people and injuring a further 128. This was the last airship raid on Britain in 1915.

When operations resumed in January 1916, they were directed against targets spread along the whole length of Britain. The first raid of the year, on 31 January, was made on Liverpool by nine naval airships. One of them, the L19, suffered engine failure and came down in the North Sea. The crew escaped, but the British trawler King Stephen refused to pick them up, her skipper fearing that the Germans would take over his ship. As a result, the Zeppelin's entire crew drowned, together with her commander, Odo Loewe. Edinburgh was bombed for the first time on the night of 2 April by the L14, sending £44,000-worth of whisky up in flames when a warehouse suffered a direct hit.

In May 1916 the Naval Airship Division received the first of the new super-Zeppelins, the L30. Together with her sister ships, she formed the spearhead of a renewed air offensive against Britain in July 1916. With 18 airships at his disposal, Strasser was able to plan the raids from a position of moderate

Above: Kapitänleutnant Heinrich Mathy. Below: Heinrich Mathy's L13, which he commanded before the advent in May 1916 of the new super-Zeppelins. The L13 was one of the 10 Type P Zeppelins and was commissioned on 25 July 1915. The Type P airships were powered by four 210hp Maybach CX six-cylinder water-cooled piston engines and had a maximum speed of 59mph. With a service ceiling

Oberleutnant zur See Klaus Hirsch, veteran of the early North Sea reconnaissance flights. Hirsch was therefore on board when the airship set out on a similar mission on 3 September. On her way back to Nordholz, L10 exploded near Neuwerk Island, and crashed with the loss of its 19 crew members.

Hirsch was the first of the Naval Airship Division's renowned commanders to die. He was one of a select band of men who, under the direction of the fiery Korvettenkapitän Peter Strasser, had pioneered the Zeppelin as an instrument of war. Their names were household words in Germany, and might have been plucked from a roll-call of the German nobility: Horst von Buttlar-Brandenfels, Hans Fritz, Magnus von Blaten-Hallermund, Werner Peterson, Alois Böcker, Joachim Breithaupt, Odo Loewe, Max Dietrich, Helmut Beelitz – and Heinrich Mathy. Almost all of them had had narrow escapes, but had survived. Their luck was not to last.

Army airships were active in early September 1915, bombing Milwall, Deptford, Greenwich and Woolwich docks. Then came Heinrich Mathy's devastating incendiary raid of 8/9 September, the success of which eclipsed all previous raids. Mathy's triumph was followed by a raid on 13 October which, although inflicting less material damage, was the most devastating of the whole war in terms of human casualties. Five airships took part: Mathy's L13, in

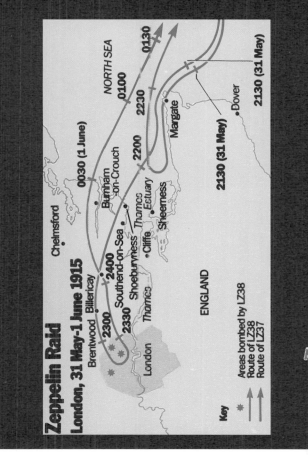

Zeppelin Raid
London, 31 May-1 June 1915

NORTH SEA

0130
0100
0030 (1 June)
2330
2300
2400
2330
2200
2230

Chelmsford
Brentwood
Billericay
Burnham-on-Crouch
Southend-on-Sea
Shoeburyness
Thames
Cliffe
Thames
Sheerness
Margate
Dover
London

2130 (31 May)
2130 (31 May)

ENGLAND

Key
* Areas bombed by LZ38
→ Route of LZ38
→ Route of LZ37

L13

Below left: The interior of the control cabin of the L59, the airship that became known as 'The African Ship' and made the epic 4200-mile round voyage from Bulgaria in a bid to ferry supplies to General von Lettow-Vorbeck in German East Africa. Below: The machine-gun and lookout position on the outer envelope of a German airship.

strength, and this was demonstrated on 24 August when 13 airships set out to attack southern England. The striking force included two Schütte-Lanz craft, the *SL8* and *SL9*. Used by the army, the Schütte-Lanz airships were about the same size as their Zeppelin counterparts, but their hulls were constructed of laminated plywood girders instead of aluminium. The Schütte-Lanz firm was absorbed into Luftschiffbau Zeppelin (Zeppelin Airship Company) on the outbreak of war, but the ships retained their SL designation. On this raid, only Heinrich Mathy reached London in his *L31*.

On 2 September the largest raiding force of airships assembled during the entire war set course for England. There were 16 of them, comprising 11 navy craft and five army. As the ships droned out over the sea, their crews could not know that this mission would mark the death-knell of the hope so fondly cherished by Peter Strasser and other airship advocates – that England could be brought to her knees by Zeppelin-borne fire from the skies.

Two of the attackers – the *L17* and the army's *LZ97* – ran into bad weather and were forced to turn back. The remaining army ships crossed the English coast at various points ahead of the navy craft; the *LZ90* dropped her bombs on Norfolk before sheering off seawards, while the *LZ98* and the *SL11* approached London from the south and north re-

spectively. Flying over the capital's northern suburbs, the *SL11*'s commander, Hauptmann Wilhelm Schramm, released his bombs on landmarks that, as a boy, he had known well – London had been his birthplace. Shortly before the *SL11* dropped the last of her load, she was sighted by Lieutenant William Leefe Robinson and Second-Lieutenants J.I. Mackay and B.H. Hunt of No.39 (Home Defence) Squadron, Royal Flying Corps (RFC). All three pilots went after the ship, and Leefe Robinson was the first to catch up with her. From a range of 800ft, he emptied two drums of explosive ammunition into the silvery envelope. Away in the distance, the crews of the Navy airships droning towards London saw a sudden brilliant light burst across the sky. Horrified, they watched the burning mass that had been the *SL11* slide towards the darkened earth. The wreckage of the *SL11* fell at Cuffley, where the remains of her crew were buried with full military honours. Her passing was marked with the end of the German Army's participation in the raids on Britain.

The loss of the *SL11*, although failing to deter the Navy from mounting further raids, nevertheless persuaded Strasser to act with more caution. From now on, attacks on London were to be carried out only by the new super-Zeppelins, operating in small numbers. On 23 September, 12 navy Zeppelins – including Heinrich Mathy's *L31* and Alois Böcker's *L33* – set out to attack London and the midlands. The *L33*, damaged by anti-aircraft fire and air attack, crash-

AFRICAN ADVENTURE

In the autumn of 1917, in an attempt to ferry much-needed supplies to the isolated garrison of General von Lettow-Vorbeck in German East Africa, the Navy Zeppelin *L59* was re-built to increase her capacity to two and a half million cubic feet.

On the morning of 21 November 1917, *L59* took off from Yambol in eastern Bulgaria and set out across the Sea of Marmara.

Commanded by Kapitänleutnant Ludwig Bockholt, the airship had been extensively renovated to allow maximum use of its parts by the beleaguered garrison. The Zeppelin's engines would be used to power the garrison's radio transmitter, the cotton envelope would be cannibalised for clothing, the metal girders could be employed in the construction of buildings, and the catwalks were lined with leather suitable for making boots. Finally, 'The African Ship' was laden with a precious 13-ton cargo of medical and military equipment.

Passing over eastern Turkey, *L59* struck out across the Mediterranean on the night of 21 November. The crew struggled to keep the airship on course in the face of violent storms and, in the early hours of the 22nd, *L59* crossed the shore of Africa and headed inland across the Sahara Desert.

At midnight on 22 November, with *L59* south of Khartoum, Bockholt received a radio message ordering him to return to Yambol. German intelligence had been duped by the British into believing that von Lettow-Vorbeck's garrison was beyond help. *L59* arrived back at base on 25 November, having covered 4200 miles and with sufficient fuel left for a further 3000 miles. Although the relief mission may have failed, *L59*'s epic journey constituted the Zeppelin's greatest wartime achievement. In addition, it provided a glimpse into the role the airship would later play in fostering intercontinental flight.

landed almost intact in a field near West Mersea, in Essex. Böcker and his 21 crew were taken prisoner.

Another veteran, Werner Peterson in the *L32*, was not so fortunate. His airship was shot down in flames near Billericay by Second-Lieutenant Frederick Sowrey. All 22 crew members perished. Heinrich Mathy, in *L31*, still seemed to bear a charmed life. He bombed London, killing 22 people and injuring 74, before making his escape pursued by heavy gunfire.

On the night of 1/2 October 1916, Mathy and the *L31* set out as part of an 11-strong Zeppelin force. The orders issued by Strasser to the airship commanders were simple: 'Attack London if possible according to weather conditions.' At 2100 hours Mathy made landfall at Lowestoft, and from there steered on a compass heading until he was able to pick up the Great Eastern Railway that ran to the capital through Chelmsford, in Essex. It was then that he made the biggest, and the last mistake of his distinguished career. Instead of following the railway directly to London, dropping his bombs and escaping before the RFC had time to intercept, he detoured to the northeast of the capital, presumably in an attempt to avoid the brunt of the anti-aircraft defences. It was a manoeuvre that cost Mathy vital extra minutes. As the *L31* was tracked moving towards London from the north, four RFC pilots took off to chase her. One of them was Second-Lieutenant W J Tempest, who climbed away from North Weald, near Harlow, in Essex, in his BE2C biplane. His combat report tells the rest of the story.

'As I drew up to the Zeppelin, to my relief I found that I was quite free of AA fire for the nearest shells were bursting quite three miles away. The Zeppelin was now nearly 12,700ft high and mounting rapidly. I therefore started to drive at her, for, though I had a slight advantage in speed she was climbing like a rocket and leaving me standing. I

accordingly gave a tremendous pump at my petrol tank and dived straight at her, firing a burst into her as I came. I let her have another burst as I passed under her and then banking my machine over, sat under her tail, and flying along underneath her, pumped lead into her for all I was worth. I could see tracer bullets flying from her in all directions, but I was too close under her for them to concentrate on me.

'As I was firing I noticed her begin to go red inside like an enormous Chinese lantern and then a flame shot out of the front part of her and I realised she was on fire. She shot up about 200ft, paused, and came roaring straight down on me before I had time to get out of the way. I nose-dived for all I was worth, with the Zepp tearing after me, and expected every minute to be engulfed in the flames. I put my machine into a spin and just managed to corkscrew out of the way as she shot past me, roaring like a furnace. I righted my machine and watched her hit the ground with a shower of sparks.'

The wreckage of *L31* fell in a field at Potter's Bar, near Barnet on the Great North Road. Some distance away from the tangled, fire-blackened aluminium girders, local villagers found the broken body of a German officer, sunk into the ground. Kapitänleutnant Heinrich Mathy had jumped from the inferno of his blazing hydrogen to meet a quick, clean death. His crew of 18 died with him. Before the end of the year,

Right: Portraits of two of the great Zeppelin commanders — Alois Böcker (left) and Max Dietrich (right).

two more German airships were destroyed over England. Max Dietrich, who like Mathy had seemed indestructible, was shot down in *L34* on 29 November. On that same night, *L21*, commanded by Kapitänleutnant Frankenburg, was attacked and shot down in flames with the loss of all hands.

The era of the large-scale Zeppelin raids was over, and from the beginning of 1917 the offensive against southern England was progressively taken over by bomber aircraft such as the Gotha. Nevertheless, operations against more distant British targets were still carried out by the Navy's Zeppelins. The majority of raids were made with a new generation of Zeppelins known as 'height climbers'. These were nearly 700ft long and could climb to over 20,000ft. The Zeppelins had failed to bring London to its knees, but their crews' commitment was never in doubt. Between January 1915 and August 1918, German airships made a total of 51 raids on Britain, dropping 196 tons of explosives. They killed 557 people and injured 1358, as well as inflicting damage amounting to one and a half million pounds.

The last Zeppelin attack of the war was made on 5/6 August 1918, and was intercepted by aircraft from Great Yarmouth air station. Zeppelin *L70* was shot down by Egbert Cadbury, flying a DH4, and fell blazing into the sea with the loss of all 22 crew. Among those who perished was the man who had led the Naval Airship Division through four years of war, the architect of the first Blitz on Britain – Korvettenkapitän Peter Strasser.

Although the airships had not achieved Strasser's aim of inflicting crippling material and psychological blows on Britain, the Zeppelin crews had nevertheless made a significant contribution to the German war effort. By the end of 1916, the Zeppelin threat had tied down 12 RFC squadrons and hundreds of guns and searchlights – at a time when Allied manpower and equipment were desperately needed in France.

THE AUTHOR Robert Jackson is a professional aviation historian and the author of over 50 books, including *Airships – In Peace and War.*

Main picture: *L12* lies broken in the sea, a victim of the Royal Flying Corps. Below: Zeppelin commanders Horst von Buttlar-Brandenfels (seated) and von Schiller. Bottom: The last moments of Max Dietrich's *L34*, captured by an amateur photographer in Hartlepool. Bottom far left: *L42* and *L63* in their shed at Nordholz. Bottom centre: British troops survey the tangled mass of girders that once were an airship.

Kapitänleutnant Joachim Breithaupt, commander of Zeppelin *L15*

Breithaupt wears a German naval officer's jacket, with stripes on the cuffs indicating the rank of Kapitänleutnant, and a naval officer's peaked cap. Under the jacket he wears a polo-neck sweater (Zeppelin crews had to withstand extreme cold), and the leather trousers of a foul-weather suit. Leather gaiters and boots complete the uniform and he wears the ribbon of the Iron Cross, 2nd Class, and the Iron Cross, 1st Class.

Sailing into the Indian Ocean in late August 1914, the German cruiser SMS Emden left a trail of destruction unsurpassed in the annals of surface raiding

AT 1800 HOURS on 5 August 1914 SMS *Emden*, a cruiser attached to the Imperial German Navy's Far East Squadron, set sail from the colony port of Tsingtao in China for the second and final time. Britain had been at war with Germany for little more than 48 hours, and *Emden* was putting to sea as a commercial raider. As the ship's crew took their last look at their former base, their spirits raised by the martial music played by *Emden's* band, the cruiser's charismatic captain, Commander Karl Friedrich Max von Müller, ordered his helmsman to steer towards a pre-arranged rendezvous with three other

vessels, including the former British steamer SS *Markomannia. Emden* and the other ships were making for the German island of Pagan in the Marianas to link up with the rest of the Far East Squadron. The journey passed without incident, allowing one of Müller's officers, Reserve Lieutenant Julius Lauterbach, to give lessons on the correct procedure for seizing merchantmen.

At Pagan, Müller and the commander of the Far East Squadron, Vice-Admiral Maximilian Graf von Spee, discussed *Emden's* deployment options. On 13 August Müller received his orders: 'You are hereby allocated the *Markomannia* [as a collier] and will be detached with the task of entering the Indian Ocean and waging cruiser warfare as best you can... This order will come into force tomorrow morning.' After a night of feverish activity, *Emden* and the rest of the squadron put to sea at 1730 hours; next day, at 0800 on the 15th, *Emden* and her collier turned southwards on a heading that would take them to the German Palau Islands, where *Emden* would take coal from *Markomannia*. The transfer went smoothly and the cruise was resumed through the Molucca Strait to reach Timor on the 25th.

As the voyage continued, attempts were made to disguise the cruiser. At the suggestion of the ship's first officer, Kurt Hellmuth von Mücke, a dummy smokestack was built out of canvas and wood. Like the rest of the ship, it was painted in British naval grey. As the changes were effected, the cruiser successfully negotiated the dangerous narrows

Below: The beauty of SMS *Emden* belied her deadly purpose, as 16 British merchantmen and two warships learned to their cost. During her lone three-month cruise she became a legend, successfully evading searching warships of the British, French and Japanese Navies and mounting raids of increasing daring. Bottom: Photographed on the day of the demise of the warship, 10 November 1914, a landing party from *Emden* boards launches in order to reach the schooner *Ayesha* and escape from the Cocos Islands.

CRUISE OF THE EMDEN

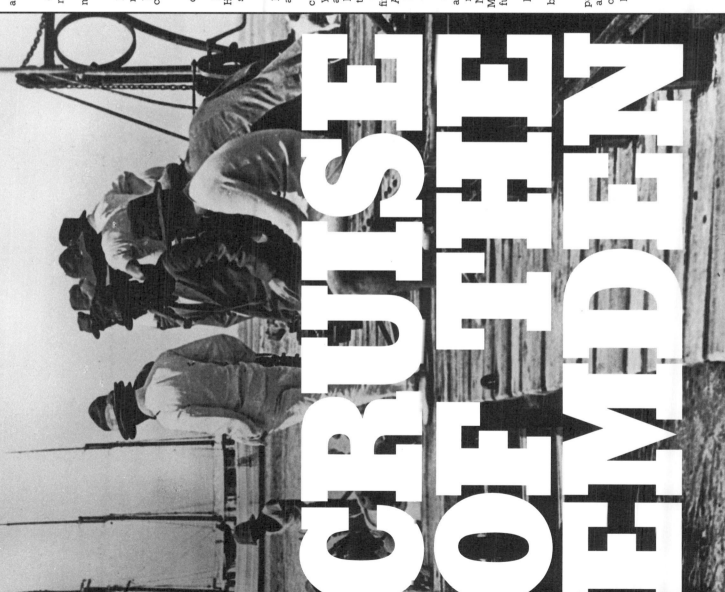

between the islands of Bali and Lombok and crossed the equator off Sumatra during the night of 28/29 August.

By 5 September the ship was ready to begin operations in the Bay of Bengal. Her first victim was a neutral vessel, the Greek *Pontoporos*, sighted on the 9th. However, the steamer was carrying some 6500 tons of British coal. Müller made the Greek captain an offer he could not refuse and *Pontoporos* joined *Markomannia* as one of *Emden's* supply ships. On the 10th, the cruiser sighted a distant smoke cloud and set off in pursuit. At 24 knots the cruiser quickly overtook the sluggish steamer and identified her as the *Indus*, a 3393-ton transport on the way to Bombay to pick up horses. Though in ballast, the vessel did provide *Emden's* crew with some much-needed provisions. At 1600 Müller ordered the ship sunk; the valves were opened to the sea and six close-range shots were pumped into her hull to complete the job.

Indus' crew were placed aboard *Markomannia*. A similar coup took place on the following day when *Emden* intercepted the *Lovat*, a troop transport bound for Bombay. Again a sinking party was organised to open the ship's valves, and *Emden* delivered the final blow.

Müller now considered his next move, and he finally decided to go into action against the busy sea lanes to the south of Calcutta, near the mouth of the Hooghly river. Close to 2300 hours on the 12th, Müller forced a merchantman to halt. The vessel, the 4657-ton *Kabinga*, was British but carrying cargo for a neutral country. Not wishing to cause an international incident, Müller contented himself with transferring the crews of his previous victims to the ship and destroying her wireless. Four hours later *Emden's* crew again went to action stations as another unidentified steamer was spotted. The ship was the *Killin*, carrying a 6000-ton cargo of low-grade coal that was

CRUISER COMMANDER

The officer in charge of SMS *Emden* on her epic voyage, Commander Karl Friedrich Max von Müller, was born into a military family on 16 June 1873. After spells at two grammar schools he was accepted at the Plön military academy, from where he joined the army's officer-cadet corps. In an unusual move, Müller transferred to the navy in 1891, and by mid-1896 he was attached to a battleship as a sub-lieutenant.

Müller received excellent reports from his superiors, yet promotion was slow in coming. In 1903, after a two-year stint in German East Africa, during which he contracted malaria, Müller was given the rank of lieutenant on a battleship. His time was spent between several tours of duty and a series of staff courses. In 1907 he joined the staff of Prince Heinrich of Prussia and won further promotion to the rank of lieutenant-commander in the following year. After a spell in Berlin at the Imperial Navy Office between 1909 and 1912, at the comparatively late age of 39 Müller received his first command, SMS *Emden*. Awarded the coveted Pour le Mérite for his cruise in *Emden*, Müller spent the remainder of the war in captivity, firstly in Britain and then, shortly before his repatriation in 1918, in the Netherlands. After the war Müller was given the rank of full captain and took a desk job in the Navy Office. However, due to ill-health brought on by recurrent bouts of malaria, he retired in 1919. During his retirement, Müller participated in local politics and was elected to the post of deputy to the Brunswick provincial parliament. He died on 11 March 1923.

SMS EMDEN

SMS *Emden* was not a purpose-built commercial raider and her role had been envisaged as a cruiser, deployed in the North Sea to screen the manoeuvres of the Imperial German Navy's High Seas Fleet. Displacing 3600 tons, *Emden* was 387ft long with a beam of just under 44ft. Powered by two three-cylinder coal-fired engines, she was capable of reaching a top speed of 24 knots; at the more economical cruising speed of 12 knots, however, her range rose from 1226 to 3790 miles.

For her size, *Emden* packed sufficient punch to deal with any light opposition. The ship's primary armament consisted of 10 4.1in guns situated in pairs fore and aft, and two three-gun batteries placed on each side of the hull. In action, *Emden* was able to unleash a five-gun broadside out to a maximum distance of 13,500yds. The ship also carried a pair of underwater torpedo tubes sited independently amidships on either side of the hull. Five 17.7in torpedoes were available for use, each with a maximum range of some 3600yds.

Emden had two great disadvantages as a commercial raider. Although her armour was of a better quality than most and her rangefinding equipment superior, the cruiser was unlikely to stand much chance in a direct battle with any British ship of the same class, for they were better armoured and more heavily armed. As a lone raider, *Emden* suffered from her limited fuel-carrying capacity (790 tons), which necessitated frequent meetings with supporting collier ships – a factor that curtailed her ability to carry out long-term independent action.

---

of no value to the German raider. As there seemed to be no immediate danger, Müller refrained from sinking *Killin*, and *Emden*, now at the head of *Kabinga*, *Markomannia*, *Pontoporos* and *Killin*, sailed forth. However, a squall blew up and Müller saw the danger of losing his prizes. At 0100 on 13 September, *Killin* was sent to the bottom.

Emden's next victim, sighted at 1500, was the *Diplomat*, a 7615-ton vessel loaded with 10,000 tons of the finest tea. So valuable a catch could be shown no mercy and Müller ordered a boarding party to open the vessel's sea valves. To make sure that *Diplomat* succumbed, explosive devices were positioned in her holds. While the fate of *Diplomat* was being sealed, *Emden* set off in pursuit of another sighting which proved to be a neutral Italian vessel. Müller was unwilling to deal with the vessel and allowed her to escape. The Italian captain wasted no time in radioing the British with *Emden's* last-known position. Several Allied warships were alerted to the threat.

Emden, however, maintained her watch on the

Müller then sailed on in search of more targets.

Below: When *Emden* raided Penang harbour at dawn on 28 October 1914, her foremost funnel was false, a dummy constructed to disguise her as the British cruiser HMS *Yarmouth*. Right: One that survived. Because her cargo was destined for a neutral country, the merchantman *Kabinga* was taken in tow.

Bay of Bengal sea lanes and was able to intercept the *Trabboch* on the morning of the 14th and the *Clan Matheson* in the evening. In five days of almost continuous action, *Emden* had sunk six ships, allowed one to continue her voyage, and kept another as an auxiliary collier. The British were well aware of *Emden's* presence and Müller opted to move further afield in search of a quiet anchorage in which to refuel before seeking out new targets. The cruiser headed southeastwards in the direction of

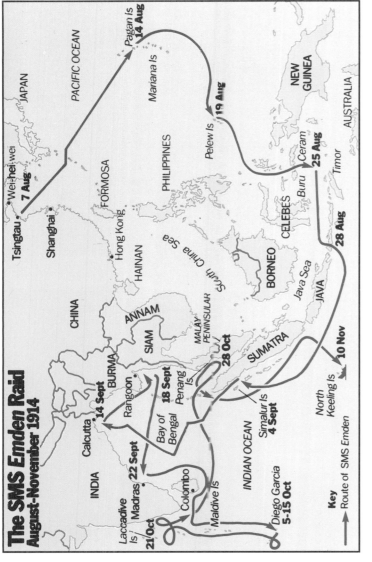

The SMS *Emden* Raid
August–November 1914

JAPAN

PACIFIC OCEAN

Tsingtau Wei-hei-wei
7 Aug

Shanghai

FORMOSA

Hong Kong

HAINAN

CHINA

ANNAM

BURMA

SIAM

MALAY
PENINSULAR

Rangoon

Calcutta
14 Sept

Penang
Is
18 Sept

Bay of
Bengal

Madras 22 Sept

INDIA

Laccadive
Is 21 Oct

Colombo

Maldive Is

Diego Garcia
5-15 Oct

INDIAN OCEAN

Simalur Is
4 Sept

SUMATRA

28 Oct

South China
Sea

Java Sea

BORNEO

JAVA

PHILIPPINES

Mariana Is

Pelew Is
19 Aug

Pagan Is
14 Aug

CELEBES

Buru
Ceram
25 Aug

Timor

28 Aug

10 Nov

North
Keeling Is

NEW
GUINEA

AUSTRALIA

Key
→ Route of SMS *Emden*

Rangoon, but no enemy vessels were sighted and *Emden* turned westwards back across the Bay of Bengal. Despite British naval activity in the area, Müller decided to make a daring night attack on the Indian port of Madras.

At 0200 hours on 22 September Müller gave the final attack order. Cutting through the calm waters at 24 knots, with the crew at action stations, *Emden* closed on her unsuspecting target: the port's fuel dump. Some 3000yds from shore the cruiser halted and her four searchlights were directed at the dump. In 10 minutes, the ship unleashed 25 salvoes, scoring hits on five of the six white-painted storage tanks. Before the harbour defences could react, *Emden* was steaming to safety. The ship and her crew had carried out the attack with surgical precision: 350,000 gallons of fuel had been destroyed with very few casualties among the population ashore.

After being reunited with *Markomannia* off Pondicherry on the 23rd, Müller planned his next move, a manoeuvre that would take *Emden* into the western Indian Ocean and result in the sinking of even more merchantmen. Shortly after noon on the 25th, a few miles off the southwest coast of Ceylon, the cruiser overhauled a 3650-ton British steamer, the *King Lud*. The ship was in ballast but did yield some useful provisions before being sent to the bottom. The day's action was only just beginning for the *Emden* and her crew. At 2200, at a point between Colombo in Ceylon and Minicoy Island in the Laccadives, she caught up with the *Tymeric*. Of 3314 tons, the vessel was loaded with a valuable cargo of sugar bound for Britain. Her master proved to be troublesome and Müller dispensed with the usual niceties, allowing *Tymeric's* crew only 10 minutes to abandon ship. His gunners then dealt with the steamer. The *Emden* resumed

Above: The fuel depot at Madras becomes a blazing inferno after *Emden's* attack on 22 September. Note the shell holes of the tank in the foreground. *Above left:* The instrument room of the British cable station on Direction Island, thoroughly devastated after a visit by *Emden's* landing party.

her cruise at 0030 on the 26th, less than two hours after first sighting *Tymeric*. A few hours later, a third vessel was spotted on the horizon; *Emden* picked up speed and quickly overtook her prey. The steamer, the *Gryfevale*, was en route to Colombo from Aden and was in ballast. However, the vessel proved a useful prize: Müller was able to transfer his captives.

This, the most fruitful stage of *Emden's* cruise, continued into the following day, Sunday, 27 September. Lookouts spied what was to be the most valuable prize of the voyage for the running of the German warship. This was the 4350-ton *Buresk*, a collier carrying some 7500 tons of high-grade coal. Müller put a boarding party on the vessel. After lunch, another smoke cloud was spotted on the horizon and the crew prepared for action as the distance between *Emden* and her target closed. On closer inspection the vessel was identified as the *Ribera*, a 3500-ton steamer on her way from Alexandria to Batavia. The crew was placed aboard the recently captured *Gryfevale* while seamen from *Emden* opened *Ribera's* sea valves. Again, a handful of shots fired at close range finished the job. Shortly after nightfall, the cruiser happened upon her third victim of the day. The *Foyle*, in ballast between Aden and Colombo, was searched, her crew transferred, and then the vessel was despatched. *Gryfevale*, crowded with the crews of three ships, was set free. Müller ordered a southerly course in the direction of the Maldive Islands, where a rendezvous with the faithful *Markomannia* had been arranged for 29 September.

Müller decided that the British would react swiftly to his activities in the western Indian Ocean and decided to sail south towards Diego Garcia, where vital repairs would be carried out on *Emden's* hull. The stay on the island was brief and by 11 October the cruiser was sailing on a northbound track towards the Maldive Islands. Late on the 15th, the *Clan Grant* was detained, and, after *Emden* had dealt with the dredger *Ponrabbel*, sunk. The day's work was

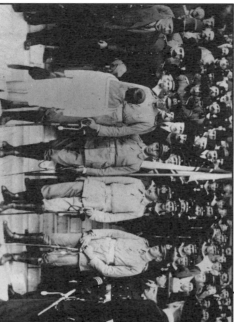

not over. At 2300 hours the *Benmohr* was sighted. Forced to halt, her crew were evacuated and the 4806-ton steamer was sunk with explosive charges. Cruising off Minicoy Island in search of fresh pickings, *Emden* gave chase to a cargo liner, the *Troilus*, whose mixed, 10,000-ton cargo was the most valuable taken on the cruise. Müller put a boarding party on the ship and ordered *Troilus* to fall in behind *Emden*. Over the next 24 hours the raider detained two further ships: the *St Egbert*, which was used as a prison ship, and the 4542-ton *Exford*. To

complete the remarkable work of the last five days, a seventh steamer, the *Chilkana*, was taken on the 19th. Five of the ships were either immediately or subsequently sunk; and one, *Exford*, was used to hold prisoners.

Müller now planned the most daring attack of *Emden's* cruise: a night attack against the ships at anchor in the harbour of Penang's capital, Georgetown. After sailing eastwards for several days, the commander gave his final orders at dusk on 20 October. The onslaught was to begin at dawn on the 27th and, to confuse the enemy, *Emden* was to be disguised as the British cruiser HMS *Yarmouth* by the erection of its dummy funnel. At 0500 hours, at a distance of 1300yds, lookouts spotted a target of a similar size to *Emden*; the Russian cruiser *Zhemchug*. Manoeuvring with great skill in the confines of the harbour, *Emden* made two torpedo runs. Both achieved hits; the second, striking home beneath the Russian cruiser's bridge, was accompanied by a tremendous explosion that ripped *Zhemchug* apart. Satisfied with the morning's work, Müller headed for open waters and safety.

The destroyer's captain refused to strike his colours, preparing to go down with his ship

At 0700, as *Emden's* crew stood down, a smoke cloud was spotted to the stern. On investigation, the ship was identified as an old French destroyer, the *Mousquet*. Though no match for *Emden*, the destroyer gamely offered battle. As the distance between the two adversaries dropped to 4500yds, *Emden* opened fire. One of the cruiser's salvoes stopped the Frenchman dead in the water, and although clearly sinking by the bow, the destroyer's captain refused to strike his colours, preparing to go down with his ship. Some 40 survivors were picked up by *Emden's* launches.

After the action, *Emden* made full speed to escape a lone pursuer from Penang, a second French destroyer, the *Pistolet*. Despite all efforts to jam the French radio transmissions, *Pistolet* managed to get off the message: '*Emden* at Penang...*Emden* at Penang'.

On the last day of October, *Emden* made a refuelling rendezvous with *Buresk* off the coast of Simaloer. It was a timely meeting as the cruiser was low on coal and *Emden's* two other colliers, *Markomannia* and *Pontoporos*, had both been taken by *Yarmouth* on 16

October. By making a feint down the west coast of Sumatra in the direction of the seas off Western Australia, Müller hoped to draw off some of his pursuers. He would then turn westwards for a meeting with the captured British collier *Exford* at North Keeling Island, part of the Cocos group of islands, on the evening of 7 November. Müller also resolved to destroy a British radio and wireless station on Direction Island, believing that there were no ships in the immediate vicinity capable of coming to the station's rescue.

The destruction of the station began at 0630 hours on 10 November when a 50-strong landing party mustered on the deck of *Emden* for its final orders. *Emden* was well within sight of the wireless station staff and a series of distress signals was sent out. Unfortunately for Müller and his men, the message was picked up by an unsuspected British convoy less than 100 miles from Direction Island. One of its escorts, an Australian cruiser, HMAS *Sydney*, was sent to investigate the distress call. Unaware of the danger, Müller waited offshore for the arrival of *Buresk*. Thus, when a ship with two masts and one funnel appeared on the horizon, it gave no immediate cause for alarm. However, a quick calculation of her closing speed clearly showed that she could not be *Buresk*. Müller ordered his remaining crew to action stations and got up steam.

To give those crewmen remaining a better chance of survival, *Emden* was run aground

Müller correctly identified the vessel as a light cruiser and knew that he would be outgunned in a stand-up fight. Nevertheless at 0940, at a distance of 10,500yds, he gave the order to open fire. Early, accurate salvoes put *Sydney's* foremost and aft rangefinders out of action, but the Australian ship kept her distance, using her heavier broadsides to inflict massive damage on *Emden*, rapidly turning the German cruiser into a shattered hulk. At 1115 Müller gave the order to cease fire. His ship was sinking and his crew had suffered terrible losses. To give those crewmen remaining a better chance of survival, *Emden* was run aground on North Keeling Island. Some 65 per cent of *Emden's* crew were either killed or wounded in the unequal struggle. The members of the landing party, under Kurt Hellmuth von Mücke, managed to escape from the island on the schooner *Ayesha*, and after many adventures they ended up in Turkey, where they were fêted as heroes.

The cruise of the *Emden* lasted little more than three months, yet the damage inflicted on British ships was enormous. Since departing Tsingtao, the ship had covered 30,000 miles and sunk 16 British merchantmen. Three colliers had been detained as supply ships, while two other steamers had been allowed to go free after taking on board prisoners captured in other actions. One Russian cruiser and one French destroyer had been sent to the bottom. The total value of these losses was estimated at about five million pounds, some 15 times the cost of building *Emden*. Fighting with great skill and gallantry, *Emden* and her remarkable crew had punched a large hole in the British merchant fleet in the Indian Ocean.

THE AUTHOR William Franklin is a military writer who has a particular interest in the elite forces of the 20th century.

Above: The once-proud *Emden* lies beached on North Keeling Island, her superstructure blown apart by the superior armament of HMAS *Sydney*. Left: One of *Sydney's* boats is prepared for a landing on Direction Island.

Below: Marooned by *Emden* when she sailed to face the approaching threat of *Sydney*, members of the German cruiser's landing party are reduced to anxiously watching the battle from a rooftop. Far left: *Emden* crew members are welcomed as heroes in Constantinople.

SACRIFICE AT WALCHEREN

For sheer heroism, no episode in Royal Navy history equals the self-sacrifice of the SSEF's landing-craft crews at Walcheren

Below: 1 November 1944. Norwegians of No.10 (Inter-Allied) Commando en route for Fortress Walcheren. Right: An LCT joins the assault flotilla. Below right: An Oerlikon crew, Able Seamen Nicholson, Ardern and McCabe, who survived the ordeal by fire at Walcheren.

TWO WEEKS AFTER the Normandy landings of 6 June 1944, the western beaches were more or less secure from attack from the sea. However, on the eastern flank, the supply anchorages were still highly vulnerable to the German Navy based at Le Havre and to its use of such unorthodox weapons as explosive motor boats and human torpedoes.

It was therefore decided to reinforce the eastern beaches, and on 23 June the Support Squadron Eastern Flank (SSEF) was formed, its personnel drawn from the various naval units that had provided inshore fire support to the British forces on D-day. The squadron had a dual role to play: to safeguard the beaches and their supply lines, and to give support fire to infantry ashore. To undertake these tasks, 76 vessels, manned by 240 officers and 3200 men of the Royal Navy and Royal Marines, were assembled under the overall command of Captain A.F. Pugsley, DSO. Mostly LCGs (Landing Craft, Gun), LCFs (Landing Craft, Flak), and LCSs (Landing Craft, Support), these craft had been converted from LCTs (Landing Craft, Tank) for a close-support role during the landings and were now under Commander K.A. Sellar, DSO, DSC.

Three types of support fire were put down by the squadron. Every day, two of the LCGs harassed the enemy's positions and lines of communication in the Franceville area, while the other LCGs carried out indirect bombardments requested by forward observation officers ashore. Finally, LCSs carried out frequent daylight hit-and-run raids on enemy positions between Franceville and Cabourg.

However, it was during the hours of darkness that the SSEF carried out its most valuable role. Each night it created an armed barrier, which became known as the 'Trout Line', to protect the Allied anchorages from attack from the sea. The line stretched about six miles out from Ouistreham and then about two miles in a northwesterly direction to an area covered by Pugsley's other patrols. The main line, consisting of LCGs and LCFs anchored about 700yds apart, was stationary, while a second, mobile, line of motor boats patrolled the gaps.

On the nights of 5/6 and 7/8 July the Germans launched their first attacks with one-man torpedoes, 27 of these being thrown against the Trout Line on the

CAPTAIN A.F. PUGSLEY

A three-times winner of the DSO, A.F. Pugsley was one of the Royal Navy's truly great commanders of small ships during World War II. Educated at the Royal Naval College, Dartmouth, his burning ambition from the start was to command a destroyer, an opportunity that eventually came to him in 1934 after a career which included a spell on a Yangtse River gunboat and the command of an antiquated submarine chaser. In 1936 he was promoted to commander and in September 1939 he became captain of one of the Navy's newest and most powerful destroyers. He was in the thick of the Norwegian campaign, took part in Dunkirk, and then served in Admiral Somerville's Force H in the Mediterranean, and in the Indian Ocean. He was promoted to captain in 1943, and on D-day commanded the assault force that landed the British troops on Juno Beach. This accomplished, he assumed the appointment of Captain (Patrols), which included overall command of the Support Squadron Eastern Flank. Then, in September 1944, he was ordered to form Force T, whose task it was to deliver the Commandos safely ashore at Westkapelle. He carried out this tricky operation with great brilliance and panache, for it was his decision and his alone to order the SSEF to engage the German batteries at point-blank range. Awarded the OBE for his part in the Walcheren operation, he finished his career as a rear-admiral and was made a CBE.

first night and 31 on the second. Some got through and there were Allied casualties; but the Germans suffered losses too, and they subsequently used ingenious decoys to divert the patrols' fire. For example, dummy human-torpedo cockpit domes, with the head and shoulders of a man painted on the inside, were dropped to confuse the defences while real torpedo operators tried to creep through.

On the night of 9/10 July the first German midget submarine was sighted, but these were never very successful. A much more deadly device was a very long-range circling torpedo. It could travel for up to 10 hours at a speed of between six and nine knots and had a device that enabled it to start circling once it had reached the anchorages off the beaches. If it ran out of power, it acted as a lethal mine.

Another equally dangerous weapon was the explosive motor boat. These first appeared on the night of 2/3 August when the Germans launched their first all-out attack on the Trout Line. About 16ft long, each boat was driven at about 30 knots by two Ford V8 engines and carried a 250lb explosive charge which was triggered when the bows hit a target. For over two hours the Germans tried to pilot wave upon wave of these infernal machines through the double line, following them up with a mass attack by human torpedoes.

'Any explosive motor boats that managed to penetrate the Trout Line were set on and destroyed'

Commander Sellar later reported:

'A furious battle was waged. When the enemy retired he left 32 explosive motor boats certainly sunk, two probably sunk and one possibly sunk. The Trout Line had lost only one craft – LCG 764, which had sunk one explosive motor boat before being hit by two others. Any explosive motor boats that managed to penetrate the Trout Line were set on and destroyed by the motor launches.'

The human torpedoes suffered equally heavy casualties, 21 being certainly destroyed, three probably and 11 possibly.

A week later the Germans mounted another all-out attack, again with disastrous results to themselves. For an hour the explosive motor boats vainly tried to penetrate the Trout Line, but they were almost totally wiped out with no loss to the SSEF. From that time the attacks were sporadic and unco-ordinated and, after Le Havre and the surrounding coastline had been captured, they petered out altogether. On 11 September the SSEF left the area, its mission satisfactorily accomplished. Off Normandy its casualties had been light – only four craft had been lost – but it was soon to suffer severe losses during an even more hazardous mission.

As the winter of 1944 approached, it became of paramount importance to have the use of Antwerp which had been captured with its docks intact on 4 September, in order to supply the massive Allied formations poised to strike into Germany. But

although Antwerp was in Allied hands, any entry to it was blocked by the heavily fortified island of Walcheren standing at the mouth of the Scheldt river. In September it was decided that Walcheren must be stormed.

The attack was to be a three-pronged affair, but the most hazardous part of the operation was the proposed landing of three Royal Marine Commandos, and half of No 10 (Inter-Allied) Commando, at Westkapelle, right under the guns of the German coastal batteries. To render the defences as ineffective as possible, the dyke at Westkapelle was bombed, flooding a large part of the island.

To protect the landing force an elaborate fire plan was arranged. Pugsley, with his newly formed Force T, was charged with putting the commandos safely ashore. The fire plan included bombardment of the main German batteries, from the sea by the battleship HMS Warspite and two monitors, and from the air, while the SSEF engaged the smaller strongpoints. On paper it looked as if this fearsome display of firepower would pulverise the defences and render them incapable of harming the commandos in their vulnerable landing craft. It was not to be so. Adverse weather conditions on the morning of the attack, on 1 November 1944, made it impossible for the RAF to send in their heavy bombers, and the massive naval guns were only partially effective. This spelt disaster, and Pugsley had no alternative but to order the SSEF – now a much smaller force of 27 craft – to divert the attention of the shore batteries away from the commandos' landing craft and onto themselves, a tactic that proved so successful that the SSEF was to be almost wiped out. Afterwards Pugsley wrote: 'Nelson, whose favourite signal, invariably to be seen at his masthead in battle, was "Engage the enemy more closely", would have been pleased with them.'

At 0847 hours the SSEF deployed into two groups to attack the German defences to the north and south of a gap in the dyke. The northern group, commanded by Lieutenant-Commander L.C.A. Leefe in LCH

Top right: Landing-craft commanders (from left) Carmaine, Gurnsey and Bain are photographed with Sergeant-Major Leure of an RM Commando before the Walcheren raid. Top left: Members of No 5 Commando struggle ashore at Westkapelle while the SSEF diverts enemy fire. Above right: LCG(M) 102, one of two vessels deployed of this type. Right: Commandos head for a Buffalo LVT on the Westkapelle waterfront. Below: Men and machines go in under a lowering black cloud caused by the preliminary shell and rocket bombardment.

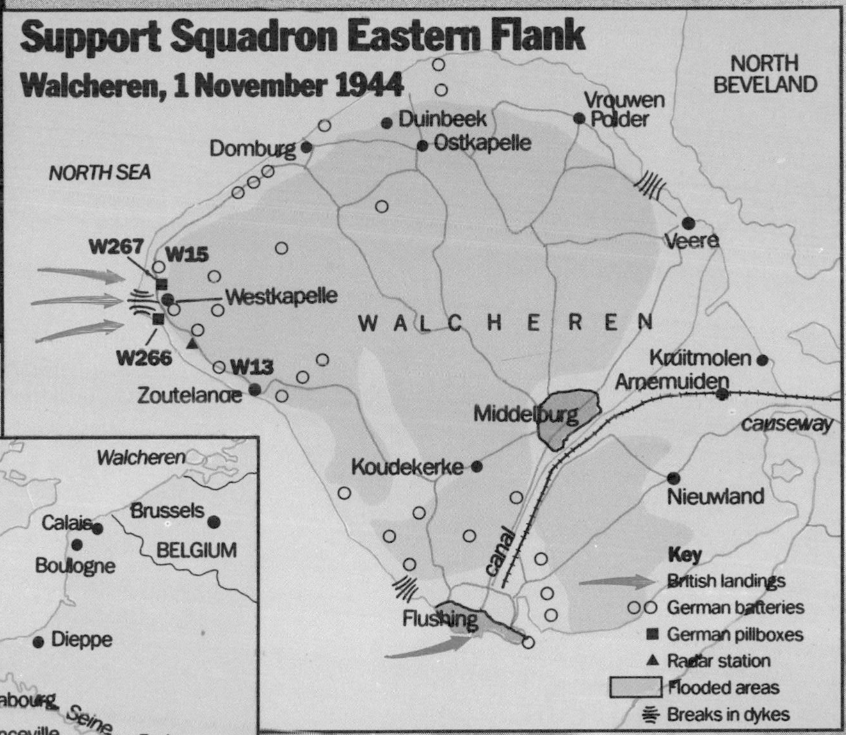

Support Squadron Eastern Flank
Walcheren, 1 November 1944

NORTH BEVELAND

WALCHEREN

NORTH SEA

Veere
Vrouwen Polder
Kcoitmolen
Arnemuiden
Nieuwland
Duinbeek
Ostkapelle
Middelburg
Koudekerke
Domburg
Westkapelle
Zoutelande
Flushing
W15
W267
W266
W13

canal
causeway

Key
○ British landings
● German batteries
■ German pillboxes
▲ Radar station
▢ Flooded areas
≋ Breaks in dykes

Walcheren
Brussels
BELGIUM
Calais
Boulogne
Dieppe
London
Le Havre
Cabourg
Franceville
Caen
Ouistreham
English Channel
Southampton
Cherbourg
Seine
Paris
ENGLAND
FRANCE
- - - Trout Line

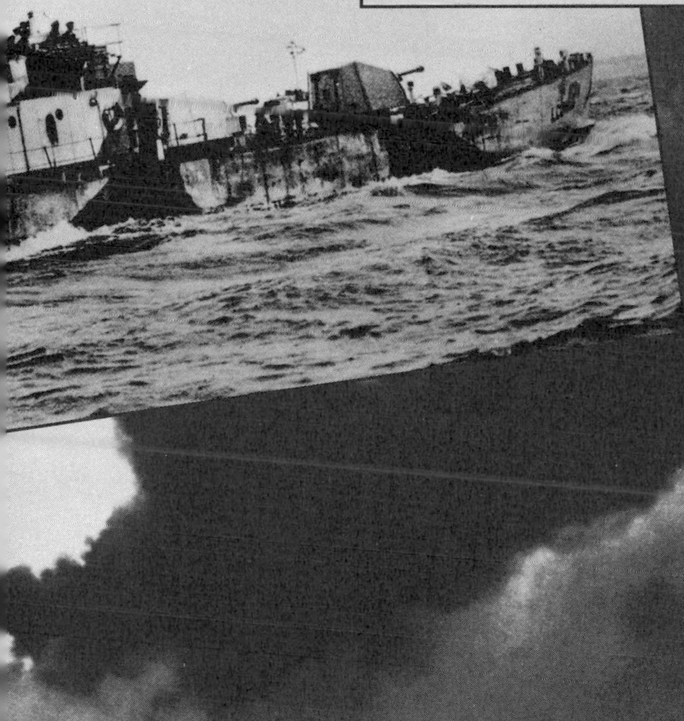

(Landing Craft, Headquarters) 98, consisted of three LCG(L)s (Landing Craft, Gun (Large)), three LCFs, three LCS(L)s (Landing Craft, Support (Large)), and three LCT(R)s (Landing Craft, Tank (Rocket)), while the southern group, led by Commander K.A. Sellar aboard LCH 269, had the same except for one less LCT(R). Additionally, each group had an LCG(M) (Landing Craft, Gun (Medium)), a new type of craft designed to run aground and engage enemy fortifications from the shore line.

The first craft of the squadron to be hit was LCF 37, the one leading the southern group, when one of the main German batteries, W15, switched its fire from the main force and scored a hit on the water-line. The hole was successfully plugged but then she came within range of another major German battery, W13. She was hit astern and a near miss filled the bridge and upper deck with water. Two shells then blew away the bows and the forward magazine, before a third hit the main magazine, detonating 100,000 rounds of 2-pounder and Oerlikon ammunition. Most of the crew were blown into the sea, and many were killed.

Between 0941 and 0955 the three rocket ships to the north of the gap fired their broadsides. Of these, two fell short of the targets, one of them hitting LCF 42. Then, after laying down a smokescreen to conceal the landing beaches, they returned to Ostend. The two rocket ships in the southern group did better. LCT(R) 363 struck the German radar station W154, and LCT(R) 334, despite being hit, smothered the beach defences well clear of the waterline. However, at 1009 hours 363 was hit and had to be towed clear by 334.

Meanwhile, the three LCGs in the northern group started pounding W15 with their broadsides. Of these, two fell short of the targets, one of them hitting LCF 42. Then, after laying down a smokescreen to conceal the landing beaches, they returned to Ostend.

They engaged a pillbox at point-blank range, but their armament could not penetrate the concrete

All three of the LCFs in the northern group were also hit. Her CO reported afterwards:

'At 0945 the shore batteries began registering hits on both sides of the ship [LCF 38]. Between 800-1000yds from the beach a 90 degree turn was made, so as to engage enemy machine-gun nests and batteries. By this time we had been hit by about 10 heavy shells... the magazine [was] on fire, the forward mess-deck about a foot under water, the wheelhouse a shambles, the steering jammed, one engine gone, five gun positions smashed, and the wardroom on fire. Still, all available armament maintained constant fire on the enemy'.

LCF 36 came alongside and took LCF 38 in tow, but the latter received more direct hits and was abandoned just before she blew up and sank.

The smaller and more vulnerable LCS(L)s in the northern group displayed the same tenacity when they engaged a pillbox and adjacent targets at point-blank range, but their armament could not penetrate the German concrete. One of the craft was soon hit and set on fire and the two survivors were sent to support the incoming landing craft.

Meanwhile, the three LCGs in the northern group started pounding W15 with their breech-loading 4.7in guns, but they were soon suffering hits from the German batteries. LCG(L) 1 was set on fire and later sank. LCG(L) 2 was hit and severely damaged, and when LCG(L) 17 turned to help she, too, was holed. An LCS(L) tried to tow LCG(L) 17 but found her too heavily flooded, so Lieutenant-Commander Leefe's LCH turned her so she could continue to fire on W15. She was later taken in tow but was sunk by a mine.

Meanwhile LCG(M) 101 had opened fire on her target at about 2000yds from the beach. During the last mile to the shore she came under fire from W15 and was eventually hit just before beaching. Once aground, the forward part of the ship was out of W15's arc of fire but she continued to be hit on the port side. Not more than 50ft separated the LCG(M) 101 from the nearest enemy positions and, with the decks being raked by 88mm and machine-gun fire, both gun turrets received such damage that they could only fire by local control, and this became very sporadic. After 20 minutes the captain ordered the craft out in order to move to a secondary target further down the beach. But by this time LCG(M) 101 was riddled with holes and within minutes of regaining deep water

Meanwhile LCG(M) 101 had opened fire on her target at about 2000yds from the beach. During the last mile to the shore she came under fire from W15 and was eventually hit just before beaching. Once aground, the forward part of the ship was out of W15's arc of fire but she continued to be hit on the port side. Not more than 50ft separated the LCG(M) 101 from the nearest enemy positions and, with the decks being raked by 88mm and machine-gun fire, both gun turrets received such damage that they could only fire by local control, and this became very sporadic. After 20 minutes the captain ordered the craft out in order to move to a secondary target further down the beach. But by this time LCG(M) 101 was riddled with holes and within minutes of regaining deep water

But perhaps the most outstanding acts of heroism in the face of the enemy's withering fire were performed by the two LCG(M)s. LCG(M) 101's target was a pillbox, W267, on the north edge of the gap in the dyke, while 102's was a similar pillbox, W266, on the south edge. At 0943 hours, 102 beached and engaged her target, but her 17-pounder guns could not penetrate the 10ft-thick concrete and within 15 minutes she was observed to be on fire. Later, she was seen as a blazing wreck on the beach opposite W266. There was only one survivor.

Carlton's fortitude was typical of the Royal Navy that day, as was the almost suicidal bravery of the three LCS(L)s in the southern group. These were simply wiped out within the space of half an hour as they pressed home their attack on the beach defences. But perhaps the most outstanding acts of heroism in the face of the enemy's withering fire were performed by the two LCG(M)s. LCG(M) 101's target was a pillbox, W267, on the north edge of the gap in the dyke, while 102's was a similar pillbox, W266, on the south edge.

It was impossible to get down to the engine-room and we were ploughing round in circles

The three LCFs were also damaged, though only LCF 37 was sunk. Her captain, Commander Carlton, stated afterwards:

'After we had been holed I started to zig-zag, but it was hopeless – another shell killed the crew of the aft guns, and the next, forward, started a fire in the smaller magazine. Again the damage control party did a good job, but then came the shell that hit the main magazine and blew us up. I heard the shell but remembered nothing more, I must have passed out for a few minutes. When I came to, the only survivor left with me was my Marine officer. There was just nothing left, the wheelhouse had gone and so had the guns. We were well down in the sea with the engines still racing ahead but it was impossible to get down to the engine-room and we were ploughing round in circles. I could see a raft with survivors clinging to it some 20yds away, and decided to swim out to it. The tide was swift, I was very dazed, probably with shell-shock, bleeding badly, and felt weak, with my left hand useless, but I managed to get there.'

The southern group fared no better. Besides the damage done to one of the LCT(R)s, two of the LCG(L)s were hit, though both managed to resume firing. The gunnery officer of LCG(L) 10 was Lieutenant J.W. Harvie, RM: 'We received a direct hit from a 6in shell on the gun-deck abaft "B" gun. It killed my sergeant-major, injured several of the gun crew, detonated one of the ready-use cordite lockers and started a fire just for'ard of the bridge. Despite this terrible damage, Harvie kept both his guns in action. During that desperate day the fire from LCG(L) 10's guns was so intense that she expended one and a half times more ammunition than she had used on D-day and the five days following it.

THE LCG(M)

The Landing Craft Gun (Medium) broke all the rules of conventional warfare. It deliberately ran itself aground, and it ignored the golden rule of anyone involved in combined operations: get off the waterline as quickly as possible, either by advancing inland or withdrawing out to sea.

Over 150ft long and displacing 380 tons, the LCG(M) had a crew of three officers and 28 men, some of whom were Royal Marine gunners in charge of two 17-pounder guns mounted in 5in armoured turrets. Unlike the other ships in the Support Squadrons, which were converted to carry various armaments, the LCG(M) was purpose-built for amphibious warfare in the Pacific. Its armour plating was designed to withstand Japanese 6in projectiles, but it proved vulnerable to German 88mm high velocity armour-piercing shells. Additional armament included two single Oerlikons on aft bandstands, and twin Paxman Riccardo 500hp diesels produced a top speed of nearly 12 knots.

The technique for using these unusual vessels was partially to flood their buoyancy tanks just before running ashore. When they beached, a kedge anchor was thrown out from the stern and the buoyancy tanks were then fully flooded. This firmly grounded the hull which now provided a stable gun platform for engaging enemy fortifications. When the time came to withdraw, a powerful pump, which expelled nearly 16,000lb of water a minute from the tanks, was activated. Once refloated, the LCG(M) was winched off to the kedge and then tried to beat a hasty retreat. The LCG(M) only ever saw action at Walcheren.

she heeled over and sank.

Miraculously, only two of the LCG(M)'s crew had been killed and four wounded, and the rest were picked up. But the overall casualties suffered by the SSEF in protecting the landing force were horrifyingly high: 172 killed or missing and 125 wounded, and only seven ships remained fit for action. However, the Marine Commandos stormed ashore with a minimum of losses and within a few days Allied shipping was sailing up the Scheldt. Just as it had in Nelson's day, the Royal Navy had done its duty.

THE AUTHOR Ian Dear served as a regular officer in the Royal Marines, 1953-56. He is now a professional writer on military and maritime subjects and is author of *Ten Commando*, to be published by Leo Cooper Ltd later in 1987.

Left: Holed by German gunfire, LCG(M) 101 steadily sinks as she pulls away from the shore.
Above, far left: Commandos and crew are rescued from the doomed vessel. Above left: Among the specialist vehicles deployed on the raid were flail tanks (left) and Churchill AVREs.

The lead ship of a 20,000-ton aircraft carrier class that was also to include USS *Enterprise*, and later USS *Hornet*, USS *Yorktown* was laid down at Newport News Naval Yard in May 1934. Her 809ft by 83ft hull was protected by an armoured belt up to four inches in thickness over a layer of special tensile steel 0.75in thick. The flight deck was 824ft long by 109ft wide, and the conning-tower was given four inches of armour with a roof two inches thick.

Defensive armament consisted of eight 5in guns with 16 1.1in and 24 0.5in anti-aircraft guns, but the ship's fighting strength lay in her 96 aircraft – 18 fighters, 36 torpedo bombers, 37 dive bombers and five utility aircraft. *Yorktown* was commissioned on 30 September 1937 and entered service with the Pacific Fleet. However, the threat of German U-boats led to her being ordered to the Atlantic Fleet in April 1941 to carry out Neutrality Patrol operations and convoy escort duties.

When the Japanese bombed Pearl Harbor on 7 December she was awaiting a refit in the Atlantic Fleet's main base at Norfolk, Virginia. She was transferred to the Pacific Fleet and deployed as escort to a convoy carrying the 2nd Marine Brigade to American Samoa. Joining the convoy at San Diego on 30 December, she and other support ships were organised into Task Force 17. Sailing on 6 January, the convoy reached Samoa on the 19th. *Yorktown* then conducted air raids on the Japanese-held Marshall and Gilbert Islands before making for Pearl Harbor. Task Force 17 left Pearl on 16 February to conduct a raid on Lae and Salamaua in New Guinea with USS *Lexington*. This action was followed by the Battle of Coral Sea on 7-8 May, when her aircraft damaged the carriers *Shokaku* and *Shoho*. After this battle *Yorktown* was recalled to Pearl Harbor in readiness for the defence of Midway.

Landing Signals Officer, US Pacific Fleet 1942

A landing signals officer works to ensure that aircraft touch down on the carrier as safely and efficiently as possible. This man is clad in the light khaki summer uniform of an officer in the US Navy, with which he wears a jersey and cap in bright yellow for maximum visibility. Pilots are trained to operate according to the signals that he gives with his coloured 'bats'.

CARRIER ACTION

Although the Battle of Midway lost the Americans their carrier USS *Yorktown*, four Japanese carriers were sunk in a single day

IN LATE APRIL 1942, Lieutenant-Commander John S. Thach found himself at Naval Air Station Kaneohe Bay in Hawaii with 21 spanking-new Grumman F4F Wildcats – but no pilots. Thach, officer in command of VF-3 (Fighting 'Three'), spent his time test-flying each new aircraft until, at the end of the month, a replacement arrived at Pearl Harbor and was assigned to Kaneohe. Ensign Robert 'Ram' Dibb received a couple of days' personal tuition from his commander before two more pilots turned up –

Machinists Doyle Barnes and Tom Cheek. Now Thach could put a whole flight into the air! He borrowed two more pilots from VB-5 and the six men practised a new manoeuvre he had developed in the summer of 1941, using matches for aeroplanes on his kitchen table in San Diego. Evaluating the nimble Japanese Zero fighter, Thach had realised that his table-top musings might provide a valuable counter-move for his heavier and slower F4Fs. He called it the beam defence position and it proved very effective

in a test against some Army pilots also stationed at Kaneohe.

Seven more pilots arrived on 20 May 1942, all rookies like Dibb. Thach's VF-3 squadron had been stripped of pilots and maintenance crews to strengthen Fighting Two aboard USS *Lexington*, leaving Fighting Three with only 11 pilots, 16 below its official complement. Thach hoped that there would be time to bring the squadron up to strength.

The Japanese, however, moved first. On 5 April 1942 their Naval General Staff approved a Combined Fleet operation to capture the atoll of Midway, an American possession since 1867. As the name suggests, the island lies almost at the centre of the Pacific Ocean. The Japanese hoped to force the remnants of the US Pacific Fleet to the atoll for a decisive battle in which the superior weight and morale of their navy would crush the Americans. Throughout April, Japanese ships began to assemble at bases in the home islands and on Saipan.

Three Japanese bombs had hit the carrier, bending bulkheads and watertight doors out of true

Unknown to the Japanese, the US Navy's cryptanalysts on Hawaii had managed to decipher parts of the Imperial Navy's JN-25 code, and much of what was transmitted by radio from Japanese ships was intercepted by the Americans. Therefore, as the Japanese fleet began to reassemble from the far reaches of the Greater East Asia Co-Prosperity Sphere, the US Navy became aware that something big was in the offing. Midway was thought to be the most likely target, so Admiral Chester Nimitz, the CinCPac (Commander-in-Chief, Pacific), organised his forces to counter such a move.

The aircraft carrier USS *Yorktown* was rushed to Pearl Harbor for the repair of damage sustained at the Battle of Coral Sea, and Fighting Three received orders to join *Yorktown* as soon as she arrived in Hawaiian waters. The carrier arrived at Pearl on 27 May, went into Dry Dock No.1 on 28 May, and 1400 men went to work to repair the battle damage. Three Japanese bombs had hit the carrier, bending bulkheads and watertight doors out of true, as well as causing an oil leak. In just over 48 hours *Yorktown* was made ready for sea, although she was still unable

to sail at full speed.

Despite the fact that the *Yorktown* air group was one of the most combat experienced in the Pacific Fleet, ComCarPac (Commander, Carriers, Pacific) had decided to break up the old team. Fighting Forty-Two would be combined with Thach's Fighting Three. *Yorktown's* scouting and torpedo squadrons were sent ashore, to be replaced by VB-3 (Bombing Three) and VT-3 (Torpedo Three). *Yorktown's* own Bombing Five was temporarily redesignated Scouting Five. On 30 May, *Yorktown* left Pearl for a rendezvous with her sister carriers, USS *Enterprise* and USS *Hornet* in Task Force 16 (TF16). *Yorktown* herself formed the nucleus of Task Force 17 (TF17). Her fighters flew aboard from Kaneohe, while the other aircraft flew in from Ford Island.

Yorktown steamed from the Hawaiian islands towards her pre-arranged meeting point with TF16 at 32 degrees north latitude, 173 degrees west longitude, a position designated Point Luck by Admiral Nimitz. The commander of TF17, Rear-Admiral Frank Jack Fletcher, would take charge of the operations around Midway by virtue of his seniority over the commander of TF16, Rear-Admiral Raymond Spruance. He knew that the Japanese had four or five aircraft carriers, two battleships, six cruisers and 22 destroyers, plus submarines. Fletcher was outnumbered in every category except heavy cruisers.

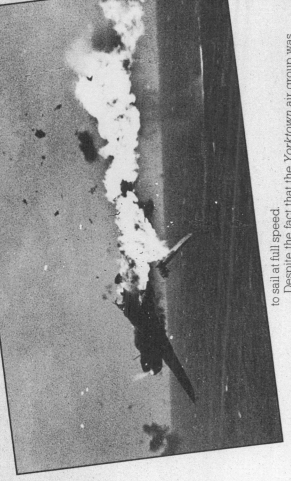

Below left: A Douglas SBD Dauntless dive bomber comes in to land on USS *Yorktown*. Its perforated dive-brakes, seen here lowered for landing, were also dropped in the full bombing dive. Above: A Nakajima B5N attack bomber (codenamed 'Kate' by the Allies) disintegrates after a hit by *Yorktown's* guns. Below: *Yorktown's* ordeal by fire. Anti-aircraft shells burst high above the carrier as she sustains bomb attacks from Kates. The black smoke beginning to pour from her superstructure indicates that her boiler has already been hit.

The Japanese and US Navies differed only slightly in their fighter tactics in the period preceding their involvement in World War II, both of them employing the traditional three-aircraft vee formation. The Americans then began to experiment with a two-aircraft section in which the leader was responsible for manoeuvring while the wingman, flying up to 50m below him, conformed to his flight and guarded his tail. The preferred method of attack was a dive from above, the pilot firing on the target as he swept past it.

The organisation of squadrons into two-aircraft sections was approved in July 1941.

The Japanese retained the three-aircraft formation, the aircraft flying 50m apart at the same level. When combat was likely, the vees were deployed into echelon with a 100-200m interval, or a loose vee with one aircraft 200m back and the other 300m back. The Japanese also preferred to attack from above, diving one at a time. This technique worked only as long as the pilots were experienced, however, and in 1943 the Japanese adopted the US two-aircraft section.

Lieutenant-Commander John Thach, who had gained some knowledge of Japanese tactics from Naval Intelligence Reports and from Claire Chennault, the commander of the 'Flying Tigers' in China, saw that the two-aircraft section could be used to organise squadrons into four-plane elements which flew abreast. In an attack from above or behind, the two sections would turn towards one another, spoiling the attacker's aim and possibly setting up a shot at him. First used at Midway and widely adopted by 1943, this manoeuvre became known as the 'Thach weave', and it may be regarded as the precursor of the 'loose deuce' tactic used by the US Navy in Vietnam.

Both sides retired that night knowing that a major action would be fought the next day

At 1600 on 2 June, the two US task forces rendezvoused at Point Luck. Yorktown took up air patrol duty for both task forces the next day, and 20 aircraft searched for the Japanese carriers on a northerly arc out to a range of 200 miles. Unfortunately, the weather was overcast and they saw nothing.

However, the clouds did not stop a PBY Catalina from finding the ships of the Midway invasion force. This Catalina was based at Midway atoll itself, along with other Army, Navy and Marine aircraft. It was patrolling southeast at its maximum range, in the general direction of Wake Island, when it observed the enemy vessels. The PBY sighting led to an unsuccessful raid by B-17s based at Midway on the Japanese ships. A madcap night torpedo attack by PBY Catalinas damaged a Japanese oiler, and both sides retired that night knowing that a major action would be fought the next day.

At about the same time that the Catalina pilots were making their attack, the crew of Yorktown was woken by reveille. Pilots went to their ready rooms and began to eat breakfast in shifts. Some were quiet in anticipation, others chattered away as if 4 June 1942 would be just another routine day. All knew that the enemy was nearby, in strength. At 0430 hours Yorktown launched its CAP (combat air patrol) of six F4Fs, plus 10 SBD Dauntlesses from Scouting Five. The latter were to begin the search for the Japanese carriers.

One hour later, the carrier's radio received a voice transmission – 'Enemy carriers'. It came from a Midway-based PBY flying a reconnaissance mission. The sky over Nagumo's ships was still overcast, and it was not until 20 minutes later that the PBY pilot was able to get a good look at them. At 0552 the American force received the message: 'Two carriers and battleships, bearing 320 degrees, distance 180 (miles), course 135 (degrees), speed 25 (knots)'.

The Battle of Midway was on – Japanese bombers and fighters were already en route for the island. They tangled with the Marine fighters based there at 0615 hours, the Japanese escorts shooting most of these down while the bombers worked over the atoll. The bombing raid was only a partial success, however, for although many buildings were damaged or destroyed, the airstrips were untouched. The flight leader recommended that the carriers make a second attack.

The raids on Midway were followed 30 minutes later by a counter-attack from Midway on the Japanese aircraft carriers. Bombers flown by Marine and Army pilots made a gallant effort to damage the enemy but their attacks were a complete failure. Nagumo, responding to the threat posed by these attacks, had already ordered his second wave to equip for another raid on Midway when he received a report of American ships in the area. The preparations for the second attack were halted until the situation could be clarified.

Fifteen minutes after Fletcher received the PBY's report aboard Yorktown, he ordered Spruance to strike with TF16's aircraft at the Japanese fleet. Fletcher's TF17 was to wait and recover the 10 dive bombers that had been sent up earlier. Spruance's force set

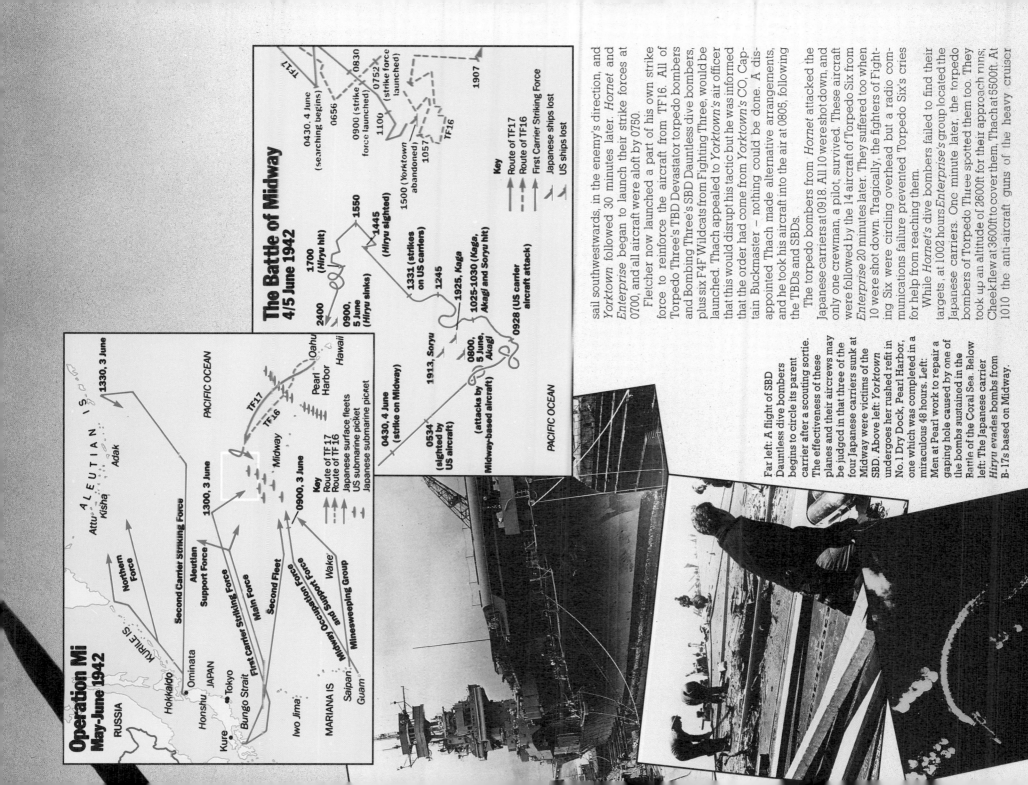

Operation Mi
May–June 1942

RUSSIA

KURILE IS

ALEUTIAN IS
Attu Kiska
Adak

Northern Force

Second Carrier Striking Force

Aleutian Support Force

1330, 3 June

PACIFIC OCEAN

1300, 3 June

Midway

TF 17

TF 16

Pearl Harbor

Oahu

Hawaii

Hokkaido

Honshu JAPAN

Ominata

Tokyo

Bungo Strait First Carrier Striking Force

Kure

Iwo Jima

MARIANA IS
Saipan
Guam

Main Force

Second Fleet

Midway Occupation Force

Minesweeping Group

Wake

0900, 3 June

Key
Route of TF 17
Route of TF 16
Japanese surface fleets
US submarine picket
Japanese submarine picket

The Battle of Midway
4/5 June 1942

TF 17

0430, 4 June
(searching begins)

0656

0830

0752
(strike
force launched)

0900 (strike
force launched)

1100

1057

TF 16

1907

2400

1700
(Hiryu hit)

1550

1445
(Hiryu sighted)

1331 (strikes
on US carriers)

1245

1925, Kaga

1025–1030 (Kaga,
Akagi and Soryu hit)

0928 (US carrier
aircraft attack)

1500 (Yorktown
abandoned)

0900,
5 June
(Hiryu sinks)

0534
(sighted by
US aircraft)

1913, Soryu

0800,
5 June, Akagi

0430, 4 June
(strike on Midway)

(attacks by
Midway-based aircraft)

PACIFIC OCEAN

Key
Route of TF 17
Route of TF 16
First Carrier Striking Force
Japanese ships lost
US ships lost

sail southwestwards, in the enemy's direction, and *Yorktown* followed 30 minutes later. *Hornet* and *Enterprise* began to launch their strike forces at 0700, and all aircraft were aloft by 0750.

Fletcher now launched a part of his own strike force to reinforce the aircraft from TF16. All of Torpedo Three's TBD Devastator torpedo bombers and Bombing Three's SBD Dauntless dive bombers, plus six F4F Wildcats from Fighting Three, would be launched. Thach appealed to *Yorktown's* air officer that this would disrupt his tactic but he was informed that the order had come from *Yorktown's* CO, Captain Buckmaster – nothing could be done. A disappointed Thach made alternative arrangements, and he took his aircraft into the air at 0805, following the TBDs and SBDs.

The torpedo bombers from *Hornet* attacked the Japanese carriers at 0918. All 10 were shot down, and only one crewman, a pilot, survived. These aircraft were followed by the 14 aircraft of Torpedo Six from *Enterprise* 20 minutes later. They suffered too when 10 were shot down. Tragically, the fighters of Fighting Six were circling overhead but a radio communications failure prevented Torpedo Six's cries for help from reaching them.

While *Hornet's* dive bombers failed to find their targets, at 1002 hours *Enterprise's* group located the Japanese carriers. One minute later, the torpedo bombers of Torpedo Three spotted them too. They took up an altitude of 2600ft for their approach runs; Cheek flew at 3600ft to cover them, Thach at 5500ft. At 1010 the anti-aircraft guns of the heavy cruiser

Far left: A flight of SBD Dauntless dive bombers begins to circle its parent carrier after a scouting sortie. The effectiveness of these planes and their aircrews may be judged in that three of the four Japanese carriers sunk at Midway were victims of the SBD. **Above left:** *Yorktown* undergoes her rushed refit in No.1 Dry Dock, Pearl Harbor, one which was completed in a miraculous 48 hours. **Left:** Men at Pearl work to repair a gaping hole caused by one of the bombs sustained in the Battle of the Coral Sea. **Below left:** The Japanese carrier *Hiryu* evades bombs from B-17s based on Midway.

147

Chikuma opened fire on the approaching torpedo bombers, alerting 43 Zero fighters flying CAP which immediately flew into the attack.

The first thing that the Zeroes hit was Thach's division of four planes. Two ganged up on the F4F in tail position, piloted by Ensign Edgar Bassett, who was an import from Fighting Forty-Two and a veteran of the Coral Sea. He was shot down in flames and perished. Between 15 and 20 Zeroes now began firing passes from above. Thach led his three surviving planes in a series of turnaways from any Zero coming in on an attack sweep. The new tail pilot, Lieutenant Brainard Macomber, also a Fighting Forty-Two import, was unaware of Thach's beam defence manoeuvre. Since Macomber's radio was out of action, Thach was forced to improvise – he followed each turn with a reverse turn that set up a reflection shot on the attacking Zero. As a result, he shot a Zero down.

Thach then got his wingman, Ensign Dibb, to act as a section leader. Dibb flew out to the right and was immediately attacked by a Zero. Thach implemented the beam defence: Dibb turned sharply left, while Thach, followed by Macomber, turned right. The Zero continued to pursue Dibb and became an easy target for Thach's gun, giving him his second kill. Although the Zero pilots did not always follow the tail of their quarry, the manoeuvre kept the Americans alive. Thach scored a third kill, while Dibb and Macomber got one each.

Down below, Cheek and Sheedy were struggling in a scrambling fight with Zeroes intent on attacking Torpedo Three. The first Zero to attack was shot down by Cheek. The Devastator tail-gunners got another. Although seriously wounded, Sheedy caused another Zero to crash into the sea. But the Japanese took another heavy toll of TBDs and only two of them survived.

Above: Lieutenant-Commander John S. Thach at the controls of F-1, his Grumman F4F Avenger. His wingman in this photograph is Lieutenant Edward H. O'Hare, who was credited with shooting down five Japanese bombers during the defence of USS *Lexington* in the Battle of the Coral Sea. This battle was similar to that of Midway in that it was a struggle between two forces of aircraft carriers, and was notable as the first naval action in history in which two fleets engaged without coming within sight of each other. Below: Holed by torpedoes from Japanese aircraft, *Yorktown* lists to port. By now all her aircraft have transferred to her sister carriers *Enterprise* and *Hornet*.

The attack on Torpedo Three and the dogfight with Thach's men had absorbed the entire attention of the Japanese CAPs. The Zero pilots did not notice the approach of the SBDs above, and the lookouts on the carriers *Akagi* and *Kaga* did not spot them until they were lining up for the attack. At about 1022, the dive bombers from *Enterprise* began their attack, and both vessels were turned into burning wrecks as fuel and aircraft caught fire. Bombs were stacked on the flight decks and fuel lines had been left open by maintenance men still working to re-equip bombers and attack aircraft. Bombing Three scored three hits on *Soryu*, putting 18 armed and fuelled aircraft on the flight deck to the torch. In five minutes, the cream of Japanese naval aviation was wiped out.

During the torpedo-bomber attacks the last Japanese carrier, *Hiryu*, had become separated from the other three while attempting violent evasive manoeuvres, and she managed to escape. *Hiryu* was the flagship of Nagumo's second-in-command, Admiral Yamaguchi. He decided to send a strike group after the American carriers and at 1050 a force of 18 D3A1 dive bombers and six Zero fighters took off in their general direction. Shortly afterwards, two Japanese seaplanes made contact with Task Force 17 and directed the strike group towards *Yorktown*.

Thach and his men landed on *Yorktown* ahead of the SBDs. Cheek crashed his F4F but survived. At about 1150, *Yorktown's* radar picked up the approaching Japanese aircraft. The carrier's CAP had only just taken off after refuelling and had to race against time to reach the altitude of the Japanese aircraft. Fighters from *Hornet* and *Enterprise* also joined the fray. Hit just after 1200, the Japanese formation broke up in the face of determined attacks by aircraft of Fighting Three. Ten of the D3A1s were shot down, and another was bagged by a pilot from

Fighting Eight. The remaining seven bombers began their dive on *Yorktown*. One group of three came out of the west and scored one hit; a group of four sweeping in from the south scored two hits, one of which damaged the ship's boiler.

Hiryu launched a second wave at 1315, just a few survivors of the first attack returned. This wave consisted of 10 B5N torpedo bombers and six Zero escorts. Meanwhile, Fighting Three regrouped, with the CAP pilots landing on *Enterprise* to rearm, refuel and grab some food. Those aircraft that remained aboard the damaged *Yorktown* were re-equipped and readied for take-off. The damage, which at first had seemed severe, was now under control. Fires were put out and power restored as the boilers were brought back into operation. It looked as if *Yorktown* had passed the worst.

When *Hiryu's* second wave spotted Task Force 17 at 1430 they thought it a different carrier group, for *Yorktown* seemed undamaged. Four of the six CAP aircraft from *Yorktown* and *Enterprise* failed to see the Japanese bombers as they began their run, but the other two shot down a B5N, before being shot down themselves by the fighter escort. As the emergency deepened, Thach and seven other Fighter Three pilots took off from *Yorktown*. Thach turned his aircraft right and proceeded to shoot down a B5N – the bomber still managed to get off its torpedo, but fortunately it missed. Two more were brought down by Fighter Three pilots without gaining torpedo hits, and anti-aircraft fire claimed another.

The attack had cost the Japanese five B5Ns and two Zeroes, but it had achieved its purpose

The remaining five bombers came at *Yorktown* from the northeast. These had better fighter escort and Fighting Three's Wildcats were kept at bay. Four dropped their torpedoes and the carrier sustained two hits. *Yorktown* lost all electrical power and came to a dead stop. The attack had cost the Japanese five B5Ns and two Zeroes, but it had succeeded.

But now *Hiryu's* luck ran out. She was spotted at 1445 by a Dauntless of Scouting Five that had been launched three and a half hours previously from *Yorktown*. Immediately, *Enterprise* launched 25 SBDs, 14 of them from *Yorktown's* Bombing Three, to destroy her. Finding *Hiryu* shortly before 1700, they dive-bombed the carrier. Bombing Three could take credit for some of the four hits, but the exact number is uncertain. *Hiryu* was turned into another burning wreck.

For *Yorktown* and the men of Fighting Three the Battle of Midway was over. The order to abandon ship was given at 1445 and the pilots of Fighting Three transferred to *Enterprise* and *Hornet*. Their claims amounted to 69 per cent of the total number of enemy aircraft shot down and credited to US pilots. Thach was awarded a Distinguished Service Medal. *Yorktown* survived until 6 June, when Captain Buckmaster and a small crew returned to conduct salvage operations. Things went well and the carrier was taken under tow by a tug. However, a Japanese submarine that had been diverted to the area put two torpedoes into her, as well as sinking a destroyer. *Yorktown* finally capsized on 7 June.

THE AUTHOR Paul Szuscikiewicz is an American writer, based in London, who has published several articles on naval and military affairs.

Above: In order to reduce *Yorktown's* list to port, on 6 June a salvage crew was landed on the carrier to reduce the weight on that side by cutting away the 5in gun mountings. A short time after, however, the Japanese submarine *I-168* sent two torpedoes into her starboard side and one into the escorting destroyer USS *Hammann*. The destroyer broke in half and *Yorktown* sank the next day, fortunately without casualties. Left: The torpedoing of *Yorktown* at Midway spelled the end of that illustrious ship, but not of her name. CV-10, a member of the great US Essex aircraft carrier class that finally included 24 vessels, was commissioned in 1943 and named *Yorktown* after her predecessor.

STEEL-CLAD SURVIVOR

ORDEAL BY FIRE

In late 1940 the crack dive-bomber formation Fliegerkorps X was transferred from Norway to the Mediterranean, and on 10 January 1941 it mounted its debut operation against the British Mediterranean Fleet. Just after noon, a force of 36 Ju 87 Stukas and Ju 88s appeared above the escorts of an eastbound Allied convoy, flying at 12,000ft. While six aircraft peeled away to attack the battleships HMS *Warspite* and *Valiant*, the main body of 30 planes headed straight for HMS *Illustrious*.

The Germans were very skilful at avoiding the aircraft carrier's defences and their bombing was extremely precise. A gun platform on the forward deck was obliterated, another bomb struck the bow, a third dislodged another gun platform. One bomb destroyed an

aircraft as it came up on the after elevator, while another penetrated the closed hangar. The forward elevator was hit and the steering gear was severely damaged. Only then did *Illustrious's* Fulmar aircraft succeed in driving off the attackers. Then, steering with the engines and with fires raging below the flightdeck, *Illustrious* made for Malta, fighting off a second wave of bombers on the way.

While *Illustrious* was temporarily crippled by the attack, it is probable that any one of Britain's older carriers would have been sunk outright. She had sustained six direct hits by 1000lb bombs, yet her heavy armour and superb fire parties saved her from disaster. The decision taken to sacrifice hangar space for adequate armour had been fully vindicated, and the ship survived to play a major role in the campaign against Japan.

150

Above: HMS *Illustrious*, screened by the powerful guns of a cruiser escort. Right: *Illustrious* takes heavy punishment during her first attack off Malta. Far right: Seen astern of the carrier's crammed flightdeck, the battleship HMS *Valiant* tests her guns. Inset: Commander of the *Illustrious*, Captain C. E. Lambe.

HMS ILLUSTRIOUS

The Royal Navy's aircraft carriers in the late 1930s included only two which had been designed specifically for their task – HMS *Hermes*, launched in 1919, and HMS *Ark Royal*, launched in 1937. The remaining five carriers were conversions of World War I vessels and were fast becoming obsolete.

Seeing the threat of war with Germany in 1937, Britain ordered two new carriers, to be named HMS *Illustrious* and *Victorious*, as reinforcement for her carrier fleet, and another pair, HMS *Formidable* and *Indomitable*, were ordered in the same year. While their design was broadly that of *Ark Royal*, the decision to armour them to the same degree as the big-gun ships brought about a substantial reduction in length and hangar capacity, since their maximum displacement was limited by international treaty.

Though *Illustrious* was launched on 5 April 1939, a shortage of armour plating delayed her sailing from the Vickers-Armstrong yard at Barrow until a year later. Featuring *Ark Royal's* full-length flightdeck and a larger island superstructure, her main armament lay in 16 4.5in guns mounted in eight turrets located below the flightdeck on each side, while her anti-aircraft weapons consisted of 48 two-pounders and 38 20mm guns. She was powered by three shaft-geared turbines and achieved 31 knots at sea.

The armoured hangar and design of *Illustrious* limited her aircraft capacity to 36 planes. The types of aircraft varied throughout the war, and during her career she carried Fairey Fulmars, Swordfish and Barracudas, Grumman Martlets and TBF Avengers, Supermarine Spitfires and Vought F4U Corsairs.

In January 1944, HMS *Illustrious*, the world's first armoured aircraft carrier, set sail for the Pacific where the British Eastern Fleet awaited her to join in the fierce battle with the Japanese

WHEN THE AIRCRAFT carrier HMS *Illustrious* left Greenock in January 1944, bound for Gibraltar, she was already one of the most famous ships in the Royal Navy. She had dealt the Italian battle fleet a severe blow at Taranto in November 1940, and then had been savagely mauled only two months later by Fliegerkorps X off Malta. After a lengthy rebuilding in the United States, she had taken part in the Madagascar and Salerno landings. She was then taken in hand for modifications that would enable her to operate the new Vought F4U1B Corsair II.

When the ship began her work-up in the Clyde in November 1943, a new air group had been allocated, with the fighter and strike aircraft newly organised in wings, along US Navy lines. Each wing was led by an experienced officer responsible for tactical doctrine, training and combat efficiency, while each squadron CO retained responsibility for the administration of his unit. By the end of December, No. 21 Torpedo-Bomber-Reconnaissance Wing, comprising a dozen Fairey Barracudas of No. 810 Squadron and another nine of No. 847 Squadron, had been joined by No. 15 Naval Fighter Wing, which comprised the 28 Corsairs of No. 1830 and 1833 Squadrons.

Illustrious arrived at Trincomalee, Ceylon (now Sri Lanka) on 31 January 1944, where the British Eastern Fleet awaited her. Her air group was an important reinforcement, and on 8 March she sailed on her first operation, a search for three Japanese cruisers in the Indian Ocean. No trace was found, as the cruisers had already returned to Singapore, but it gave the carrier a much-needed chance to exercise with the fleet. On 21 March *Illustrious* met the famous US carrier USS *Saratoga*, giving the inexperienced Fleet Air Arm (FAA) aircrews a chance to learn something of American carrier doctrine.

Operation Cockpit, a carrier strike against the island of Sabang at the northern end of Sumatra, started on 16 April 1944, when 27 Allied warships sailed from Trincomalee. The Japanese had established a small base with supply and storage facilities

at Sabang, and that was the target. On 19 April a strike of 17 FAA Barracuda torpedo-bombers and 13 escorting Corsairs, accompanied by 29 American Grumman Avengers and Douglas Dauntlesses escorted by a total of 32 Grumman Hellcats, swept in over the harbour. The *Saratoga's* strike force attacked the small number of ships in the harbour while the Barracudas dropped 500lb and 250lb bombs on the shore installations. No fighter opposition was encountered and all the aircraft returned safely to their carriers, but it had been a rather disappointing raid.

For the next strike, against the oil refineries at Soerabaya in Java, the slow and clumsy Barracudas were exchanged for Avenger torpedo-bombers of No. 832 and 851 Squadrons. The low-altitude Barracuda could not hope to cover the 240 miles to Soerabaya and climb over the 10,000ft mountains in central Java, nor would the carriers find it easy to hit a target 1800 miles from Trincomalee, and it was necessary to steam first to Exmouth Gulf in Australia. The escorting destroyers were to refuel there before the attack, and again on the way home.

The attack on Soerabaya on 17 May was only partially successful. *Illustrious* launched 18 bombers but two crashed shortly afterwards. Although none of the surviving aircraft met hostile fighters, there were again few targets in the harbour. Nor did an American strike achieve any significant hits on the oil refinery.

As 18 of the aircraft needed to land urgently, there was a grave risk of a flightdeck accident

When the *Saratoga* returned to Pearl Harbor, the weakness of *Illustrious's* small air group became more apparent. Her normal complement of 21 strike aircraft and 28 fighters allowed her to mount a strike or to provide air defence for the Eastern Fleet, but not both. When, on 21 June, she mounted a solo strike against Port Blair in the Andaman Islands, it took 15 Barracudas and 23 Corsairs to strafe the airfield and sink one small craft. Recovering the strike force was a very risky business, for most of the aircraft left behind had remained airborne, on patrol, until the last minute. As the latter now needed to land urgently, there was a grave risk of a flightdeck accident causing sufficient delay to result in the ditching of half the air group. The carrier was well within range of Japanese airfields, and it was only a matter of luck that the operation did not end in total disaster.

Background: *Illustrious* ploughs through a heavy swell towards her next area of operations against the Japanese in the Pacific. The forward aircraft elevator has been lowered to the armoured aircraft hangar below the flightdeck.

The War in the Pacific 1944-45

Key
→ Allied forces
● Raids by British carrier force
•••• Front line, March 1944
- - - Front line, October 1944
— Front line, August 1945

P A C I F I C

SOVIET UNION

MANCHURIA

JAPAN

KOREA

CHINA

RYUKYUS
OKINAWA
SAKISHIMA GUNTO
FORMOSA
PHILIPPINES
LEYTE
Manila

MARIANA IS

CAROLINE IS

MARSHALL IS

GILBERT IS

SOLOMON IS

NEW GUINEA

CELEBES

Brunei

BURMA
THAILAND
FRENCH INDO-CHINA
Hanoi
Saigon
MALAYA
Singapore
SUMATRA
Palembang
Batavia JAVA Soerabaja
Port Blair
Sabang
ANDAMAN IS

(Inset map)

CHINA
JAPAN
INDIA
DUTCH EAST INDIES
Pearl Harbor HAWAII
CEYLON
Trincomalee
INDIAN OCEAN
Exmouth Gulf
AUSTRALIA
Sydney

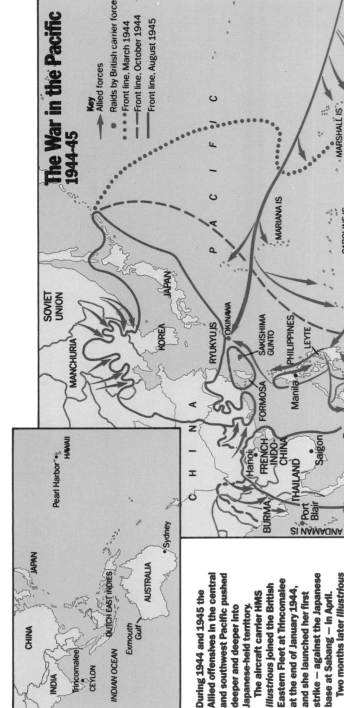

During 1944 and 1945 the Allied offensives in the central and southwest Pacific pushed deeper and deeper into Japanese-held territory.

The aircraft carrier HMS *Illustrious* joined the British Eastern Fleet at Trincomalee at the end of January 1944, and she launched her first strike – against the Japanese base at Sabang – in April.

Two months later *Illustrious* was joined by *Victorious* and *Indomitable*. The British carrier force continued to mount intensive operations against the enemy as the Pacific campaign moved into its final phase.

FORTIFIED WITH STEEL

In 1936, Britain finally acknowledged that a rearmament programme was unavoidable, and the largest naval shipbuilding programme since World War I was authorised: two battleships, two aircraft carriers and seven cruisers.

The aircraft carriers, to be named *Illustrious* and *Victorious*, were initially designed as two repeats of *Ark Royal*, but slightly enlarged to bring displacement up to the maximum of 23,000 tons permitted by international disarmament treaties. It was then proposed by the Comptroller of the Navy, Sir Reginald Henderson, that the light armour featured in *Ark Royal's* design should be heavily reinforced. The new carriers were to incorporate an armoured 'box' which clad the flightdeck and the sides of the hangar, thus protecting the aircraft as well as the ship.

Given the 23,000-ton displacement limit, the massive topweight of armour plating carried

well above the waterline meant that a complete hangar had to be omitted, cutting the ships' aircraft complement from *Ark Royal's* 72 to only 36. This severe cut in aircraft capacity was also imposed by the Navy's insistence on a closed hangar, in order to minimise damage caused by fire and explosions from fuel leaks.

Although Henderson's proposals undoubtedly created a safer ship, many believed that he had erred on the side of caution, as the Americans and Japanese were building carriers with air groups of up to 90 planes. However, the Luftwaffe attack on *Illustrious* off Malta, on 10 January 1941, confirmed his priorities in two ways. First, the Stukas demonstrated that they could easily out perform the British Fairey Fulmars, highlighting the vulnerability of the ship. Second, the heavy armour proved its worth in withstanding the worst that the German dive-bombers could throw against it. Given the aircraft available to him, Henderson's decisions were justified.

Below: The proud profile of *Illustrious*. Although her displacement of 23,000 tons exceeded the 22,000 tons of *Ark Royal*, the inclusion of 5000 tons of armour necessitated the loss of nearly 60ft in overall length. The main armour on the waterline and hangar side was four-and-a-half inches thick.

The arrival of two sister ships, HMS *Victorious* and *Indomitable*, at the end of June meant that the Eastern Fleet could resume the offensive, and on 25 July the fleet's battleships bombarded Sabang, leaving the Corsairs to protect the fleet and neutralise the nearby airfields, *Illustrious* deployed her No.15 Fighter Wing on a combat air patrol over the battleships, spotting the fall of shot and carrying out photographic reconnaissance in order to determine the results of the bombardment. Japanese opposition did not appear until late that afternoon, and it was roughly handled by the ship's combat air patrol. The Japanese lost four aircraft without getting near the carriers.

Another refit followed, this time at Durban. *Illustrious* returned to service at the beginning of November 1944, and by mid-December she had joined the First Aircraft Carrier Squadron. With *Indomitable*, *Victorious* and HMS *Indefatigable*, a sister ship launched in 1942. Their first target was to be another oil refinery in the East Indies, this time Pangkalan Brandan. Low cloud obscured the target and an attack on the port of Belawan Deli yielded little result. It was, however, a curtain-raiser for the first real success, the attack on the refineries at Palembang in Sumatra. Operation Meridian halved the output of the Pladjoe refinery on 24 January 1945, and five days later the Soengi Gerong refinery was put out of action completely. *Illustrious* launched 24 Avenger and 52 Corsair sorties during these two attacks, accounting for five Japanese aircraft, but losing five of her own to anti-aircraft fire and fighters. During a Japanese air attack on the carrier on 29 January the ship was damaged slightly by two shells from an Allied cruiser.

As he climbed up the nearest ladder, the entire ship shook as if she had been torpedoed

While the damage was being repaired at Sydney, the ship's engineers took the opportunity to investigate some persistent machinery defects which were clearly the legacy of the terrible ordeal she had suffered off Malta in 1941. So serious was the trouble that her centre propeller was removed, reducing her power plant to two shafts and cutting speed to 24 knots. In this less than satisfactory state the carrier was about to enter a much more dangerous phase of the war in the Far East.

The US Navy and Marine Corps were in the final stages of the planned assault on Okinawa, and the British carrier squadron had been given the task of neutralising the airfields on Sakishima Gunto, 200 miles northeast of Okinawa. *Illustrious* rejoined the 1st Aircraft Carrier Squadron at Manus Island in mid-March 1945, and shortly after the whole British Pacific Fleet (or BPF, designated Task Force 57) left for the Sakishima Gunto area.

One of the Corsair pilots embarked in *Illustrious* remembered the atmosphere of tiredness in the ship. Fatigue brought in its wake lethargy and carelessness, which meant more bad landings. The daily routine began at 0330 hours when all aircrew, squadron ratings and flight deck parties were given a 'shake'. Between 0430 and 0500 the carrier closed up to action stations in readiness for any kamikaze attacks. Gun crews closed up, watertight doors were shut, and ventilating fans were shut down. Typical rations during action stations were an endless round of tea and bully-beef sandwiches. Intensive operations normally lasted three days.

Top: Diving towards *Illustrious*, this Japanese suicide plane was hit by anti-aircraft fire and it grazed the superstructure, causing only slight damage (above left). Above right: A kamikaze plane lies shattered on the flightdeck.

forward base at Leyte, US Navy divers reported that the near-miss had split the outer plating and cracked several internal transverse frames on both sides. The extent of the damage was still unknown, however, when on 11 April *Illustrious* was readied for a raid against the kamikazes based on Formosa.

On 12 April a strong force of Avengers with Corsair escorts attacked Shinchiku airfield on the northwest corner of Formosa. Cloud level was down to about 2500ft and visibility was poor over the island. Next day was the ship's last day of involvement in Operation Iceberg, codename of the invasion of the Ryukyu Islands, and she then sailed for Leyte in the Philippines, with two destroyers for escort. It was there that the bad news was learned about the underwater damage, and the *Illustrious* was taken out of battle. During the whole of Iceberg her aircraft had flown 234 offensive sorties and 209 defensive sorties. Losses amounted to three Avengers and nine Corsairs.

Captain Lambe allowed his exhausted but lively ship's company the privilege of a *feu de joie*

As the ship passed through the Bismarck Sea, heading for Sydney, it was learned that the war in Europe had ended. Captain Lambe allowed his exhausted but lively ship's company the privilege of a *feu de joie* (a gun salute), with every gun firing for half a minute, followed by the traditional order of 'splice the mainbrace'. The hull damage had reduced her maximum speed to 19 knots, and she took some time to reach Sydney. After disembarking her remaining Avengers, and removing the crash barriers and arrestor wires to provide spares for the other BPF carriers, she headed for home on 24 May.

An aircraft carrier without aircraft is a depressing sight, and the ship's company felt uncomfortably like passengers. After brief stops at Port Said and Gibraltar, the ship returned to Rosyth, where she paid off for a major refit. Everyone assumed that the war in the Far East would go on for months or even years, and it was taken for granted that the ship would soon be back in the Pacific. But on 15 August the news of the Japanese surrender came through, and all work was suspended.

The refit was completed in the middle of 1946, but *Illustrious* would never again see frontline service, even under the less exacting conditions of peacetime. Apart from a trooping run to Cyprus in 1951 she remained in home waters, carrying out all the humdrum tasks of training aircrew. She was also used for the early trials of jet-propelled carrier aircraft and other prototypes. When she was finally paid off at the end of 1954 she had seen such hard service that it was considered that she was not worth the cost of further modernisation, despite having been in service for only 14 years.

The ship's remarkable war career apart, she represented a uniquely British contribution to aircraft-carrier design. As the world's first armoured carrier she was a break with all carrier traditions, and that unusual feature, among others, was to ensure her survival, despite some of the heaviest punishment inflicted on an aircraft carrier throughout World War II.

THE AUTHOR Anthony Preston is naval editor of the military magazine *Defence* and is author of numerous publications, including *Battleships*, *Aircraft Carriers* and *Submarines*.

On 26 March the British carriers struck at the airfields on the islands of Miyako, Ishigaki and Mihara, hitting airfields, coast defences, barracks and any shipping which could be found.

On 1 April the first kamikazes appeared from Formosa (Taiwan). At first light aircrew standing on the flightdeck were startled to hear a scream as an enemy aircraft dived close overhead and slammed into the superstructure of the *Indefatigable* 300yds away. A week later an Aichi D4Y3 came out of the cloud on the port beam, in a fast shallow dive, and this aircraft chose the *Illustrious*. One eye witness was in his cabin when the blast from the 4.5in guns above blew every single item off the shelves. As he climbed up the nearest ladder, the entire ship shook as if she had been torpedoed, but the vibrations were caused by the explosion of the D4Y3's bomb detonating in the water after her wing-tip had clipped the radome forward of the bridge. Fortunately for *Illustrious*, a 40mm Bofors gunner had scored hits on the 'tail section, thus deflecting the aircraft from the carrier's most vulnerable point, the angle between its flightdeck and the 'island' superstructure.

Although the attack had lasted only seven seconds, two Corsairs parked on deck were destroyed by the blast of the bomb. At the time it seemed that the ship had suffered only superficial damage, but when she was examined subsequently at the US

Above: Explosions from blazing aircraft mark a successful kamikaze strike to the carrier's stern.

FIRE

FROM THE SEA

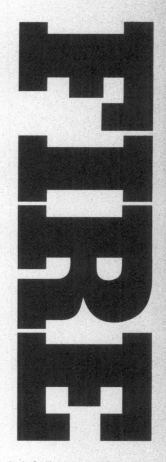

Controlled by the highly skilled personnel of the Bombardment Units, naval gunfire was a dreaded and terrifying weapon in World War II

IN THE FALKLANDS campaign of 1982, the 4.5in guns of the Royal Navy were directed onto their targets with deadly accuracy by the Naval Gunfire Forward Observation teams of 148 Commando Forward Observation Battery, Royal Artillery. 148 Battery is the surviving remnant of the Combined Operations Bombardment Units of World War II, which grew

BOMBARDMENT UNITS

from one unit in 1942 to five by 1944. Nos. 1 and 4 were based at HMS *Dundonald*, a shore-based training establishment near Troon in Scotland, No. 2 in North Africa and the Mediterranean, No. 3 at Vestis, Isle of Wight, and No. 5 in the Far East. The modern-day successor to these units continues to develop the techniques they initiated over 25 years ago.

Formed on 26 April 1942, the Forward Observation and Bombardment Liaison Unit was 'blooded' in combat between 7 and 30 May 1942 in the attack on the French port of Diego Suarez in Madagascar. The Forward Observer Bombardment (FOB) attached to No. 5 Commando, Captain W. S. Knight, and his team encountered a heavily armed 120-man crew who had come ashore from a damaged French sloop. Receiving machine-gun fire, the team set off into the jungle to establish a forward observation post. On the way, they captured a French admiral's barge, laden with wine, chocolate, cigarettes and ham, but they were ordered to return to Diego Suarez before they could sail it away!

The first major test of the new unit – now called simply the Bombardment Unit – was the raid on Dieppe of 19 August 1942. The basic aim of the raid was to learn in battle the lessons of an assault on a heavily defended port, as an early preparation for the Normandy landings. It was a reconnaissance in force and for the Bombardment Unit it was to be a tragedy.

The first attempt to mount this operation, in July, failed because of bad weather. For security reasons, the troops were kept 'under lock and key' until they embarked a second time. The plan was to land the

2nd Canadian Division on four main beaches with Nos. 3 and 4 Commandos assaulting on the east and west flanks. Six FOB teams controlled the fire of eight Hunt-class destroyers and one gunboat. On the ships, seven liaison officers, with a headquarters staff split between the destroyers HMS *Calpe* and *Fernie*, controlled the bombardment. The first troops landed between 0430 and 0500 hours.

During the fighting that followed, the destroyer HMS *Albrighton* sailed up to the harbour entrance to deal with enemy gun positions firing from the breakwater onto the beaches. On the sea front every house was packed with machine guns that pinned down the assault troops, but *Albrighton*'s 4.5in shells lacked the penetration necessary to destroy the strongly fortified buildings. Captain T. K. Hanson's FOB team, caught under fire in the centre of the four landing beaches, suffered heavy casualties. Two of the FOBs were killed, two were wounded, and two were taken prisoner. (One, Captain G. A. Browne of the Royal Canadian Artillery, later escaped to England via France and Spain, to be awarded the DSO.) Captain Hanson himself escaped capture by swimming to safety. Meanwhile, FOB Captain Carswell was wounded attempting to get into position to control fire onto a radar station half a mile to the east of the town. His telegraphists requested *Albrighton*

A typical forward observation 'watch' might include three telegraphists and a captain (far left). Messages from the observer (left) would be relayed by radio to a forward HQ (bottom), from where they would be transmitted to liaison officers aboard offshore warships such as HMS *Rodney* (below).

In the winter of 1940, only months after the evacuation from Dunkirk, groups of Royal Artillery officers attended courses at Whale Island to learn how to adjust naval gunfire and act as liaison officers on board bombardment ships. The Forward Observation and Bombardment Liaison Unit was officially formed on 26 April 1942 with Royal Artillery Observation Post Assistants (OPAs) and Royal Navy telegraphists and signalmen.

Originally known as Forward Observation Officers (FOOs), the men were subsequently renamed Forward Observers Bombardment (FOBs). They and their teams had no transport and on operations they used anything available, from armoured cars to pack animals. They carried telephone and line, radio sets and Aldis lamps for communication between themselves and with the bombarding ships. Carrier wave (morse code) was always used because of its increased range and narrow band width.

FOB training varied from group to group. Some underwent parachute training, others attended the Commando course at Achnacarry, and some trained with the Special Boat Squadron, learning how to go ashore from submarines in collapsible boats and mastering navigation at sea. Each FOB team was self-contained, able to defend and fend for itself. Each man carried about 60lb, including ammunition, grenades (Mills bombs carried in chest pouches or on the belt), sand bags, rations, blankets and spare radio batteries. Most carried both a 0.303in rifle and a 0.38in revolver, with trench daggers and concealed weapons in their clothing. Personal escape packs were sewn into their garments and some individuals carried poison for use if captured.

BOMBARDMENT UNITS: WORLD WAR II

to engage the station by direct fire and it was destroyed.

At about 1100 hours the order came to withdraw. Several ships were badly damaged as they came in to fire and pick up troops. The Luftwaffe came in to bomb the ships and the air strikes continued as the damaged ships limped back to England.

On 6 and 7 June 1944 the Allies landed 176,000 men and 20,111 vehicles on the Normandy beaches. The invasion was supported by 84 bombarding ships and 27 landing craft with guns mounted. To co-ordinate the naval fire, 42 FOB teams and 78 Bombardment Liaison Officers (BLOs) were used. Seven FOB teams landed with the Commandos and six with the 6th Airborne Division as they attacked on the eastern flank of the Allied front.

The massive armada sailed from ports around the south of England on 5 June. At dawn on the 6th, the RAF bombed enemy defensive positions, an awe-inspiring spectacle. As the aircraft departed, cruisers of the Royal Navy and the US Navy took over, engaging pre-arranged targets by direct observation and by spotting from aircraft. The quiet and peaceful coast suddenly and sensationally erupted with the power of the vast quantities of high explosive being applied to it. There seemed to be little reaction from the shore, as if the enemy was unaware of the enormous forces about to land.

Direct fire observation soon became difficult because of smoke from burning buildings. The tall, graceful spires of churches stood, seemingly inviolate amid the fire and smoke. As the landing craft grounded, the gunfire lifted from the beaches onto targets further inland. Rocket craft fired into the enemy positions until the sea-going tanks were

Right: Captain F. Vere Hodge, MC, directs naval gunfire onto a German battery of 105mm guns at Franceville from the elevated vantage point of Ouistreham lighthouse (far right). Bottom left: Captain Geoff Burgess (seated on a half-track) briefs an observation team in Colleville-sur-Orne on the first day of the Normandy invasion. Bottom: French civilians pose with men of the Bombardment Units at Colleville. Note the parachute wings worn by several men.

It may be considered a general guideline in the conduct of infantry warfare that attackers must outnumber defenders by at least three to one, and there must be accurate artillery fire support if an attack is to succeed. In the case of an amphibious assault, when the attackers are at a much greater disadvantage as they struggle under fire from ship to shore, the ratio should be very much higher. The attackers require an advantage of at least seven to one, and it is vital that the assault troops are given covering fire before they can land and deploy their arms.

In World War II the British Bombardment Units combined the very best advantages of the Army and the Navy, making certain that the power of naval gunfire was channelled intelligently into the land battle. On board the ships the Battery Liaison Officers (BLOs) had to win the confidence of the naval staff, explaining the progress of ground operations and putting into context the great risk of coming inshore to bombard.

Looking back on the events of 1944, the Chief of Combined Operations, Major-General R.E. Laycock, wrote that: 'Without the full and terrible effect of the guns of the Royal Navy upon a determined enemy ashore, their resistance in the early stages of our landings could never have been overcome in what was the most critical phase of these historic operations.' It is not an exaggeration to state that without the fire support of the Allied navies, the D-day landings and the invasion of Europe could never have taken place.

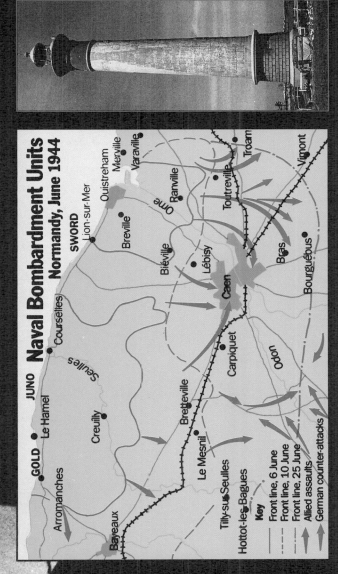

Naval Bombardment Units
Normandy, June 1944

GOLD JUNO SWORD

Key
— Front line, 6 June
–·– Front line, 10 June
···· Front line, 25 June
↑ Allied assaults
↑ German counter-attacks

Arromanches · Le Hamel · Courseulles · Ouistreham · Lion-sur-Mer · Merville · Varaville · Bayeux · Creully · Breville · Ranville · Toutteville · Troarn · Bieville · Lébisy · Bras · Caen · Carpiquet · Bourguébus · Vimont · Bretteville · Le Mesnil · Tilly-sur-Seulles · Hottot-les-Bagues · Seulles · Odon · Orne

landed and in action. Enemy artillery pieces fired back at the bombarding ships, but were themselves put out of action as naval fire was returned. Although an expected Luftwaffe attack never materialised, on the beaches the teams were not so lucky. One BLO said later: 'There was nothing for us to do now but wait for our FOB to come up on the air. He never did – the enemy saw to that.'

On Omaha beach in the American sector, German mobile artillery batteries and multiple mortars, tucked away safe from the preparatory bombardment, pinned the assault troops down on the shoreline. The first wave foundered. As the Rangers scaled the cliffs at Pointe du Hoc to destroy an enemy artillery battery, the Shore Fire Control Party (SFCP) brought down accurate naval gunfire, keeping up the bombardment for 24 hours. The American admiral motivated the gunnery teams on board his bombarding ships with pithy 'off the record' remarks, maintaining fierce competition in speed of response and accuracy of fire.

A FOB team with 1st Special Service Brigade landed in the Sword beach area at H+75. The left-hand ramp of their landing craft was blown away by heavy fire. The men saw their marker house just off the beach and made a dash for it. Their mission was to take out a German artillery battery. Pausing only to readjust their equipment, they crossed barbed-wire defences into a marsh lying to the west of Ouistreham. This natural obstacle was mined and subjected to enemy artillery and mortar fire, but nevertheless the men 'quietened down' the battery despite a poor observation position.

After assaulting an occupied house and almost shelling No.6 Commando in an attempt to hit enemy positions in Breville Wood, some 300yds away (a ticklish shoot') they established themselves in a skylight of a farmhouse, from where they brought down further fire. On D+1, with two Troops of No.6 Commando, they attacked Breville Wood and removed the breech blocks and dial sights of an artillery battery of 10cm field guns.

Other FOBs going into Sword were not so lucky. OP Assistants and telegraphists. Several were killed in the landing craft on the run in, and on the beaches during the assault. Captain Geoff Burgess, the Brigade FOB landed just

west of Ouistreham at H+60 to find that fire was still coming from houses which had yet to be mopped up.'

The next morning, Captain Burgess occupied the top room of a house near Blainville which commanded a good view of enemy territory. The 2nd Battalion, Warwickshire Regiment, was to attack Lébisey Wood with gunfire support from HMS *Warspite*. Burgess was to be the anchor OP and Captain J. Lee went forward with the Warwicks to control the fire. Unfortunately, the attack did not go in immediately after the artillery and naval gunfire finished and the Warwicks assaulted virtually unsupported, sustaining heavy losses (only 80 of the battalion returned). Captain Lee and his team were killed. They were last seen in a blazing half track with Lee himself standing in the back firing a Bren gun at the enemy.

'Using phosphorus hand grenades we had to bomb and burn the building to the ground'

Meanwhile, the enemy had spotted Burgess OP and was busy trying to mortar and machine-gun the team out. After an attack by aircraft, the owner of the house (a woman whose husband had been a prisoner since 1940) became hysterical and confronted him. Burgess pacified her as best he could, concluding that the OP was getting very unhealthy. At dusk the team moved to the village of Biéville, finding it under fire and burning, with snipers too numerous to mop up. Burgess reported: 'At 1145pm an enemy machine gun opened fire from a barn. Using phosphorus hand grenades we had to bomb and burn the building to the ground. The Germans did not surrender. We dug in for the night at 2am. Captain Burgess continued to bombard Lébisey Wood and the Germans, demoralised by the fire, began to desert. The wood was reported to look like a 'butcher's shop'.

On the boundary of the British and American sectors, Captain A. Todd, the FOB with the US 1st Infantry Division, was to co-ordinate the naval gunfire. His job was to ensure that the British bombarding ships did not endanger American troops, and also to engage targets in the British sector that were not visible to the British FOBs. Heavy opposition on the beaches delayed his landing for 12 hours. The D-day landings were also to be a very costly

The broken, hilly terrain of Normandy, criss-crossed by hedgerows concealing German defensive positions, often made observation from the air an essential in order to secure accurate ranges for naval gunfire. Left: Captain H. Orr, RA, climbs aboard an Auster IV spotter plane.

Captain Orr was a member of the 652nd Air Observation Squadron, a unit of Royal Artillery officers trained to pilot the Auster at very slow speeds very close to the enemy lines, at the same time radioing fire co-ordinates to officers controlling naval guns or field artillery batteries. Far left: Captain F.E. Shaw reports his observations to his squadron intelligence officer. Below left: The pilot's gunfire corrections are relayed to HMS *Exeter* by telegraphists. Below right: The invasion of Normandy left a trail of destruction to which the rain of naval shells made a handsome contribution.

operation for the officers of the Bombardment Unit who accompanied the 6th Airborne Division as they dropped inland of Sword beach. Emplaning just before midnight on D-1 (5 June), the tasks of the paratroopers and glider soldiers were to seize bridges over the Orne River and Caen Canal, capture a coastal defence battery at Sallenelles, blow up the bridges at Troarn, and hold Varaville until joined by 1st Special Service Brigade.

Many of the Bombardment Unit men were despatched incorrectly, jumping into the darkness miles from the correct drop zone. Lance-Bombardier Clegg and Leading Telegraphist Cutler, having already survived the crash of their Stirling as its port engine failed on take-off, arrived late over the French coast and were dropped several miles south of their destination of Troarn. Finding themselves behind enemy lines, they attacked a German position in a copse, received mortar fire and took two prisoners. Cutler was killed in a German counter-attack and Clegg, attempting to skirt round a group of vehicles, found himself trapped in a ditch in the middle of an enemy mortar emplacement.

Escaping from this predicament, at noon on D+4 he ran into some British paratroops who had spent the night trying to capture an enemy-occupied château. They were without a gunner, so he observed for their artillery, enabling them to take the building. Shortly after, he made contact with his unit and resumed more regular work until, sadly, he too was killed.

Captain J.K. Thompson – already a veteran of the Salerno landings – had been dropped near Caen and was ambushed in a small copse. His Observation Post Assistant (OPA), Sergeant Cumper, and one telegraphist were captured. Later, having run into No. 6 Commando, he took part in an attack on a defended house, capturing 80 Russians serving with the Wehrmacht.

One of his naval gunfire targets was a group of eight tanks, all of which were put out of action in the shoot. Near Toutreville, ordered to engage a particular target, the only way to a decent observation position was through a wood stiff with enemy snipers. The FOB team got through in a purloined jeep, with

one man sitting on the bonnet and spraying the trees ahead with a Bren gun. On D+2 they beat off an enemy counter-attack on 3rd Paratroop Brigade, using gunfire from HMS *Sirius*.

Bombardier Luggar and Telegraphist Peters, also dropped in the wrong place, were on their own for nine weeks behind German lines. Joining up with two others of their parachute 'stick' and a downed RAF pilot, they rejoined the British forces after 11 weeks, in time for the advance to the Seine.

Communications from land to the bombarding ships were not always by radio. On D+4 a carrier pigeon landed on the deck of the Canadian destroyer HMCS *Sioux*. The message contained information from the French underground about ammunition dumps and movements of German armour. As the advance inland proceeded, a mobile Bombardment Control Unit was deployed as an intermediate radio station to extend the communications of the FOBs to the ships. This vital team was known as the 'Mobile Bath Unit'.

On 11 June, HMS *Nelson* successfully engaged troop concentrations in Hottot-les-Bagues village. The range was 33,100yds, the village being well over 15 miles inland.

Enemy gun batteries were located by using sound-ranging equipment and by flash-spotting at night

The FOB teams found themselves fighting through close and often heavily wooded country, which made observation from the ground very difficult and sometimes impossible. The lighthouse at the mouth of the Orne, the church tower at Ouistreham and Ranville church tower were all used as observation posts. Enemy gun batteries were located by using sound-ranging equipment and by flash-spotting at night.

The brickworks chimney at Le Mesnil, about 100ft high, was the only vantage point in the area and subsequently received much German mortar, gun and sniper fire. It was in constant use; the FOB climbed the steel rungs on the outside, taking care at the top not to expose his head too much. He shouted his fire corrections down to his OPA inside the chimney, who relayed the messages to the telegraphist in the brickyard. Despite the additional worry of a live German sea mine, dropped into the yard instead of the Orne River anchorages, this OP continued to be used.

Aircraft spotting was also successful. The BLO in HMS *Roberts*, Captain S.W.T. Musto, was impressed: 'Communications were excellent, procedure correct and all pilots very keen, in many instances observing under heavy anti-aircraft fire and staying on the spot until dangerously short of petrol.'

At times, the observers' enthusiasm overcame procedure. The Polish cruiser *Dragon* was shifted from firing upon an artillery battery onto a column of tanks moving up from Caen to Lébisey. After the third salvo the pilot reported: 'So near the tank it didn't matter.' Then: 'Direct hit on the forward end of one tank.' Finally, after *Dragon* had damaged several tanks and blown one clean off the road: 'Yippee, you've hit it on the cupola!'

A vast volume of naval ordnance was expended during the Normandy invasion. Between 6 June and 12 September a total of 58,621 rounds were fired; 3371 from the mighty 16in and 15in guns of the battleships, 1034 from their 6in secondary armament, 30,216 from the 7.5in and 5.25in guns of the cruisers and 24,000 from the 4.7in and 4in guns of the destroyers. The fire was reliable, accurate and devastatingly effective. 'All prisoners,' wrote one of the FOBs in his report, 'spoke of the dread the Germans had of the naval gunfire.' Another noted very much the same thing. 'In the words of some prisoners, the weight and high velocity of naval gunfire was most terrifying.'

On land the FOBs fought their own wars, often having to decide for themselves what needed to be done and how best to do it. They pushed quietly forward to engage the enemy, often working up to and beyond the FEBA (forward edge of the battle area). Many were captured or killed as a result. After Normandy the survivors (and members of other Bombardment Units not involved in D-day) took part in the assault on Walcheren, the landing on Elba, as well as operations in the south of France, the Adriatic and Greece and in the war against the Japanese.

The sailors and soldiers of the Bombardment Units were tough, determined, independent and individualistic; but above all they lived up to the Combined Operations motto of 'United we conquer', combining the best of the Royal Navy with the best of the Royal Artillery. Their work was vital to the success of the Normandy landings – in the same way that the work of their successors in 148 Commando Forward Observation Battery, Royal Artillery, was vital to the success of Operation Corporate, 38 years later.

THE AUTHOR Major Hugh McManners, as a captain, was one of the Naval Gunfire Forward Observers of 148 Commando Forward Observation Battery during the Falklands campaign of 1982. The author and publishers would like to thank Geoff Burgess, Stanley Reed, Malcolm Fordyce and the Bombardment Unit Association for their invaluable help in the preparation of this article.

Top right: In flat country such as this, forward observation was particularly hazardous. Operating close to enemy lines, the observer was obliged to poke his head above cover in order to see the shells fall. Here, Captain Burgess (with pipe) is on watch, with Sergeant Len Sherry on guard with a Thompson sub-machine gun and Telegraphist Winch as radio operator. Above right: The fluidity of battle often demanded a mobile Forward Observation HQ – here a half-track has been specially converted into a communications vehicle. Below: Supplied with pinpoint targets by forward observers, the enormous firepower of HMS Rodney is let fly.

EXOCET!

Armed with the fearsome Exocet missile, the pilots of the Argentinian 2nd Naval Escuadrilla joined battle with the ships of the Task Force

AT THE OUTBREAK of hostilities between Britain and Argentina, the Argentinian commanders wasted no time in planning attacks against the British fleet. Carrier task forces on both sides launched probes to find each other. Just before dawn on 2 May the Argentinian navy carrier, *25 de Mayo*, arrived in position to launch an airstrike, about 200 miles to the northwest of the British warships.

Much to group commander Rear Admiral Juan Lombardo's dismay, the wind, normally very strong, was calm, which meant that the Skyhawks could not launch with a full load of bombs and fuel. As it was getting light, Lombardo ordered the carrier and her escorts to turn back for safer waters nearer the Argentinian mainland until the weather improved. Later in the day, after the sinking of the cruiser *General Belgrano* by the British nuclear-powered submarine *Conqueror*, the Argentinian fleet was permanently recalled for the duration of the war.

With the Argentinian naval forces 'bottled up', the great hope for hitting the British fleet lay in the use of the French-built Exocet missile/Super Etendard jet combination. However, the 2nd Naval Fighter and Attack Escuadrilla, under Commander Jorge Colombo, had only been formed in November 1981 after the pilots had each flown a total of about 45 hours familiarisation with the aircraft. Initial training in France had not included operation of the weapons system. Little more had been done by Colombo and his pilots before 31 March when, as the Argentinian Marines were preparing to land on the Falklands, he suddenly received orders to get his unit ready for operations with the Exocet missile.

The squadron had only five missiles, and the French technicians who were supposed to help get aircraft and missile mated were embargoed from coming to Argentina. That left Colombo and his men

COMANDO DE AVIACION NAVAL ARGENTINA

The Comando de Aviacion Naval Argentina (naval air arm) order of battle for the Falklands consisted of the following units and aircraft: the 2nd Naval Fighter and Attack Escuadrilla (four operational Super Etendards and one to provide spares); the 3rd Naval Fighter and Attack Escuadrilla (11 A-4Q Skyhawks); the 1st Naval Attack Escuadrilla (four Beech T-34C Turbo-Mentors); the 1st Naval Reconnaissance Escuadrilla (two SP-2H Neptunes); the 1st Naval Anti-submarine Escuadrilla (six S-2E Trackers); the 1st Naval Helicopter Escuadrilla (seven Alouette and two Lynx helicopters); the 2nd Naval Helicopter Escuadrilla (four SH-3D Sea Kings); the 1st Naval Logistics Escuadrilla (three Electras); and the 2nd Naval Logistics Escuadrilla (3 Fokker F-28s). The insignia of the 2nd Naval Fighter and Attack Escuadrilla, the unit tasked with the Exocet missions, is shown above.

Left above: The entire pilot corps of the 2nd Escuadrilla, photographed during the Falklands conflict. Fourth from the left is the unit CO, Commander Jorge Colombo. Left: A Super Etendard of the 2nd Escuadrilla comes in to land.

to fend for themselves.

Using French manuals and working around the clock, the squadron became operational within two weeks. Pilots trained out of Puerto Belgrano against all types of vessels, including Type 42 destroyers. Colombo investigated the possible use of the 4100ft runway at Puerto Argentino (Stanley) by marking off this same length at Espora airfield. Take-off and braking distances were tested with the aircraft in attack configuration. With the runway dry, the planes could have landed with a very narrow margin of safety. Landings were impossible, however, on a wet runway, though the Super Etendards could just take off from the runway in any condition. This was also the case for the air force attack jets. As a result, the critical airfield at Stanley was considered usable only as an emergency alternative.

On 19 April, the first two Super Etendards took off from Espora for Rio Grande in Tierra del Fuego, their

2ND NAVAL FIGHTER AND ATTACK ESCUADRILLA: FALKLANDS 1982

operational base if armed conflict were to break out with Britain. During the same period, other air force and naval squadrons departed for bases in southern Argentina, including Rio Gallegos, Santa Cruz, San Julián, Puerto Deseado, Comodoro Rivadavia and Trelew.

The first Exocet mission was launched on 2 May, when Commander Colombo led a pair of Super Etendards of the 2nd Escuadrilla from Rio Grande. After climbing for altitude off the coast, the first link-up with the Hercules refuelling tankers failed and the two aircraft returned to base with the missiles still on their launchers. With only five Exocets available, Colombo was not about to risk his assets until a kill could be reasonably assured.

Early on the morning of 4 May an SP-2H Neptune of the 1st Naval Reconnaissance Escuadrilla began shadowing the British warships. At 0710 the crew made its first radar contact and reported the main concentration of ships to be about 100 miles south of Stanley. The Argentinian Naval Air Command immediately ordered a Super Etendard strike.

At 0945, Lieutenant Commander Augusto Bedacaratz and Lieutenant Armando Mayora took off from Rio Grande. Each aircraft carried external fuel tanks under the port wing and fuselage, and a single Exocet missile under the starboard wing. Fifteen minutes after take-off, the attack aircraft topped up their fuel tanks from a KC-130 tanker, then continued east at medium altitude. As they approached the

target area, the two pilots used their radar warning gear to determine the radar horizon, then began a slow descent beneath that horizon until they were only 50ft above the water. During the descent, attack and position information was radioed to the fighters from the shadowing Neptune.

The two pilots maintained visual contact with each other, but kept strict radio and radar silence, relying on infrequent broadcasts from the Neptune to update their position on the target. At 1050 the Neptune made its last transmission – the fighters could easily bear in to the target on their own from this point. Shortly thereafter, the Super Etendards pulled up to 120ft, switched on their radars for a moment in order to locate the exact positions of the targets in front of them, launched their Exocets, and withdrew at high speed. This was modern war at its most impersonal: neither pilot had any idea at which ship he had aimed his missile.

One of the missiles struck HMS *Sheffield* amidships and set her ablaze, though the warhead did not

The Argentinian Exocet missions were a grim illustration of the highly impersonal quality of modern warfare. Launching their missiles miles from the target meant that the pilots of the 2nd Escuadrilla (above left) only learnt that they had scored a hit from news bulletins put out by the BBC. During the conflict, two ships – HMS *Sheffield* (left) and the *Atlantic Conveyor* (above) – were destroyed by air-launched Exocet attacks.

In 1979 Argentina's naval air arm placed an order for 14 Dassault Super Etendard single-seat carrier-based strike aircraft and a supply of AM-39 Exocets. On 26 March 1981, the first batch of five aircraft was delivered for the pilots of the 2nd Escuadrilla to commence training. In November these aircraft were delivered to the squadron's main base at Espora and, six months later, these machines were in action against the ships of the British Task Force.

During the conflict, France cut off supplies of military hardware to Argentina and the 2nd Escuadrilla was forced to cannibalise parts from one of the five aircraft to service the other four.

The French embargo also meant that the Argentinians, who had very little experience of the aircraft type, had to make do with French manuals to get the plane mated with the Exocet missile. At the time, however, there were strong rumours that the French technicians who were already in Argentina did help in the process.

The Super Etendard is powered by a 5000kg-thrust SNECMA Atar 8K-50 turbojet and, carrying a normal war load, achieves a maximum speed of 630mph at low altitude.

Armament consists of two 30mm DEFA cannon, mounted internally, and the plane is provided with mountings, one on the fuselage and four underwing, for a variety of ordnance, including rocket pods, bombs, air-to-air missiles and the AM-39 Exocet air-to-surface missile which is carried on a point under the starboard wing.

fully detonate. The fire was most probably caused by the missile's running rocket motor, and the flaring up of hot cooking fat in the ship's galley. Twenty-one of the ship's crew of 235 were killed and, six days later, the *Sheffield* foundered under tow and sank.

Both Neptunes of the 1st Escuadrilla continued to patrol in search of the British fleet, performing some anti-submarine warfare (ASW) work, until 15 May. By then, the old electronic gear aboard the aircraft had given up the ghost and was rendered useless.

Without the Neptunes, a new means of targeting for the Super Etendards had to be found. Senior naval officers, and officers from the Operations Centre at Puerto Argentino, met to devise another way of locating the British fleet. The admiral in charge of naval operations on the Malvinas (Falklands) gave radar crews at Puerto Argentino the task of analysing the tracks of Harriers seen on their screens. The

positions where Harriers first appeared on the screens, and where they disappeared on their return flights, were continually plotted. The premise was that the aircraft could not be very far from their mother carriers when they appeared and disappeared. Although this was only an approximate method, the British had anticipated just such a tactic. Sea Harrier pilots were ordered to descend below Stanley's radar horizon while within 50 miles of the carriers.

A cluster of ships was seen, targets were selected, and their co-ordinates fed to the missiles

On 17 May a pair of Super Etendards was ordered to hit the British fleet, using the information gleaned from the shore-based radars. When the fighters popped up to locate their target and launch their missiles, they found nothing. Rather than conduct a longer search on radar, which would inevitably have betrayed their presence and resulted in interception by Sea Harriers, the pair abandoned the mission and returned to Rio Grande. Six days later, another mission was attempted by two Super Etendards against British warships east of the Falklands. Again, the pilots failed to find any targets and returned to

base with their Exocets.

Undeterred by the failure of these two missions, the Argentinian pilots continued their search for targets. During the early afternoon of 25 May, as Argentinian air force Skyhawks were in the process of hitting HMS *Broadsword* and *Coventry*, Super Etendard pilots, Lieutenant Commander Roberto Curilovic and Lieutenant Julio Barraza, were half-way to their designated target area: the point just east of where the Harriers and Sea Harriers disappeared off the Puerto Argentino radar screens, and where the two British carriers *Hermes* and *Invincible* had to be.

Skirting 120 miles north of the Malvinas to keep clear of the Sea Harriers, the Argentinian fighters continued until they were northeast of the islands, then turned due south to begin their attacks. Relying on this unexpected direction, and radio silence to achieve surprise, the pair flew on until Curilovic picked up the tell-tale emissions of British ships' radars on his receiving equipment. The lead pilot eased his nose around until he was heading towards them, then the pair began descending to the target-approach altitude of 50ft.

Closing on the British force at their attack speed of 630mph, the Argentinian pilots switched on their radars and eased the aircraft into a

Above left: Super Etendards of the 2nd Escuadrilla. Above right: The Exocet attack on 30 May was a joint navy/air force effort. Lieutenant Ernesto Ureta (far left of picture) and three other Skyhawk pilots of Grupo 4 flew in to attack with the Super Etendards. Mistaking HMS *Avenger* for the carrier *Invincible*, Ureta attacked the frigate but missed her. Below: The French-built Super Etendard single-seat attack aircraft.

climb to begin a target search. Almost immediately, a cluster of ships was seen, targets were selected, and their co-ordinates fed to the missiles; each aircraft then launched its Exocet. As the missiles sped clear, the Super Etendards turned sharply and withdrew. They landed back at Rio Grande at 1838 hours and, as with the attack on the *Sheffield*, the Argentinian navy pilots had to wait for a BBC bulletin to learn what they had hit. The next morning, it was reported that *Coventry* had been sunk and that the requisitioned Cunard container-ship *Atlantic Conveyor* was hit.

Although several serious blows had been imposed upon the British fleet in the launching of four Exocets, Argentinian planners had hoped for greater prizes, namely, the Task Force carriers. With only a single missile remaining, the next mission would be carefully planned to get a carrier, preferably the *Invincible*. To add punch to the effort, the only joint air force/navy mission of the war was approved. Four Skyhawks from Grupo 4, each armed with two 500lb bombs, would fly with the navy Super Etendards to the target. After the Exocet was launched, they would follow the missile's smoke trail in, then launch their own bombing attack.

By 30 May everything was set. Lieutenant Commander Alejandro Francisco took off from Rio Grande with the sole remaining Exocet, accompanied by another Super Etendard which would provide back-up radar-attack information should Francisco's aircraft develop technical trouble. The four air force Skyhawks, flown by Captains José Vázquez and Omar Castillo, Lieutenant Ernesto Ureta and Ensign Geraldo Isaac, quickly formed up with the navy aircraft and the six planes proceeded towards the refuelling tanker, which was orbiting near Isla de los Estados, just off the Argentinian mainland. After topping up their tanks, the formation refuelled again from another KC-130, south of West Falkland. As the force approached the point just east of where the Harrier tracks disappeared on Malvinas radar, the aircraft began to descend. To achieve maximum surprise, it was planned to attack the British ships from the southeast.

Soon after 1420 hours, the Super Etendards picked up radar signals from British ships. Turning towards the source of these emissions, the two planes ran in to

AEROSPATIALE EXOCET

Exocet was developed by Nord-Aviation, now Aérospatiale, during the late 1960s in response to a French navy requirement for a surface-to-surface missile. It was designed as a long-range sea-skimming weapon, flying at high subsonic speeds. The result was the MM-38, currently in service with, among others, the British, French and Argentinian navies.

Development of an air-launched AM-38 version – essentially a standard MM-38 with a one-second delay before ignition to allow the missile to fall clear of the carrier aircraft – began in 1973. Improvements to the design led to the shorter, longer-range AM-39, which entered service on French Navy Super Frelon helicopters in 1977 and on Super Etendard fighters in mid-1978. Before their deployment by the Argentinian naval air arm in 1982, AM-39 Exocets had been used by the Iraqi Air Force to attack merchantmen off the Iranian coast during the Gulf War.

During May 1982, in a total of 12 sorties, the Exocet-equipped Super Etendard attack aircraft of the Argentinian 2nd Naval Fighter and Attack Escuadrilla stalked their prey – the ships of the British Task Force. With only five missiles and four usable Super Etendards, the squadron had to make each round, and mission, count. And yet, with the Argentinian Navy's only aircraft carrier bottled up in harbour, the Super Etendards had to operate at extreme range from their base in Tierra del Fuego in the south of Argentina, refuelling en route from Air Force KC-130 tankers. By the end of the war, the squadron's Exocets had accounted for two British ships: the destroyer Sheffield and the container-ship Atlantic Conveyor.

attack. Minutes later, at about 1430, Francisco pulled up, acquired a target on his radar, and launched his Exocet at an estimated 15-mile range. The two Super Etendards then turned back for their base, leaving the four Skyhawk fighter-bombers to follow the missile in towards the target. Just 30 seconds after launch, the Skyhawk pilots were in amongst the fleet – they were much closer than they had thought.

Almost immediately, Vázquez and Castillo, the lead pair, were shot down, according to Ureta, by Sea Dart missiles. Neither survived. Ureta, leading the second flight, caught sight of what he thought was an aircraft carrier and made straight for it. He ran in at about 30 degrees to the ship's stern, released his bombs, and after flying directly over the ship, made a turn. Looking back, he was sure that the Exocet had hit because of the thick, black column of smoke rising from the vessel. Ureta and Isaac were both convinced that serious damage had been inflicted on the vessel.

But the truth of what happened on the afternoon of 30 May lay shrouded in the 'fog of war'. From British records and interviews, it is clear that there was an attempt to launch an Exocet attack on the main body of the Task Force that afternoon. But that is about the limit of the agreement between the British and the

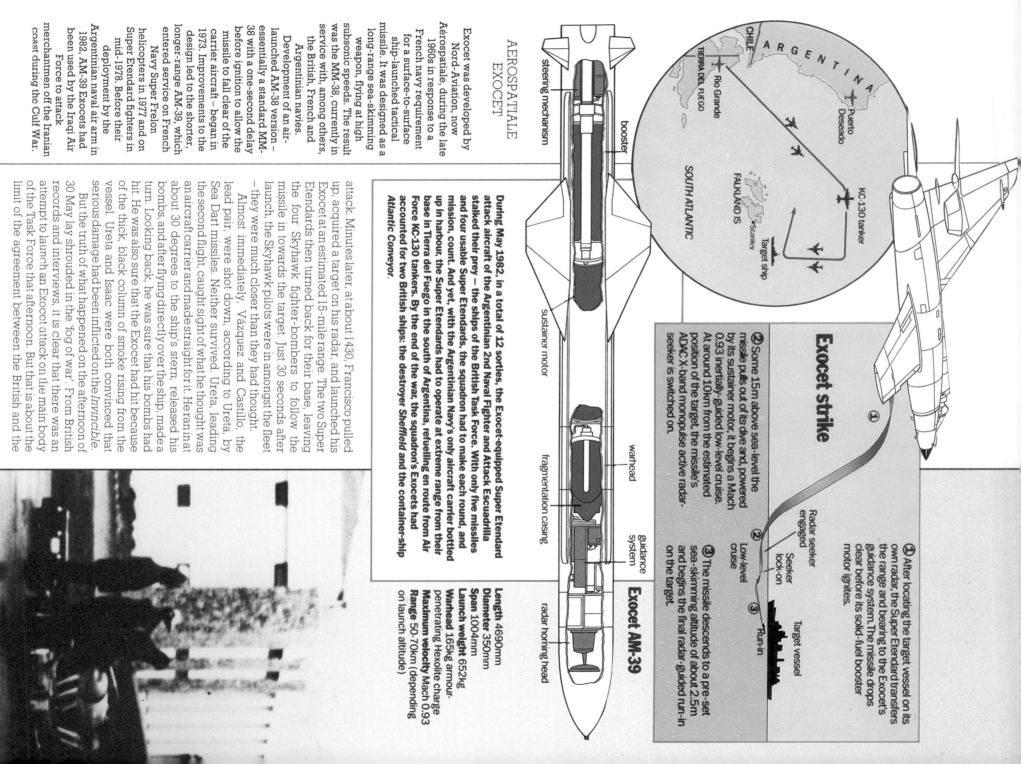

steering mechanism

booster

sustainer motor

warhead

fragmentation casing

guidance system

radar homing head

Exocet AM-39

CHILE

ARGENTINA

TIERRA DEL FUEGO

Puerto Deseado

Rio Grande

KC-130 tanker

Target ship

FALKLAND IS

Stanley

SOUTH ATLANTIC

Exocet strike

① After locating the target vessel on its own radar, the Super Etendard transfers the range and bearing to the Exocet's guidance system. The missile drops clear before its solid-fuel booster motor ignites.

② Some 15m above sea-level the missile pulls out of its dive and, powered by its sustainer motor, it begins a Mach 0.93 inertially-guided low-level cruise. At around 10km from the estimated position of the target, the missile's ADAC X-band monopulse active radar-seeker is switched on.

③ The missile descends to a pre-set sea-skimming altitude of about 2.5m and begins the final radar-guided run-in on the target.

Radar seeker engaged

Low-level cruise

Seeker lock-on

Run-in

Target vessel

Length 4690mm
Diameter 350mm
Span 1004mm
Launch weight 652kg
Warhead 165kg armour-penetrating Hexolite charge
Maximum velocity Mach 0.93
Range 50-70km (depending on launch altitude)

helicopter deck would have seemed a prominent feature. *Avenger* was also running at full power on her gas turbines, which invariably give of a lot of smoke, and she was firing every weapon that could be brought to bear and chaff rockets as well.

After the Super Etendards had returned, the pilots waited anxiously for news from the BBC to confirm their success. The confirmation never came. Since they had seen what they were sure was a crippled carrier, the opinion slowly formed among Argentinian personnel that the Royal Navy had suffered such a serious loss that it had kept it secret. The late arrival of the *Invincible* back in Britain, in pristine condition, compared to *Hermes*, seemed, in their eyes, to confirm that she had undergone extensive repairs.

Although the 2nd Naval Fighter and Attack Escuadrilla had only four usable Super Etendards and five Exocets, and flew only 12 operational sorties, it succeeded in sinking the *Sheffield* and the *Atlantic Conveyor* – and only one of the Exocet warheads detonated. Beyond this, the unit exerted great pressure on British naval operations that continued long after the last of its missiles had been fired.

Argentinian records of what happened. One thing that is certain is that neither the Exocet nor the A-4s came anywhere near the British aircraft carriers.

In fact, the action centred around the destroyer HMS *Exeter* and the frigate HMS *Avenger*, which had detached from the main body of the Task Force and were on their way to carry out a bombardment of Stanley that evening. *Exeter*, a Type 42 destroyer, reported shooting down two approaching A-4s with Sea Darts: this claim links precisely with the Argentinian record of losses. *Avenger* reported shooting down an incoming Exocet missile with her 4.5in gun. If this was so, it was a remarkable piece of shooting. Whether because of *Avenger's* first-rate gunnery, because it was decoyed by chaff, or because it simply failed, the Exocet exploded well clear.

Shortly afterwards, *Avenger* reported an attack by a pair of A-4s, whose bombs narrowly missed her. Almost certainly, this was the ship Ureta had attacked, mistaking it for *Invincible*. It might seem impossible to mistake a little Type 21 frigate (which was not hit) for an aircraft carrier on fire, but visibility was poor and the Argentinian pilots were approaching the frigate from almost astern, from which point her

LAND-LAUNCHED EXOCET

During the Falklands conflict, the use of the AM-39 air-launched Exocet was supplemented by the deployment of the surface-launched version, the MM-38. In an attempt to dissuade British warships from approaching the islands and laying down heavy bombardments on Argentinian troop positions, it was decided to improvise a land trailer-launched version of the Exocet from the system normally mounted on Argentinian warships. After days of feverish tinkering with the missiles' complex electronic systems, the Argentinian technicians succeeded in cobbling together a weapon and, by late May, the new system was ready for deployment.

On 24 May, two missiles were transported by a C-130 to Puerto Argentina (Stanley) but continuing technical hitches rendered them unserviceable. Further adjustments were made and, eventually, one missile was put back on line. This Exocet was subsequently launched at

a target but failed to hit the ship.

On 12 June, at 0300 hours, a ship entered the firing zone, an accurate bearing on her position was gained, and an Exocet was launched at a range of about 18 miles. At 0330, the missile struck the stern of HMS *Glamorgan* and, although the warhead failed to detonate, serious damage was caused and 13 crew members were killed and 17 others injured.

Because of the risk of Exocet attack after 4 May, the British carriers spent most of their time well to the east of the Falklands, with the result that Sea Harriers had to fly combat air patrols at ranges close to their operational limits, with correspondingly short times in position to block attacks. This small band of Argentinian navy pilots thus contributed directly to the destruction wrought by all other Argentinian air units throughout the conflict.

THE AUTHOR Jeffrey Ethell has written numerous articles and more than 20 books on aviation subjects. His recent books include *Air War South Atlantic*, *Fox Two* and *Pilot Maker*.

In 1981, Libyan planes tried to take on the F-14 Tomcats of US Navy Squadron VF-41 – but the US pilots were ready for action

BLACK ACES

IN AUGUST 1981 the US Navy's F-14 Tomcat interceptor fighter – arguably the most advanced aircraft of its type anywhere in the world – was blooded in combat. The action took place over the disputed waters of the Gulf of Sirte, off the coast of Libya. Two Sukhoi Su-22 Fitter-H fighters of the Libyan Arab Republic Air Force (LARAF) intercepted a pair of F-14As of the US Navy's fighter squadron VF-41, 'The Black Aces', flying from the nuclear-powered carrier USS Nimitz. The leading Fitter fired an Atoll infra-red guided missile towards the American fighters, giving them the opportunity to return the fire under the US Navy's standard rules of engagement. At the end of a fight which lasted only 45 seconds, the two Tomcat crews had each shot down one of the Libyan fighters to gain the first combat victories for the US Navy since the end of the Vietnam War.

VF-41 has had a long and eventful history as a carrier-based fighter squadron with the US Navy. It can trace its descent from the pre-World War II VF-4, which was the first unit to equip with Grumman F4F-3 Wildcats late in 1940. The following year the squadron was redesignated VF-41 and its Wildcats saw action during the North African Torch landings of November 1942, flying from USS Ranger. In 1944

Above: The formidable F-14 Tomcat interceptor, ace in the pack of USS Nimitz. Below: 'Fast Eagle 102', the Tomcat piloted by Commander Hank Kleeman over the Gulf of Sirte. The aircraft bears the Black Aces' tailplane insignia (also shown left). Right: The fliers aboard Nimitz; standing from left, James Anderson, Lawrence Muszynsky, Hank Kleeman and David Venlet.

was flying F-4B Phantom IIs. However, the possible air attacks from Cuba failed to materialise and it was not until 1965 that the Black Aces again saw action. In that year the squadron was embarked on USS *Independence*, when the ship was detached from the Atlantic Fleet for a combat cruise off Vietnam. In 1977 VF-41 exchanged its Phantoms for F-14A Tomcats and was assigned to USS *Nimitz*'s Carrier Air Wing 8 (CVW-8).

In February 1901, Commander Henry 'Hank' Kleeman relieved Commander Art Cebrowski as 'skipper' of the Black Aces. A former test pilot and a veteran of the Vietnam War, he inspired the squadron 'to fly and fight F-14s more and better than anyone else'. The squadron then embarked on a series of exercises with the whole of CVW-8. These were to culminate in an Operational Readiness Evaluation to determine CVW-8's fitness for deployment.

A Marine Corps EA-6B Prowler of VMAQ-2 miscalculated its approach during a night landing and crashed into *Nimitz*'s flight deck

However, on 26 May this carefully planned training programme was interrupted by a serious accident, which strikingly illustrates the potential hazards of carrier aviation. A Marine Corps EA-6B Prowler of VMAQ-2, which was attached to CVW-8 to provide electronic warfare support, miscalculated its approach during a night landing and crashed into *Nimitz*'s flight deck. The impact area was engulfed in flames and the job of the firefighting teams was made even more hazardous by the exploding ordnance of aircraft parked in the vicinity. Among the casualties were three of VF-41's maintenance personnel killed and three of the squadron's Tomcats were destroyed in the fire. Yet despite the intensity of the conflagration, it was brought under control and extinguished. *Nimitz* steamed back at high speed to her home port at Norfolk, Virginia, for inspection of the damage and replacement of lost and damaged aircraft. Amazingly, within 90 hours of the accident the carrier was back at sea and operating her aircraft. Nor did this accident, one of the most serious in recent naval history, interfere with CVW-8's preparations for its forthcoming operational deployment. The Wing passed its Operational Readiness Evaluation with flying colours, the Black Aces setting a new record by launching 69 sorties within a period of 72 hours with 11 of its 12 F-14As fully mission-capable throughout the period. On 3 August *Nimitz* sailed from Norfolk bound for the Mediterranean and eight days later she joined the US Sixth Fleet.

Carrier Air Wing 8's first duty with the Sixth Fleet was to carry out an Open Ocean Missile Exercise in the Gulf of Sirte on 18 and 19 August. This involved the Tomcats of VF-41 and its sister squadron VF-84, 'The Jolly Rogers', in the interception and shooting down of target drones. The mission was not as straightforward as it appeared, however, because the exercise areas was within a 300km offshore limit which Libya claimed as her territorial waters. The United States refused to countenance this claim and would only recognise a 5km limit. Therefore, it was anticipated that Libyan aircraft would attempt to interfere with the exercise and, accordingly, combat air patrols were mounted off the Libyan coast. Even so, the chances of actual fighting taking place were thought to be slight. As Vice-Admiral William Rowden, the Commander of the US Sixth Fleet said: 'We knew this was not a no-risk operation, but we felt it was a

the squadron transferred to the Pacific Theatre as VF(N)-41 and its F6F-5N Hellcat nightfighters took part in the Battle of Leyte Gulf, flying from USS *Independence*. After the end of World War II VF-41 briefly operated the composite-power Ryan FR-1 Fireball (a piston-engined fighter fitted with an auxiliary turbojet), but then reverted to more conventional equipment. From 1950-53 the squadron was embarked on USS *Midway*, flying F4U Corsairs, but as a unit of the Atlantic Fleet it saw no action in Korea.

The first pure-jet fighter to be flown by the Black Aces was the F2H-3 Banshee, which the squadron operated from 1954 until re-equipping with the F3H-2 Demon in 1956. During the Cuban Missile Crisis in October 1962, VF-41 was hastily transferred from its normal shore base at Oceana, Virginia, to Key West, Florida, in order to bolster the United States' air defences in the southeast. By that time it

Following their abortive attempt to convert the F-111 for carrier-based operations, Grumman designed an entirely new fleet defence fighter and the prototype made its maiden flight on 21 December 1970.

The F-14A is the only aircraft in naval service with computer-controlled variable-geometry wings. At slow speeds they are fully extended in a 20-degree sweepback, but as speed increases the computer adjusts their angle to a maximum of 68 degrees. Beyond the speed of sound small foreplanes are extruded ahead of the wings to reduce the shock waves of supersonic flight.

The diverse interception roles of the F-14A are reflected in its armament. Its Hughes AN/AWG-9 weapons control system tracks 24 targets and can direct the F-14A's maximum complement of six AIM-54 Phoenix missiles towards six targets simultaneously over a range of 100 miles. The F-14A may also be armed with radar-guided AIM-7 Sparrows and/or infra-red heat-seeking AIM-9L Sidewinders. An M61A1 Vulcan 20mm rotary cannon is mounted in the forward fuselage.

However, the F-14A is not without disadvantages. It is a very complex aircraft and suffers a rapid rate of systems breakdown. It has been estimated that 47 per cent of the US Navy's F-14As are 'not mission capable' at any given time, and an average of six repairs must be made after each flight.

AIM-9L SIDEWINDER

The AIM-9L air-to-air missile (AAM) was first put into production in 1977. With a length of 2.85m and a body diameter of 127mm, it weighs 85.3kg, of which 20.2kg is the annular blast fragmentation warhead. In flight it reaches Mach 2.5, powered by a solid-propellant rocket motor, and its range is 11 miles.

The missile is stabilised by four tailfins fitted with flywheels at the tips. It is guided by a telescope which detects infra-red heat generated by the target's engines; the heat is converted into electricity which directs the four pivoted fins at the nose towards the source of the heat.

low-risk one.' The Libyan Arab Republic Air Force was by no means a negligible opponent, having a strength of more than 300 combat aircraft. These included Mirage 5 and F1 fighters supplied by France; MiG-25 Foxbat, MiG-23 Flogger and Su-22 Fitter fighters supplied by the Soviet Union; plus a single squadron of Soviet-supplied Tu-22 Blinder bombers. However, a serious weakness of the LARAF was a shortage of trained pilots and fewer than 100 Libyans were thought capable of flying advanced combat aircraft. Consequently the service was to a large degree dependent on the skills of foreign pilots, especially those on loan from the Soviet Union and other Warsaw Pact nations and from Pakistan.

The first day of the missile exercise, 18 August, went much as expected. The target drone was successfully intercepted and 'splashed', while combat air patrols (CAPs) of F-14A Tomcats protected the exercise area. In addition to the potential threat from Libyan aircraft, Nimitz's air wing had to guard against interference from missile patrol boats and Soviet-supplied Foxtrot-class diesel-electric powered submarines. So the S-3A Viking anti-submarine warfare aircraft of VS-24 and the airborne early warning E-2C Hawkeyes of VAW-124 maintained a 24-hour watch for sub-surface, surface and airborne threats to the carrier. More than 40 LARAF aircraft were intercepted by Nimitz's CAPs on 18 August and these included MiG-25 Foxbats, MiG-23 Floggers and Mirages. Often the Libyan fighters would manoeuvre for an advantageous position before breaking off and returning to base. 'It was always the same,' recalled Lieutenant Larry 'Music' Musczynski, 'we would tangle with the Libyans and pretty soon everybody was low on fuel and went home.' However, the Tomcats of CVW-8 did have the advantage of in-flight refuelling from the KA-6D Intruder tankers of VA-35, 'The Black Panthers'.

The second day of the exercise began with Nimitz launching her combat air patrols, which took up station between the carrier and the Libyan coast. The first interceptions were made within 15 minutes and then, at 0715 hours, it was the turn of the southernmost CAP. This was mounted by the Black Aces' skipper, Commander Hank Kleeman, with Lieutenant David Venlet as his 'backseater' in 'Fast Eagle 102'. Kleeman's wingman was 28-year-old Lieutenant Musczynski and his Radar Intercept Officer (RIO), Lieutenant (junior grade) Jim 'Amos' Anderson, flying in 'Fast Eagle 107'. Musczynski and Anderson were an experienced team; they had been flying together for over a year and Musczynski had nearly 1000 hours' flying time on the Tomcat. Flying at an altitude of 20,000ft, the two Tomcats picked up a pair of Libyan fighters on their own radars. This was somewhat unusual, because generally the E-2C Hawkeye airborne early warning aircraft would

GROUND-CONTROLLED INTERCEPTION

Usually operating over friendly territory, the role of the interceptor is to locate, intercept, identify and, if appropriate, destroy aircraft intruding into defended air-space. They work in close collaboration with ground or ship-borne radar stations, and these make the first contact with the target, identify it as closely as the radar system allows, and then guide the interceptor close enough for its own radar to take over the tracking process.

Observation of Soviet tactics of interception in the postwar years has indicated that in most incidents the tactical thinking has been done at the radar post on the ground, the decisions being relayed by radio as commands to the interceptor's 'puppet' aircrew. As late as 1970, Soviet pilots had to request permission from Ground-Controlled Interception (GCI) to make a simple turn in flight, and thus were denied a degree of flexibility in airborne tactics long taken for granted by Western pilots.

However, the introduction of Soviet supersonic, all-weather air superiority fighters, equipped with look-down/shoot-down weapon systems and beyond-visual-range (BVR) air-to-air missiles, is fast leading to the phasing out of GCI intervention in actual combat. While GCI now maintains constant contact with the interceptors, supplying them with reports on the situation as it develops, monitoring their co-ordination and alerting them to enemy movements, the Soviets have accepted that: 'only the pilot in the air, personally observing and evaluating everything that happens...is able to find the most advisable variation [in tactics] for performing the combat assignment at any particular moment.'

make the first contact and pass it on to the fighters. At a range of just under eight miles, Kleeman spotted the two hostile aircraft flying about 500ft apart, and when the range had closed to within two to three miles he was able positively to identify them as Su-22 Fitters. The American fighter crews noticed that the Libyans were working under close ground radar control, in accordance with the standard Soviet air interception tactical doctrine, as every move that the 'Tomcats made to intercept was promptly countered by the Fitters.

Later in the year, Musczynski and Anderson described the action to the Tailhook Association:

'At a combined closure rate of 1000 knots, the four fighters approached head-on, with Musczynski flying a 'loose deuce' about two miles to starboard and 4000ft above Kleeman. Both pilots and the lead's RIO saw the lead Libyan fire a missile at about 1000ft range. The heat-seeker went wide and was instantly gone from sight. "There was a brief period of astonishment," said Amos. "In thousands of intercepts I don't think many of us really thought we'd be shot at, let alone have to shoot back." But then the hours of training and

Below: A Black Aces F-14 Tomcat tears down the *Nimitz* flight deck to begin a Combat Air Patrol.

LT DAVE VENLET

CDR. HANK KLEEMAN

102

RESCUE

Dogfight
US Navy VF-41 Squadron, Gulf of Sirte
19 August 1981

The US Sixth Fleet sailed into the disputed waters of the Gulf of Sirte, off Libya, on 17 August 1981. For two days the fighters of Nimitz and Forrestal intercepted Libyan intruders and escorted them away from the exercise area without incident. But on the morning of 19 August a routine interception turned into a dogfight.

Carrier defence

The US Navy's Enterprise and Nimitz class nuclear-powered aircraft carriers are the most important single element in the navy's offensive capability, but their large size would make them a tempting target for air, submarine or missile attack. On-board armament is light — typically three Sea Sparrow missile launchers and three 20mm guns providing short-range anti-aircraft defence — and the big carrier relies on its escorting cruisers and destroyers, together with the defence-in-depth provided by its air group. S-3 Viking aircraft and Sea King helicopters provide anti-submarine warfare capability but air defence is normally the responsibility of the Grumman E-2 Hawkeye airborne early warning and control platform, which with the sophisticated radar and data processing electronics installed in recent variants is able to monitor up to 300 targets and handle over 40 interceptions simultaneously.

Key

- ⌢ Territorial waters claimed by Libya
- ⌢ Territorial waters recognised by United States
- ▨ Area of Sixth Fleet manoeuvres
- ○ Location of dogfight

MEDITERRANEAN
ITALY
Rome
Gaeta
GREECE
Athens
Tripoli
Sirte
LIBYA
Gulf of Sirte
Benghazi

MEDITERRANEAN
LIBYA
Tripoli
Sirte
Gulf of Sirte
Barce
Benghazi

Tomcat vs Fitter

1. Two Su-22 Fitters approach from the Libyan coast in welded-wing formation. The Su-22 leader fires an Atoll missile at Kleeman but the missile fails to guide on to its target.

2. As his leader banks away in a defensive split, the Su-22 wingman breaks away in a climbing turn.

3. Kleeman pulls round on the right.

4. Musczynski executes a climbing turn, cuts in front of his leader, and gets into position to attack the first Su-22.

5. Kleeman pulls round on the Su-22 wingman and launches his Sidewinder.

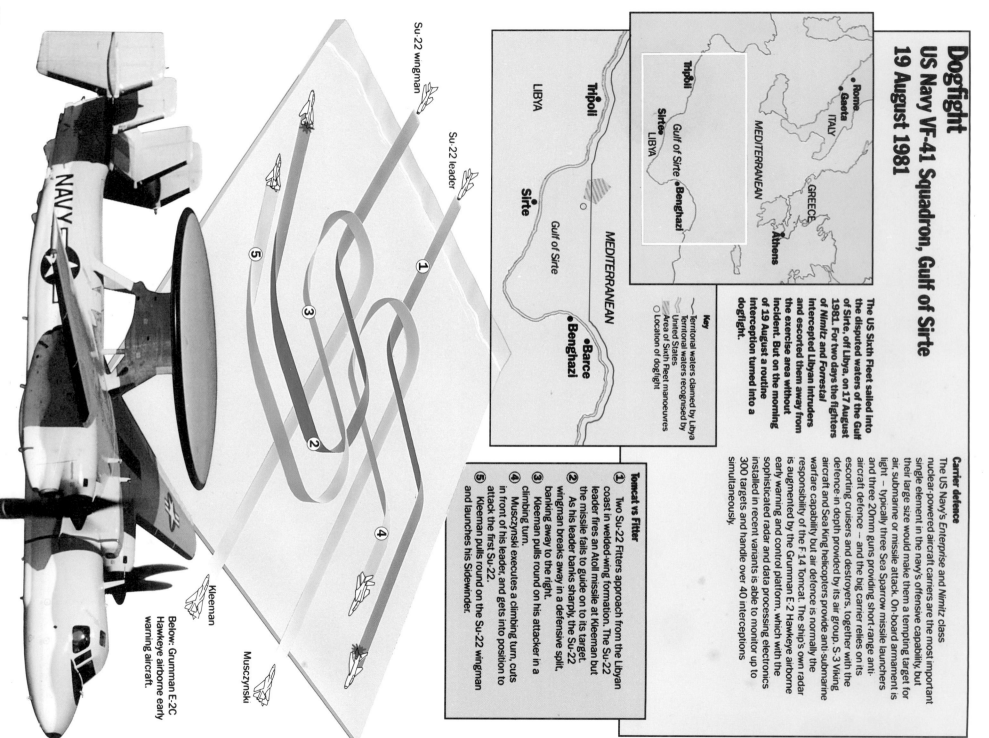

Su-22 wingman

Su-22 leader

5

1

3

2

4

NAVY

Kleeman

Musczynski

Below: Grumman E-2C Hawkeye airborne early warning aircraft.

Above: Supplied to the Libyan Arab Republic Air Force by the Soviet Union, the Sukhoi SU-22 is an export version of the SU-17. In its turn, the SU-17 was developed as a swing-wing version of the SU-7 that entered service as long ago as the late 1950s, a good example of the Soviet preference for updating existing designs to originating entirely new ones.

The designation SU-22 indicates that the revisions made by Sukhoi to the SU-17 were intended to modify its role from fighter to bomber (designation of Soviet aircraft accords even numbers to bombers, odd ones to fighters). Infra-red AA-2 ('Atoll') missiles represent its usual air-to-air armament.

Below: Lieutenant David Venlet (left) and Commander Hank Kleeman demonstrate the interception of the LARAF SU-22s for the benefit of the press.

long practice became instinctive and in a cross-over manoeuvre Music followed the Libyan leader while the CO turned and tracked the enemy wingman, who flew across the low morning sun. Kleeman told Musczynski he was going to shoot and did so, after allowing the Fitter to clear the sun. The pilot ejected as the AIM-9L Sidewinder found its mark.

'Music fired his Sidewinder from a half-mile at the lead Sukhoi's six o'clock. Half the tail came off, the pilot punched out and Music had to pitch up violently to avoid a sky filled with debris. Neither Music nor Amos saw their victim's chute open, but suggested it may have been operated barometrically. "We didn't stick around to wait for a canopy," Music said. En route to the ship, the Black Aces rendezvoused, cleared one anothers' six and reported to *Nimitz*. Kleeman called in two splashed Libyans and at least one observed parachute. The response was an understated: "The Admiral wants to talk to you, when you get back."'

A rigorous enquiry into the Black Aces' action was inevitable, but Commander Kleeman was confident that he had acted correctly.

'I decided we had been fired upon and that they were likely to do it again. The only acceptable course of action was to shoot at them myself. It did pass through my mind that it might cause a ruckus. I was aware of possible political implications. I was aware of them before we went out there, but there was no chance that I wasn't going to pull the trigger.'

In the event, Kleeman's actions were fully vindicated by his superiors, who took the view that the Libyan aircraft had made an unprovoked attack on the US Navy aircraft and that the American pilots had acted correctly and in self-defence in shooting them down. Under the Navy's standard rules of engagement they need no specific permission to return fire.

When asked to evaluate the Libyan pilots, the Black Aces' response was: 'Not as good as we were'

Although there can be no doubt that the F-14A Tomcat is considerably more technologically advanced as a combat aircraft than the Su-22 Fitter, it is ironic that the combat over the Gulf of Sirte gave little scope for the American fighter to demonstrate its most sophisticated weaponry. Conceived as a fleet air defence interceptor, the Tomcat is equipped with the AWG-9 radar and fire control system, which enables its crew to detect targets at a range of over 100 miles and furthermore to track no fewer than 24 separate targets at the same time. The F-14A's AIM-54 Phoenix missiles have a range of well over 50 miles and the Tomcat can launch up to six of these weapons in quick succession against different targets. In contrast, the Su-22 Fitter (a sparsely equipped export model of the Soviet Air Force's Su-17) is primarily a ground attack fighter, with only a short range air-to-air armament of infra-red guided AA-2 Atoll missiles. However, in a close range dogfight, individual piloting and tactical skills count for as much as technology, and when asked to evaluate the Libyan fighter pilots, the Black Aces' response was: 'Not as good as we were.'

THE AUTHOR Anthony Robinson was formerly on the staff of the RAF Museum, Hendon, and is now a freelance military aviation writer. He has edited the books *Aerial Warfare* and the *Dictionary of Aviation*.

SU-22 FITTER

NORTH

LIBYA